Applied Unsupervised Learning with R

Uncover hidden relationships and patterns with k-means clustering, hierarchical clustering, and PCA

Alok Malik and Bradford Tuckfield

Applied Unsupervised Learning with R

Authors: Alok Malik and Bradford Tuckfield

Technical Reviewer: Smitha Shivakumar

Managing Editor: Rutuja Yerunkar

Acquisitions Editor: Aditya Date

Production Editor: Nitesh Thakur

Editorial Board: David Barnes, Ewan Buckingham, Shivangi Chatterji, Simon Cox, Manasa Kumar, Alex Mazonowicz, Douglas Paterson, Dominic Pereira, Shiny Poojary, Saman Siddiqui, Erol Staveley, Ankita Thakur, and Mohita Vyas

First Published: March 2019

Production Reference: 1260319

ISBN: 978-1-78995-639-9

Published by Packt Publishing Ltd.

Livery Place, 35 Livery Street

Birmingham B3 2PB, UK

Table of Contents

Advanced Clustering Methods   51

Probability Distributions 87

Data Comparison Methods

Preface

About

This section briefly introduces the author, the coverage of this book, the technical skills you'll need to get started, and the hardware and software requirements required to complete all of the included activities and exercises.

About the Book

Starting with the basics, *Applied Unsupervised Learning with R* explains clustering methods, distribution analysis, data encoders, and features of R that enable you to understand your data better and get answers to your most pressing business questions.

This book begins with the most important and commonly used method for unsupervised learning – clustering – and explains the three main clustering algorithms: k-means, divisive, and agglomerative. Following this, you'll study market basket analysis, kernel density estimation, principal component analysis, and anomaly detection. You'll be introduced to these methods using code written in R, with further instructions on how to work with, edit, and improve R code. To help you gain a practical understanding, the book also features useful tips on applying these methods to real business problems, including market segmentation and fraud detection. By working through interesting activities, you'll explore data encoders and latent variable models.

By the end of this book, you will have a better understanding of different anomaly detection methods, such as outlier detection, Mahalanobis distances, and contextual and collective anomaly detection.

About the Authors

Alok Malik is a data scientist based in India. He has previously worked on creating and deploying unsupervised learning solutions in fields such as finance, cryptocurrency trading, logistics, and natural language processing. He has a bachelor's degree in technology from the Indian Institute of Information Technology, Design and Manufacturing, Jabalpur, where he studied electronics and communication engineering.

Bradford Tuckfield has designed and implemented data science solutions for firms in a variety of industries. He studied math for his bachelor's degree and economics for his Ph.D. He has written for scholarly journals and the popular press, on topics including linear algebra, psychology, and public policy.

Elevator Pitch

Design clever algorithms that discover hidden patterns and business-relevant insights from unstructured, unlabeled data.

Key Features

- Build state-of-the-art algorithms that can solve your business' problems
- Learn how to find hidden patterns in your data
- Implement key concepts with hands-on exercises using real-world datasets

Description

Starting with the basics, *Applied Unsupervised Learning with R* explains clustering methods, distribution analysis, data encoders, and all the features of R that enable you to understand your data better and get answers to all your business questions.

Learning Objectives

- Implement clustering methods such as k-means, agglomerative, and divisive clustering
- Write code in R to analyze market segmentation and consumer behavior
- Estimate distributions and probabilities of different outcomes
- Implement dimension reduction using principal component analysis
- Apply anomaly detection methods to identify fraud
- Design algorithms with R and learn how to edit or improve code

Audience

Applied Unsupervised Learning with R is designed for business professionals who want to learn about methods to understand their data better, and developers who have an interest in unsupervised learning. Although the book is for beginners, it will be beneficial to have some basic, beginner-level familiarity with R. This includes an understanding of how to open the R console, how to read data, and how to create a loop. To easily understand the concepts of this book, you should also know basic mathematical concepts, including exponents, square roots, means, and medians.

Approach

Applied Unsupervised Learning with R takes a hands-on approach to using R to reveal the hidden patterns in your unstructured data. It contains multiple activities that use real-life business scenarios for you to practice and apply your new skills in a highly relevant context.

Hardware Requirements

For the optimal student experience, we recommend the following hardware configuration:

- Processor: Intel Core i5 or equivalent

- Memory: 4 GB RAM

- Storage: 5 GB available space

- An internet connection

Software Requirements

We also recommend that you have the following software installed in advance:

- OS: Windows 7 SP1 64-bit, Windows 8.1 64-bit or Windows 10 64-bit, Linux (Ubuntu, Debian, Red Hat, or Suse), or the latest version of OS X

- R (3.0.0 or more recent, available for free at https://cran.r-project.org/)

Conventions

Code words in text, database table names, folder names, filenames, file extensions, pathnames, dummy URLs, user input, and Twitter handles are shown as follows: "We import a **factoextra** library for visualization of the clusters we just created."

A block of code is set as follows:

```
plot(iris_data$Sepal.Length,iris_data$Sepal.Width,col=iris_data$t_color)
points(k1[1],k1[2],pch=4)
points(k2[1],k2[2],pch=5)
points(k3[1],k3[2],pch=6)
```

New terms and important words are shown in bold. Words that you see on the screen, for example, in menus or dialog boxes, appear in the text like this: "There are many different types of algorithms for performing k-medoids clustering. The simplest and most efficient of them is **Partitioning Around Medoids**, or **PAM** for short."

Installation and Setup

Each great journey begins with a humble step. Our upcoming adventure in the land of data wrangling is no exception. Before we can do awesome things with data, we need to be prepared with the most productive environment. In this small note, we shall see how to do that.

Installing R on Windows

To install R on Windows, follow these steps:

1. Open the page dedicated to the latest version of R for Windows: https://cran.r-project.org/bin/windows/base/.

2. Click the link that says "**Download R X.X.X for Windows**", where each X is a natural number, for example R 3.5.3. This will initiate a file download.

3. The file you downloaded in *Step* 1 is an **exe** file. Double-click on this file, and a program will run that will install R on your computer.

4. The installation program that you ran in *Step* 3 will prompt you with some questions about how you want to install R. Choose the default options for each of these prompts.

5. You can open R by double-clicking on its icon wherever it was installed on your Windows computer during *Step* 4.

Installing R on macOS X

To install R on macOS X, perform the following:

1. Open the following link, which is dedicated to the latest version of R for macOS X: https://cran.r-project.org/bin/macosx/.

2. Under the **Latest release** heading, click on a file called **R-X.X.X.pkg**, where each X stands for a natural number, for example, **R-3.5.2.pkg**.

3. Open the file that you downloaded in *Step* 2. This will be a .pkg file. When you open this file, OS X will open installation wizards that will guide you through the rest of the process.

4. When the installation wizards ask you to make a decision about the installation, choose the default option.

5. After the installation wizards have completed their work, you will be able to double-click on R's icon wherever it was installed. This will open an R console.

Installing R on Linux

1. Determine which package manager your version of Linux uses. Two common examples of package managers are **yum** and **apt**.

2. Open the Terminal and type the following two commands using your package manager:

```
sudo apt update
sudo apt install r-base
```

   In this case, we wrote **apt** as the package manager, but if your version of Linux uses **yum** or some other package manager, you should replace every **apt** in these two lines with **yum** or the name of your package manager.

3. If you encounter problems, it could be that your version of Linux is not accessing the correct repository. To tell Linux where the right repository is, you should open the **sources.list** file for your version of Linux. For Ubuntu, this file is stored by default at **/etc/apt/sources.list**.

4. In the **sources.list** file, you need to add one of the following two lines if you are using either Debian or Ubuntu. For Ubuntu versions, use the following: http://cran.rstudio.com/bin/linux/ubuntu/. For Debian versions, use the following: **deb** http://cran.rstudio.com/bin/linux/debian/. If you are using Red Hat, you can run the following line in the Terminal to tell Linux which repository to use to download R: **sudo yum install epel-release**.

Introduction to Clustering Methods

Learning Objectives

By the end of this chapter, you will be able to:

- Describe the uses of clustering

- Perform the k-means algorithm using built-in R libraries

- Perform the k-medoids algorithm using built-in R libraries

- Determine the optimum number of clusters

In this chapter, we will have a look at the concept of clustering and some basic clustering algorithms.

Introduction

The 21st century is the digital century, where every person on every rung of the economic ladder is using digital devices and producing data in digital format at an unprecedented rate. 90% of data generated in the last 10 years was generated in the last 2 years. This is an exponential rate of growth, where the amount of data is increasing by 10 times every 2 years. This trend is expected to continue for the foreseeable future:

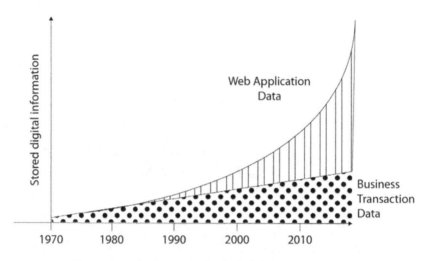

Figure 1.1: The increase in digital data year on year

But this data is not just stored in hard drives; it's being used to make lives better. For example, Google uses the data it has to serve you better results, and Netflix uses the data it has to serve you better movie recommendations. In fact, their decision to make their hit show *House of Cards* was based on analytics. IBM is using the medical data it has to create an artificially intelligent doctor and to detect cancerous tumors from x-ray images.

To process this amount of data with computers and come up with relevant results, a particular class of algorithms is used. These algorithms are collectively known as machine learning algorithms. Machine learning is divided into two parts, depending on the type of data that is being used: one is called **supervised** learning and the other is called **unsupervised learning**.

Supervised learning is done when we get labeled data. For example, say we get 1,000 images of x-rays from a hospital that are labeled as normal or fractured. We can use this data to train a machine learning model to predict whether an x-ray image shows a fractured bone or not.

Unsupervised learning is when we just have raw data and are expected to come up with insights without any labels. We have the ability to understand the data and recognize

patterns in it without explicitly being told what patterns to identify. By the end of this book, you're going to be aware of all of the major types of unsupervised learning algorithms. In this book, we're going to be using the R programming language for demonstration, but the algorithms are the same for all languages.

In this chapter, we're going to study the most basic type of unsupervised learning, **clustering**. At first, we're going to study what clustering is, its types, and how to create clusters with any type of dataset. Then we're going to study how each type of clustering works, looking at their advantages and disadvantages. At the end, we're going to learn when to use which type of clustering.

Introduction to Clustering

Clustering is a set of methods or algorithms that are used to find natural groupings according to predefined properties of variables in a dataset. The Merriam-Webster dictionary defines a cluster as "a number of similar things that occur together." Clustering in unsupervised learning is exactly what it means in the traditional sense. For example, how do you identify a bunch of grapes from far away? You have an intuitive sense without looking closely at the bunch whether the grapes are connected to each other or not. Clustering is just like that. An example of clustering is presented here:

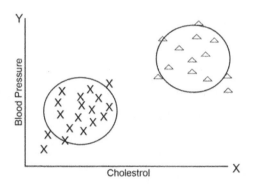

Figure 1.2: A representation of two clusters in a dataset

In the preceding graph, the data points have two properties: cholesterol and blood pressure. The data points are classified into two clusters, or two bunches, according to the **Euclidean** distance between them. One cluster contains people who are clearly at high risk of heart disease and the other cluster contains people who are at low risk of heart disease. There can be more than two clusters, too, as in the following example:

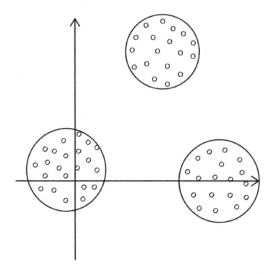

Figure 1.3: A representation of three clusters in a dataset

In the preceding graph, there are three clusters. One additional group of people has high blood pressure but with low cholesterol. This group may or may not have a risk of heart disease. In further sections, clustering will be illustrated on real datasets in which the x and y coordinates denote actual quantities.

Uses of Clustering

Like all methods of unsupervised learning, clustering is mostly used when we don't have labeled data – data with predefined classes – for training our models. Clustering uses various properties, such as Euclidean distance and **Manhattan distance**, to find patterns in the data and classify them according to similarities in their properties without having any labels for training. So, clustering has many use cases in fields where labeled data is unavailable or we want to find patterns that are not defined by labels.

The following are some applications of clustering:

- **Exploratory data analysis**: When we have unlabeled data, we often do clustering to explore the underlying structure and categories of the dataset. For example, a retail store might want to explore how many different segments of customers they have, based on purchase history.

- **Generating training data**: Sometimes, after processing unlabeled data with clustering methods, it can be labeled for further training with supervised learning algorithms. For example, two different classes that are unlabeled might form two entirely different clusters, and using their clusters, we can label data for further supervised learning algorithms that are more efficient in real-time classification than our unsupervised learning algorithms.

- **Recommender systems**: With the help of clustering, we can find the properties of similar items and use these properties to make recommendations. For example, an e-commerce website, after finding customers in the same clusters, can recommend items to customers in that cluster based upon the items bought by other customers in that cluster.

- **Natural language processing**: Clustering can be used for the grouping of similar words, texts, articles, or tweets, without labeled data. For example, you might want to group articles on the same topic automatically.

- **Anomaly detection**: You can use clustering to find outliers. We're going to learn about this in *Chapter 6, Anomaly Detection*. Anomaly detection can also be used in cases where we have unbalanced classes in data, such as in the case of the detection of fraudulent credit card transactions.

Introduction to the Iris Dataset

In this chapter, we're going to use the Iris flowers dataset in exercises to learn how to classify three species of Iris flowers (Versicolor, Setosa, and Virginica) without using labels. This dataset is built-in to R and is very good for learning about the implementation of clustering techniques.

Note that in our exercise dataset, we have final labels for the flowers. We're going to compare clustering results with those labels. We choose this dataset just to demonstrate that the results of clustering make sense. In the case of datasets such as the wholesale customer dataset (covered later in the book), where we don't have final labels, the results of clustering cannot be objectively verified and therefore might lead to misguided conclusions. That's the kind of use case where clustering is used in real life when we don't have final labels for the dataset. This point will be clearer once you have done both the exercises and activities.

Exercise 1: Exploring the Iris Dataset

In this exercise, we're going to learn how to use the Iris dataset in R. Assuming you already have R installed in your system, let's proceed:

1. Load the Iris dataset into a variable as follows:

```
iris_data<-iris
```

2. Now that our Iris data is in the **iris_data** variable, we can have a look at its first few rows by using the **head** function in R:

```
head(iris_data)
```

The output is as follows:

```
  Sepal.Length Sepal.Width Petal.Length Petal.Width Species
1          5.1         3.5          1.4         0.2  setosa
2          4.9         3.0          1.4         0.2  setosa
3          4.7         3.2          1.3         0.2  setosa
4          4.6         3.1          1.5         0.2  setosa
5          5.0         3.6          1.4         0.2  setosa
6          5.4         3.9          1.7         0.4  setosa
```

Figure 1.4: The first six rows of the Iris dataset

We can see our dataset has five columns. We're mostly going to use two columns for ease of visualization in plots of two dimensions.

Types of Clustering

As stated previously, clustering algorithms find natural groupings in data. There are many ways in which we can find natural groupings in data. The following are the methods that we're going to study in this chapter:

- k-means clustering
- k-medoids clustering

Once the concepts related to the basic types of clustering are clear, we will have a look at other types of clustering, which are as follows:

- k-modes
- Density-based clustering
- Agglomerative hierarchical clustering

- Divisive clustering

Introduction to k-means Clustering

K-means clustering is one of the most basic types of unsupervised learning algorithm. This algorithm finds natural groupings in accordance with a predefined similarity or distance measure. The distance measure can be any of the following:

- Euclidean distance
- Manhattan distance
- Cosine distance
- Hamming distance

To understand what a distance measure does, take the example of a bunch of pens. You have 12 pens. Six of them are blue, and six red. Six of them are ball point pens and six are ink pens. If you were to use ink color as a similarity measure, then six blue pens and six red pens will be in different clusters. The six blue pens can be ink or ball point here; there's no restriction on that. But if you were to use the type of pen as the similarity measure, then the six ink pens and six ball point pens would be in different clusters. Now it doesn't matter whether the pens in each cluster are of the same color or not.

Euclidean Distance

Euclidean distance is the straight-line distance between any two points. Calculation of this distance in two dimensions can be thought of an extension of the Pythagorean theorem, which you might have studied in school. But Euclidean distance can be calculated between two points in any n-dimensional space, not just a two-dimensional space. The Euclidean distance between any two points is the square root of the sum of squares of differences between the coordinates. An example of the calculation of Euclidean distance is presented here:

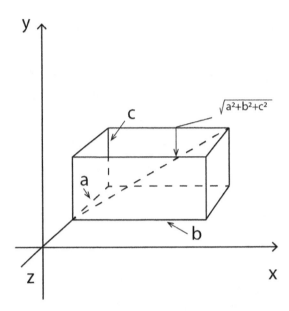

Figure 1.5: Representation of Euclidean distance calculation

In k-means clustering, Euclidean distance is used. One disadvantage of using Euclidean distance is that it loses its meaning when the dimensionality of data is very high. This is related to a phenomenon known as the curse of dimensionality. When datasets possess many dimensions, they can be harder to work with, since distances between all points can become extremely high, and the distances are difficult to interpret and visualize.

So, when the dimensionality of data is very high, either we reduce its dimensions with principal component analysis, which we're going to study in *Chapter 4, Dimension Reduction*, or we use cosine similarity.

Manhattan Distance

By definition, Manhattan distance is the distance between two points measured along a right angle to the axes:

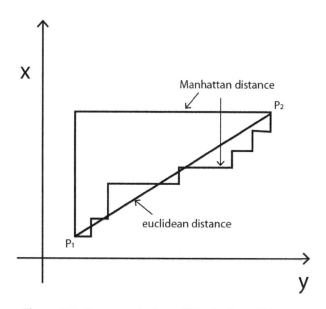

Figure 1.6: Representation of Manhattan distance

The length of the diagonal line is the Euclidean distance between the two points. Manhattan distance is simply the sum of the absolute value of the differences between two coordinates. So, the main difference between Euclidean distance and Manhattan distance is that with Euclidean distance, we square the distances between coordinates and then take the root of the sum, but in Manhattan distance, we directly take the sum of the absolute value of the differences between coordinates.

Cosine Distance

Cosine similarity between any two points is defined as the cosine of the angle between any two points with the origin as its vertex. It can be calculated by dividing the dot product of any two vectors by the product of the magnitudes of the vectors:

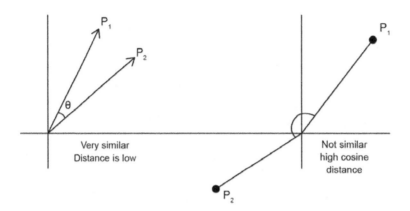

Figure 1.7: Representation of cosine similarity and cosine distance

Cosine distance is defined as (1–cosine similarity).

Cosine distance varies from 0 to 2, whereas cosine similarity varies between -1 to 1. Always remember that cosine similarity is one minus the value of of the cosine distance.

The Hamming Distance

The Hamming distance is a special type of distance that is used for categorical variables. Given two points of equal dimensions, the Hamming distance is defined as the number of coordinates differing from one another. For example, let's take two points, (0, 1, 1) and (0, 1, 0). Only one value, which is the last value, is different between these two variables. As such, the Hamming distance between them is 1:

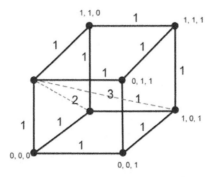

Figure 1.8: Representation of the Hamming distance

k-means Clustering Algorithm

K-means clustering is used to find clusters in a dataset of similar points when we have unlabeled data. In this chapter, we're going to use the Iris flowers dataset. This dataset contains information about the length and breadth of sepals and petals of flowers of different species. With the help of unsupervised learning, we're going to learn how to differentiate between them without knowing which properties belong to which species. The following is the scatter plot of our dataset:

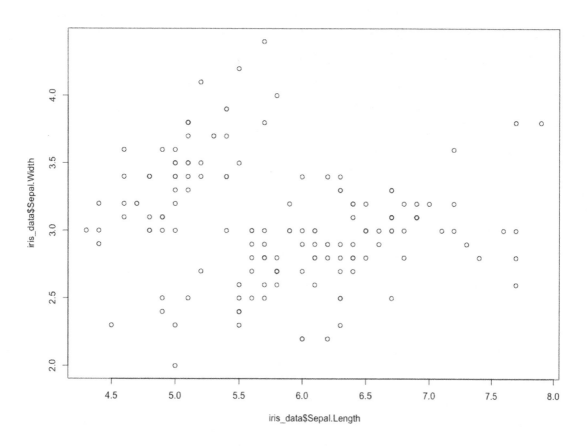

Figure 1.9: A scatter plot of the Iris flowers dataset

This is the scatter plot of two variables of the Iris flower dataset: sepal length and sepal width.

If we were to identify the clusters in the preceding dataset according to the distance between the points, we would choose clusters that look like bunches of grapes hanging from a tree. You can see that there are two major bunches (one in the top left and the other being the remaining points). The k-means algorithm identifies these "bunches" of grapes.

The following figure shows the same scatter plot, but with the three different species of Iris shown in different colors. These species are taken from the 'species' column of the original dataset, and are as follows: Iris setosa (shown in green), Iris versicolor (shown in red), and Iris virginica (shown in blue). We're going to see whether we can determine these species by forming our own classifications using clustering:

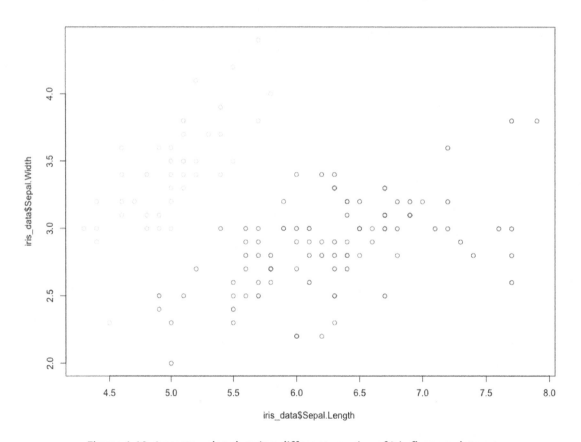

Figure 1.10: A scatter plot showing different species of Iris flowers dataset

Here is a photo of Iris setosa, which is represented in green in the preceding scatter plot:

Figure 1.11: Iris setosa

The following is a photo of Iris versicolor, which is represented in red in the preceding scatter plot:

Figure 1.12: Iris versicolor

Here is a photo of Iris virginica, which is represented in blue in the preceding scatter plot:

Figure 1.13: Iris virginica

Steps to Implement k-means Clustering

As we saw in the scatter plot in figure 1.9, each data point represents a flower. We're going to find clusters that will identify these species. To do this type of clustering, we're going to use k-means clustering, where k is the number of clusters we want. The following are the steps to perform k-means clustering, which, for simplicity of understanding, we're going to demonstrate with two clusters. We will build up to using three clusters later, in order to try and match the actual species groupings:

1. Choose any two random coordinates, k1 and k2, on the scatter plot as initial cluster centers.

2. Calculate the distance of each data point in the scatter plot from coordinates k1 and k2.

3. Assign each data point to a cluster based on whether it is closer to k1 or k2

4. Find the mean coordinates of all points in each cluster and update the values of k1 and k2 to those coordinates respectively.

5. Start again from *Step 2* until the coordinates of k1 and k2 stop moving significantly, or after a certain pre-determined number of iterations of the process.

We're going to demonstrate the preceding algorithm with graphs and code.

Exercise 2: Implementing k-means Clustering on the Iris Dataset

In this exercise, we will implement k-means clustering step by step:

1. Load the built-in Iris dataset in the **iris_data** variable:

   ```
   iris_data<-iris
   ```

2. Set the color for different species for representation on the scatter plot. This

   will help us see how the three different species are split between our initial two groupings:

   ```
   iris_data$t_color='red'
   iris_data$t_color[which(iris_data$Species=='setosa')]<-'green'
   iris_data$t_color[which(iris_data$Species=='virginica')]<-'blue'
   ```

3. Choose any two random clusters' centers to start with:

   ```
   k1<-c(7,3)
   k2<-c(5,3)
   ```

   > **Note**
   >
   > You can try changing the points and see how it affects the final clusters.

4. Plot the scatter plot along with the centers you chose in the previous step. Pass the length and width of the sepals of the iris flowers, along with the color, to the **plot** function in the first line, and then pass x and y coordinates of both the centers to the **points()** function. Here, **pch** is for selecting the type of representation of the center of the clusters – in this case, 4 is a cross and 5 is a diamond:

   ```
   plot(iris_data$Sepal.Length,iris_data$Sepal.Width,col=iris_data$t_color)
   points(k1[1],k1[2],pch=4)
   points(k2[1],k2[2],pch=5)
   ```

The output is as follows:

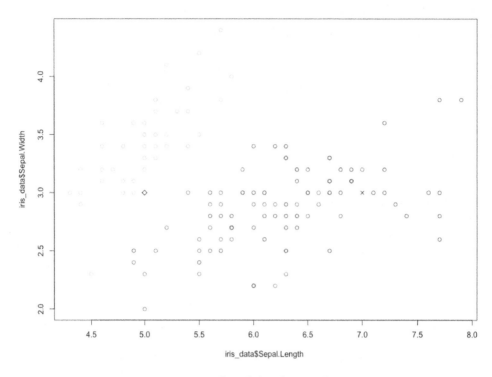

Figure 1.14: A scatter plot of the chosen cluster centers

5. Choose the number of iterations you want. The number of iterations should be such that the centers stop changing significantly after each iteration. In our case, six iterations are sufficient:

    ```
    number_of_steps<-6
    ```

6. Initialize the variable that will keep track of the number of iterations in the loop:

    ```
    n<-1
    ```

7. Start the **while** loop to find the final cluster centers:

    ```
    while(n<number_of_steps)
    {
    ```

8. Calculate the distance of each point from the current cluster centers, which is *Step 2* in the algorithm. We're calculating the Euclidean distance here using the **sqrt** function:

```
iris_data$distance_to_clust1 <- sqrt((iris_data$Sepal.Length-
k1[1])^2+(iris_data$Sepal.Width-k1[2])^2)
  iris_data$distance_to_clust2 <- sqrt((iris_data$Sepal.Length-
k2[1])^2+(iris_data$Sepal.Width-k2[2])^2)
```

9. Assign each point to the cluster whose center it is closest to, which is *Step 3* of the algorithm:

```
iris_data$clust_1 <- 1*(iris_data$distance_to_clust1<=iris_
data$distance_to_clust2)
  iris_data$clust_2 <- 1*(iris_data$distance_to_clust1>iris_data$distance_
to_clust2)
```

10. Calculate new cluster centers by calculating the mean **x** and **y** coordinates of the point in each cluster (*step 4* in the algorithm) with the **mean()** function in R:

```
k1[1]<-mean(iris_data$Sepal.Length[which(iris_data$clust_1==1)])
k1[2]<-mean(iris_data$Sepal.Width[which(iris_data$clust_1==1)])
k2[1]<-mean(iris_data$Sepal.Length[which(iris_data$clust_2==1)])
k2[2]<-mean(iris_data$Sepal.Width[which(iris_data$clust_2==1)])
```

11. Update the variable that is keeping the count of iterations for us to effectively carry out *step 5* of the algorithm:

```
n=n+1
}
```

12. Now we're going to overwrite the species colors with new colors to demonstrate the two clusters. So, there will only be two colors on our next scatter plot – one color for cluster 1, and one color for cluster 2:

```
iris_data$color='red'
iris_data$color[which(iris_data$clust_2==1)]<-'blue'
```

13. Plot the new scatter plot, which contains clusters along with cluster centers:

```
plot(iris_data$Sepal.Length,iris_data$Sepal.Width,col=iris_data$color)
points(k1[1],k1[2],pch=4)
points(k2[1],k2[2],pch=5)
```

The output will be as follows:

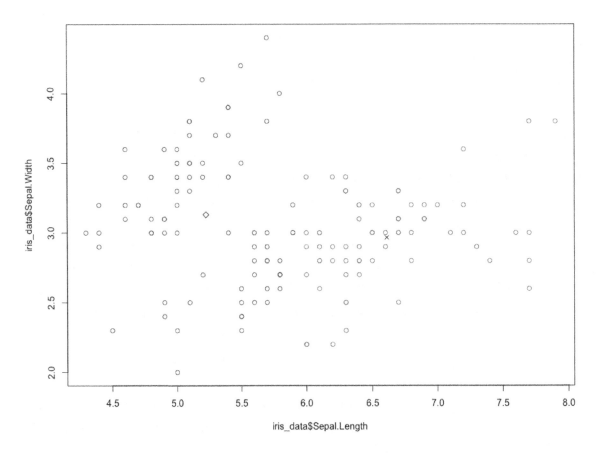

Figure 1.15: A scatter plot representing each cluster with a different color

Notice how setosa (which used to be green) has been grouped in the left cluster, while most of the virginica flowers (which were blue) have been grouped into the right cluster. The versicolor flowers (which were red) have been split between the two new clusters.

You have successfully implemented the k-means clustering algorithm to identify two groups of flowers based on their sepal size. Notice how the position of centers has changed after running the algorithm.

In the following activity, we are going to increase the number of clusters to three to see whether we can group the flowers correctly into their three different species.

Activity 1: k-means Clustering with Three Clusters

Write an R program to perform k-means clustering on the Iris dataset using three clusters. In this activity, we're going to perform the following steps:

1. Choose any three random coordinates, k1, k2, and k3, on the plot as centers.

2. Calculate the distance of each data point from k1, k2, and k3.

3. Classify each point by the cluster whose center it is closest to.

4. Find the mean coordinates of all points in the respective clusters and update the values of k1, k2, and k3 to those values.

5. Start again from *Step 2* until the coordinates of k1, k2, and k3 stop moving significantly, or after 10 iterations of the process.

The outcome of this activity will be a chart with three clusters, as follows:

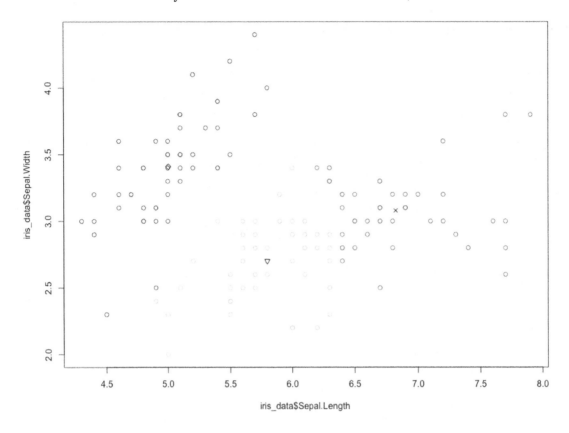

Figure 1.16: The expected scatter plot for the given cluster centers

You can compare your chart to Figure 1.10 to see how well the clusters match the actual species classifications.

> **Note**
>
> The solution for this activity can be found on page 198.

Introduction to k-means Clustering with Built-In Functions

In this section, we're going to use some built-in libraries of R to perform k-means clustering instead of writing custom code, which is lengthy and prone to bugs and errors. Using pre-built libraries instead of writing our own code has other advantages, too:

- Library functions are computationally efficient, as thousands of man hours have gone into the development of those functions.

- Library functions are almost bug-free as they've been tested by thousands of people in almost all practically-usable scenarios.

- Using libraries saves time, as you don't have to invest time in writing your own code.

k-means Clustering with Three Clusters

In the previous activity, we performed k-means clustering with three clusters by writing our own code. In this section, we're going to achieve a similar result with the help of pre-built R libraries.

At first, we're going to start with a distribution of three types of flowers in our dataset, as represented in the following graph:

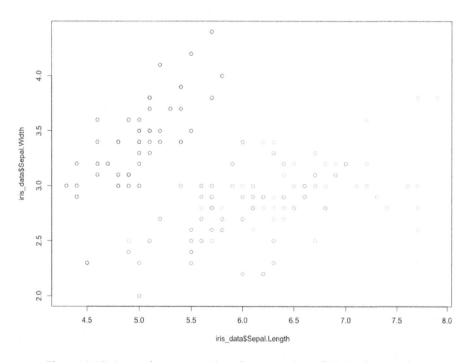

Figure 1.17: A graph representing three species of iris in three colors

In the preceding plot, setosa is represented in blue, virginica in gray, and versicolor in pink.

With this dataset, we're going to perform k-means clustering and see whether the built-in algorithm is able to find a pattern on its own to classify these three species of iris using their sepal sizes. This time, we're going to use just four lines of code.

Exercise 3: k-means Clustering with R Libraries

In this exercise, we're going to learn to do k-means clustering in a much easier way with the pre-built libraries of R. By completing this exercise, you will be able to divide the three species of Iris into three separate clusters:

1. We put the first two columns of the iris dataset, sepal length and sepal width, in the **iris_data** variable:

    ```
    iris_data<-iris[,1:2]
    ```

2. We find the k-means cluster centers and the cluster to which each point belongs, and store it all in the **km.res** variable. Here, in the **kmeans**, function we enter the dataset as the first parameter, and the number of clusters we want as the second parameter:

    ```
    km.res<-kmeans(iris_data,3)
    ```

    > **Note**
    >
    > The k-means function has many input variables, which can be altered to get different final outputs. You can find out more about them here in the documentation at https://www.rdocumentation.org/packages/stats/versions/3.5.1/topics/kmeans.

3. Install the **factoextra** library as follows:

    ```
    install.packages('factoextra')
    ```

4. We import the **factoextra** library for visualization of the clusters we just created. **Factoextra** is an R package that is used for plotting multivariate data:

    ```
    library("factoextra")
    ```

5. Generate the plot of the clusters. Here, we need to enter the results of k-means as the first parameter. In **data**, we need to enter the data on which clustering was done. In **pallete**, we're selecting the type of the geometry of points, and in **ggtheme**, we're selecting the theme of the output plot:

    ```
    fviz_cluster(km.res, data = iris_data,palette = "jco",ggtheme = theme_
    minimal())
    ```

The output will be as follows:

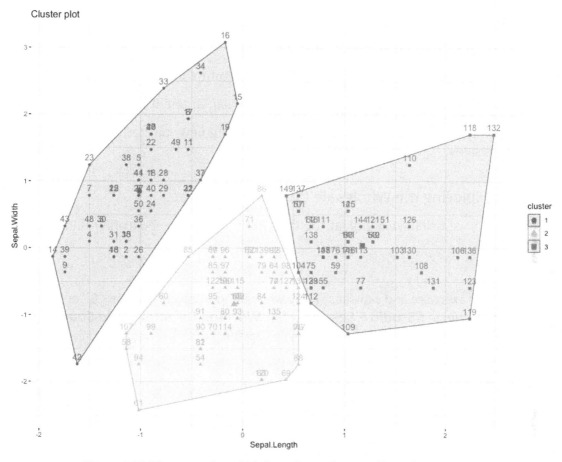

Figure 1.18: Three species of Iris have been clustered into three clusters

Here, if you compare Figure 1.18 to Figure 1.17, you will see that we have classified all three species almost correctly. The clusters we've generated don't exactly match the species shown in figure 1.18, but we've come very close considering the limitations of only using sepal length and width to classify them.

You can see from this example that clustering would've been a very useful way of categorizing the irises if we didn't already know their species. You will come across many examples of datasets where you don't have labeled categories, but are able to use clustering to form your own groupings.

Introduction to Market Segmentation

Market segmentation is dividing customers into different segments based on common characteristics. The following are the uses of customer segmentation:

- Increasing customer conversion and retention
- Developing new products for a particular segment by identifying it and its needs
- Improving brand communication with a particular segment
- Identifying gaps in marketing strategy and making new marketing strategies to increase sales

Exercise 4: Exploring the Wholesale Customer Dataset

In this exercise, we will have a look at the data in the wholesale customer dataset.

> **Note**
>
> For all the exercises and activities where we are importing an external CSV or image files, go to **RStudio**-> **Session**-> **Set Working Directory**-> **To Source File Location**. You can see in the console that the path is set automatically.

1. To download the CSV file, go to https://github.com/TrainingByPackt/Applied-Unsupervised-Learning-with-R/tree/master/Lesson01/Exercise04/wholesale_customers_data.csv. Click on `wholesale_customers_data.csv`.

> **Note**
>
> This dataset is taken from the UCI Machine Learning Repository. You can find the dataset at https://archive.ics.uci.edu/ml/machine-learning-databases/00292/. We have downloaded the file and saved it at https://github.com/TrainingByPackt/Applied-Unsupervised-Learning-with-R/tree/master/Lesson01/Exercise04/wholesale_customers_data.csv.

2. Save it to the folder in which you have installed R. Now, to load it in R, use the following function:

```
ws<-read.csv("wholesale_customers_data.csv")
```

3. Now we may have a look at the different columns and rows in this dataset by using the following function in R:

```
head(ws)
```

The output is as follows:

```
  Channel Region Fresh  Milk Grocery Frozen Detergents_Paper Delicassen
1       2      3 12669  9656    7561    214             2674       1338
2       2      3  7057  9810    9568   1762             3293       1776
3       2      3  6353  8808    7684   2405             3516       7844
4       1      3 13265  1196    4221   6404              507       1788
5       2      3 22615  5410    7198   3915             1777       5185
6       2      3  9413  8259    5126    666             1795       1451
```

Figure 1.19: Columns of the wholesale customer dataset

These six rows show the first six rows of annual spending in monetary units by category of product.

Activity 2: Customer Segmentation with k-means

For this activity, we're going to use the wholesale customer dataset from the UCI Machine Learning Repository. It's available at: https://github.com/TrainingByPackt/Applied-Unsupervised-Learning-with-R/tree/master/Lesson01/Activity02/wholesale_customers_data.csv. We're going to identify customers belonging to different market segments who like to spend on different types of goods with clustering. Try k-means clustering for values of k from 2 to 6.

> **Note**
>
> This dataset is taken from the UCI Machine Learning Repository. You can find the dataset at https://archive.ics.uci.edu/ml/machine-learning-databases/00292/. We have downloaded the file and saved it at https://github.com/TrainingByPackt/Applied-Unsupervised-Learning-with-R/tree/master/Lesson01/Activity02/wholesale_customers_data.csv.

These steps will help you complete the activity:

1. Read data downloaded from the UCI Machine Learning Repository into a variable. The data can be found at: https://github.com/TrainingByPackt/Applied-Unsupervised-Learning-with-R/tree/master/Lesson01/Activity02/wholesale_customers_data.csv.

2. Select only two columns, Grocery and Frozen, for easy visualization of clusters.

3. As in *Step 2* of *Exercise 4, Exploring the Wholesale Customer Dataset*, change the value for the number of clusters to 2 and generate the cluster centers.

4. Plot the graph as in *Step 4* in *Exercise 4, Exploring the Wholesale Customer Dataset*.

5. Save the graph you generate.

6. Repeat *Steps* 3, 4, and 5 by changing value for the number of clusters to 3, 4, 5, and 6.

7. Decide which value for the number of clusters best classifies the dataset.

The output will be chart of six clusters as follows:

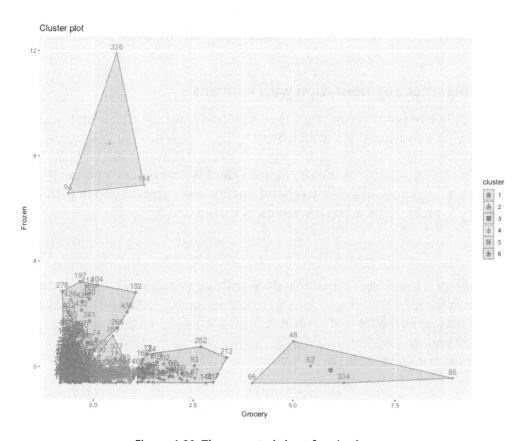

Figure 1.20: The expected chart for six clusters

Note

The solution for this activity can be found on page 201.

Introduction to k-medoids Clustering

k-medoids is another type of clustering algorithm that can be used to find natural groupings in a dataset. k-medoids clustering is very similar to k-means clustering, except for a few differences. The k-medoids clustering algorithm has a slightly different optimization function than k-means. In this section, we're going to study k-medoids clustering.

The k-medoids Clustering Algorithm

There are many different types of algorithms to perform k-medoids clustering, the simplest and most efficient of which is **Partitioning Around Medoids**, or PAM for short. In PAM, we do the following steps to find cluster centers:

1. Choose k data points from the scatter plot as starting points for cluster centers.

2. Calculate their distance from all the points in the scatter plot.

3. Classify each point into the cluster whose center it is closest to.

4. Select a new point in each cluster that minimizes the sum of distances of all points in that cluster from itself.

5. Repeat *Step* 2 until the centers stop changing.

You can see that the PAM algorithm is identical to the k-means clustering algorithm, except for *Step* 1 and *Step* 4. For most practical purposes, k-medoids clustering gives almost identical results to k-means clustering. But in some special cases where we have outliers in a dataset, k-medoids clustering is preferred as it's more robust to outliers. More about when to use which type of clustering and their differences will be studied in later sections.

k-medoids Clustering Code

In this section, we're going to use the same Iris flowers dataset that we used in the last two sections and compare to see whether the results are visibly different from the ones we got last time. Instead of writing code to perform each step of the k-medoids algorithm, we're directly going to use libraries of R to do PAM clustering.

Exercise 5: Implementing k-medoid Clustering

In this exercise, we're going to perform k-medoids with R's pre-built libraries:

1. Store the first two columns of the iris dataset in the **iris_data** variable:

    ```
    iris_data<-iris[,1:2]
    ```

2. Install the **cluster** package:

    ```
    install.packages("cluster")
    ```

3. Import the **cluster** package:

    ```
    library("cluster")
    ```

4. Store the PAM clustering results in the **km.res** variable:

    ```
    km<-pam(iris_data,3)
    ```

5. Import the **factoextra** library:

    ```
    library("factoextra")
    ```

6. Plot the PAM clustering results in a graph:

    ```
    fviz_cluster(km, data = iris_data,palette = "jco",ggtheme = theme_
    minimal())
    ```

The output is as follows:

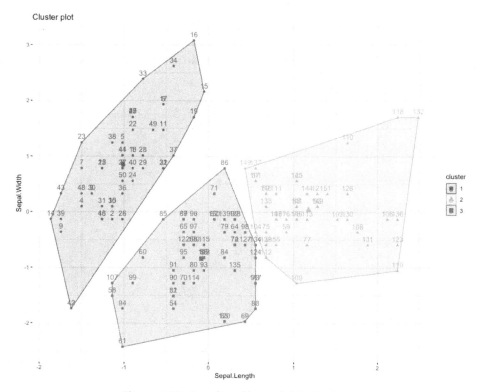

Figure 1.21: Results of k-medoids clustering

The results of k-medoids clustering are not very different from those of the k-means clustering we did in the previous section.

So, we can see that the preceding PAM algorithm classifies our dataset into three clusters that are similar to the clusters we got with k-means clustering. If we plot the results of both types of clustering side by side, we can clearly see how similar they are:

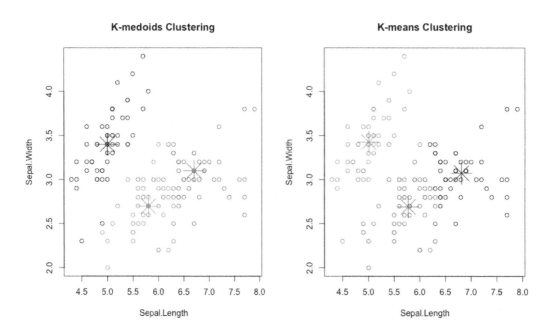

Figure 1.22: The results of k-medoids clustering versus k-means clustering

In the preceding graphs, observe how the centers of both k-means and k-medoids clustering are so close to each other, but centers for k-medoids clustering are directly overlapping on points already in the data while the centers for k-means clustering are not.

k-means Clustering versus k-medoids Clustering

Now that we've studied both k-means and k-medoids clustering, which are almost identical to each other, we're going to study the differences between them and when to use which type of clustering:

- Computational complexity: Of the two methods, k-medoids clustering is computationally more expensive. When our dataset is too large (>10,000 points) and we want to save computation time, we'll prefer k-means clustering over k-medoids clustering.

> **Note**
>
> Whether your dataset is large or not is entirely dependent on the computation power available. As computation gets cheaper over time, what is considered a large dataset will change in the future.

- Presence of outliers: k-means clustering is more sensitive to outliers than k-medoids. Cluster center positions can shift significantly due to the presence of outliers in the dataset, so we use k-medoids clustering when we have to build clusters resilient to outliers.

- Cluster centers: Both the k-means and k-medoids algorithms find cluster centers in different ways. The center of a k-medoids cluster is always a data point in the dataset. The center of a k-means cluster does not need to be a data point in the dataset.

Activity 3: Performing Customer Segmentation with k-medoids Clustering

Use the Wholesale customer dataset to perform both k-means and k-medoids clustering, and then compare the results. Read the data downloaded from the UCI machine learning repository into a variable. The data can be found at https://github.com/TrainingByPackt/Applied-Unsupervised-Learning-with-R/tree/master/Lesson01/Data/wholesale_customers_data.csv.

> **Note**
>
> This dataset is taken from the UCI Machine Learning Repository. You can find the dataset at https://archive.ics.uci.edu/ml/machine-learning-databases/00292/. We have downloaded the file and saved it at https://github.com/TrainingByPackt/Applied-Unsupervised-Learning-with-R/tree/master/Lesson01/Activity03/wholesale_customers_data.csv.

These steps will help you complete the activity:

1. Select only two columns, Grocery and Frozen, for easy two-dimensional visualization of clusters.

2. Use k-medoids clustering to plot a graph showing four clusters for this data.

3. Use k-means clustering to plot a four-cluster graph.

4. Compare the two graphs to comment on how the results of the two methods differ.

The outcome will be a k-means plot of the clusters as follows:

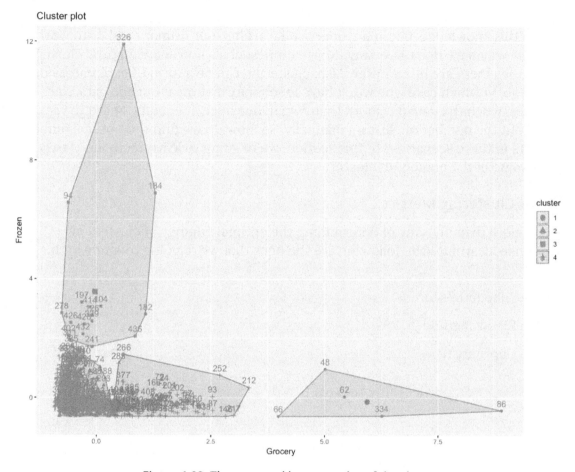

Figure 1.23: The expected k-means plot of the cluster

> **Note**
>
> The solution for this activity can be found on page 206.

Deciding the Optimal Number of Clusters

Until now, we've been working on the iris flowers dataset, in which we know how many categories of flowers there are, and we chose to divide our dataset into three clusters based on this knowledge. But in unsupervised learning, our primary task is to work with data about which we don't have any information, such as how many natural clusters or categories there are in a dataset. Also, clustering can be a form of exploratory data analysis too, in which case, you won't have much information about the data. And sometimes, when the data has more than two dimensions, it becomes hard to visualize and find out the number of clusters manually. So, how do we find the optimal number of clusters in these scenarios? In this section, we're going to learn techniques to get the optimal value of the number of clusters.

Types of Clustering Metrics

There is more than one way of determining the optimal number of clusters in unsupervised learning. The following are the ones that we're going to study in this chapter:

- The Silhouette score
- The Elbow method / WSS
- The Gap statistic

Silhouette Score

The silhouette score or average silhouette score calculation is used to quantify the quality of clusters achieved by a clustering algorithm. Let's take a point, a, in a cluster, x:

1. Calculate the average distance between point a and all the points in cluster x (denoted by **dxa**):

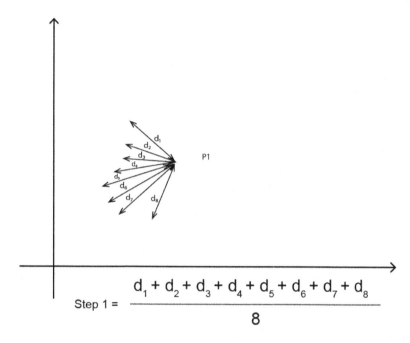

$$\text{Step 1} = \frac{d_1 + d_2 + d_3 + d_4 + d_5 + d_6 + d_7 + d_8}{8}$$

Figure 1.24: Calculating the average distance between point a and all the points of cluster x

2. Calculate the average distance between point a and all the points in another cluster nearest to a (**dya**):

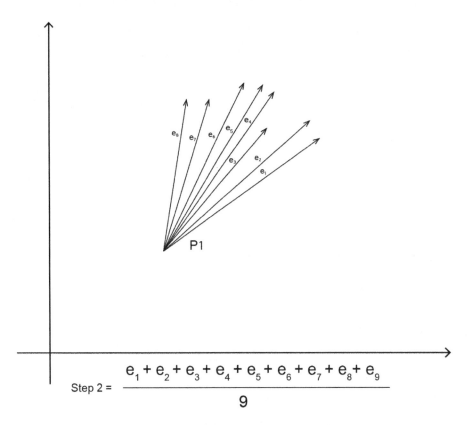

$$\text{Step 2} = \frac{e_1 + e_2 + e_3 + e_4 + e_5 + e_6 + e_7 + e_8 + e_9}{9}$$

Figure 1.25: Calculating the average distance between point a and all the points near cluster x

3. Calculate the silhouette score for that point by dividing the difference of the result of *Step* 1 from the result of *Step* 2 by the max of the result of *Step* 1 and *Step* 2 ((dya–dxa)/max(dxa,dya)).

4. Repeat the first three steps for all points in the cluster.

5. After getting the silhouette score for every point in the cluster, the average of all those scores is the silhouette score of that cluster:

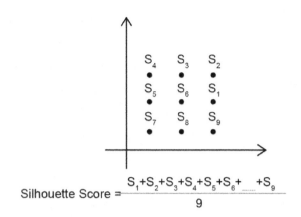

$$\text{Silhouette Score} = \frac{S_1+S_2+S_3+S_4+S_5+S_6+\ ....\ +S_9}{9}$$

Figure 1.26: Calculating the silhouette score

6. Repeat the preceding steps for all the clusters in the dataset.

7. After getting the silhouette score for all the clusters in the dataset, the average of all those scores is the silhouette score of that dataset:

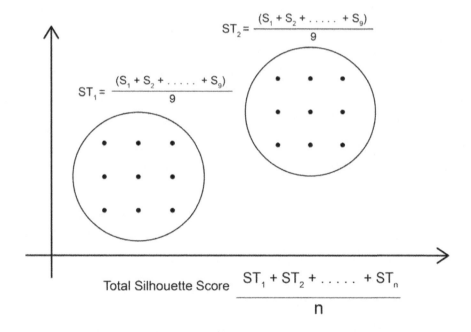

$$ST_2 = \frac{(S_1 + S_2 + \ .....\ + S_9)}{9}$$

$$ST_1 = \frac{(S_1 + S_2 + \ .....\ + S_9)}{9}$$

$$\text{Total Silhouette Score} \quad \frac{ST_1 + ST_2 + \ .....\ + ST_n}{n}$$

Figure 1.27: Calculating the average silhouette score

The silhouette score ranges between 1 and -1. If the silhouette score of a cluster is low (between 0 and -1), it means that the cluster is spread out or the distance between the points of that cluster is high. If the silhouette score of a cluster is high (close to 1), it means that the clusters are well defined and the distance between the points of a cluster is low and their distance from points of other clusters is high. So, the ideal silhouette score is near 1.

Understanding the preceding algorithm is important for forming an understanding of silhouette scores, but it's not important for learning how to implement it. So, we're going to learn how to do silhouette analysis in R using some pre-built libraries.

Exercise 6: Calculating the Silhouette Score

In this exercise, we're going to learn how to calculate the silhouette score of a dataset with a fixed number of clusters:

1. Put the first two columns of the iris dataset, sepal length and sepal width, in the **iris_data** variable:

    ```
    iris_data<-iris[,1:2]
    ```

2. Import the **cluster** library to perform k-means clustering:

    ```
    library(cluster)
    ```

3. Store the k-means clusters in the **km.res** variable:

    ```
    km.res<-kmeans(iris_data,3)
    ```

4. Store the pair-wise distance matrix for all data points in the **pair_dis** variable:

    ```
    pair_dis<-daisy(iris_data)
    ```

5. Calculate the silhouette score for each point in the dataset:

    ```
    sc<-silhouette(km.res$cluster, pair_dis)
    ```

6. Plot the silhouette score plot:

```
plot(sc,col=1:8,border=NA)
```

The output is as follows:

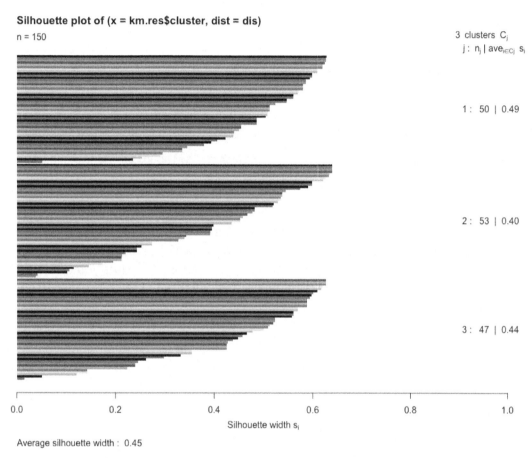

Silhouette plot of (x = km.res$cluster, dist = dis)

n = 150

3 clusters C_j

j : n_j | ave$_{i \in Cj}$ s_i

1 : 50 | 0.49

2 : 53 | 0.40

3 : 47 | 0.44

Silhouette width s_i

Average silhouette width : 0.45

Fig 1.28: The silhouette score for each point in every cluster is represented by a single bar

The preceding plot gives the average silhouette score of the dataset as 0.45. It also shows the average silhouette score cluster-wise and point-wise.

In the preceding exercise, we calculated the silhouette score for three clusters. But for deciding how many clusters to have, we'll have to calculate the silhouette score for multiple clusters in the dataset. In the next exercise, we're going to learn how to do this with the help of a library called **factoextra** in R.

Exercise 7: Identifying the Optimum Number of Clusters

In this exercise, we're going to identify the optimal number of clusters by calculating the silhouette score on various values of k in one line of code with the help of an R library:

1. Put first two columns, sepal length and sepal width, of the Iris data set in the **iris_data** variable:

    ```
    iris_data<-iris[,1:2]
    ```

2. Import the **factoextra** library:

    ```
    library("factoextra")
    ```

3. Plot a graph of the silhouette score versus number of clusters (up to 20):

    ```
    fviz_nbclust(iris_data, kmeans, method = "silhouette",k.max=20)
    ```

    > **Note**
    >
    > In the second argument, you may change k-means to k-medoids or any other type of clustering. The **k.max** variable is the max number of clusters up to which the score is to be calculated. In the method argument of the function, you can enter three types of clustering metrics to be included. All three of them are discussed in this chapter.

The output is as follows:

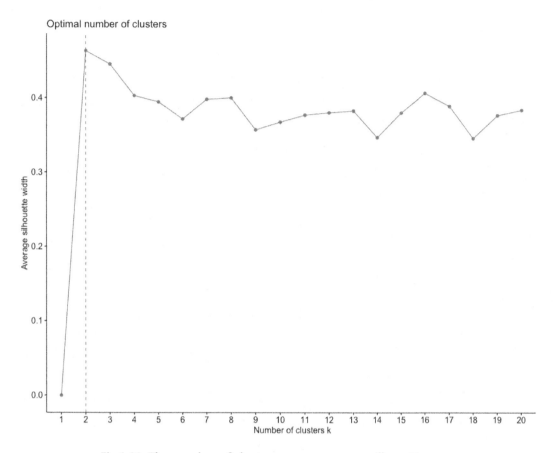

Fig 1.29: The number of clusters versus average silhouette score

From the preceding graph, you select a value of k that has the highest score; that is, 2. Two is the optimal number of clusters as per the silhouette score.

WSS/Elbow Method

To identify a cluster in a dataset, we try to minimize the distance between points in a cluster, and the **Within-Sum-of-Squares** (WSS) method measures exactly that. The WSS score is the sum of the squares of the distances of all points within a cluster. In this method, we perform the following steps:

1. Calculate clusters by using different values of k.

2. For every value of k, calculate WSS using the following formula:

$$\sum_{k=1}^{K} \sum_{i \in S_k} \sum_{j=1}^{p} (x_{ij} - \bar{x}_{kj})^2$$

where S_k is the set of observations in the *k*th cluster and $\bar{x}_{kj}$ is the *j*th variable of the cluster center for the *k*th cluster.

Figure 1.30: The formula to calculate WSS where p is the total number of dimensions of the data

This formula is illustrated here:

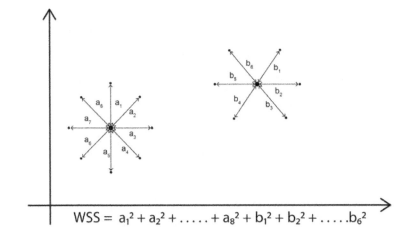

$$\text{WSS} = a_1^2 + a_2^2 + \ldots + a_8^2 + b_1^2 + b_2^2 + \ldots b_6^2$$

Figure 1.31: Illustration of WSS score

> **Note**
>
> Figure 1.31 illustrates WSS relative to two points, but in reality WSS measures sums of all distances relative to all points. within every cluster.

3. Plot number of clusters k versus WSS score.

4. Identify the k value after which the WSS score doesn't decrease significantly and choose this k as the ideal number of clusters. This point is also known as the elbow of the graph, hence the name "**elbow method**".

In the following exercise, we're going to learn how to identify the ideal number of clusters with the help of the **factoextra** library.

Exercise 8: Using WSS to Determine the Number of Clusters

In this exercise, we will see how we can use WSS to determine the number of clusters. Perform the following steps.

1. Put the first two columns, sepal length and sepal width, of the Iris data set in the **iris_data** variable:

   ```
   iris_data<-iris[,1:2]
   ```

2. Import the **factoextra** library:

   ```
   library("factoextra")
   ```

3. Plot a graph of WSS versus number of clusters (up to 20):

   ```
   fviz_nbclust(iris_data, kmeans, method = "wss", k.max=20)
   ```

The output is as follows:

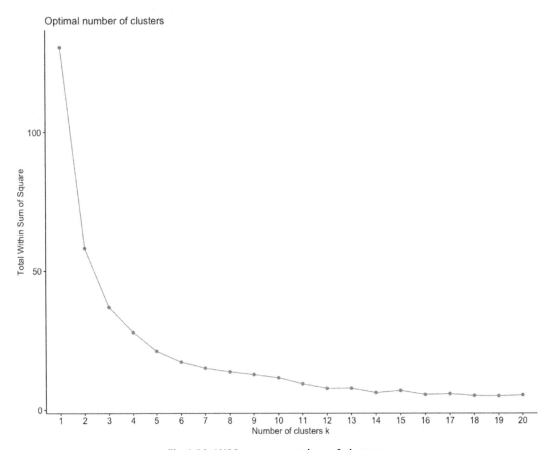

Fig 1.32: WSS versus number of clusters

In the preceding graph, we can choose the elbow of the graph as k=3, as the value of WSS starts dropping more slowly after k=3. Choosing the elbow of the graph is always a subjective choice and there could be times where you could choose k=4 or k=2 instead of k=3, but with this graph, it's clear that k>5 are inappropriate values for k as they are not the elbow of the graph, which is where the graph's slope changes sharply.

The Gap Statistic

The Gap statistic is one of the most effective methods of finding the optimal number of clusters in a dataset. It is applicable to any type of clustering method. The Gap statistic is calculated by comparing the WSS value for the clusters generated on our observed dataset versus a reference dataset in which there are no apparent clusters. The reference dataset is a uniform distribution of data points between the minimum and maximum values of our dataset on which we want to calculate the Gap statistic.

So, in short, the Gap statistic measures the WSS values for both observed and random datasets and finds the deviation of the observed dataset from the random dataset. To find the ideal number of clusters, we choose a value of k that gives us the maximum value of the Gap statistic. The mathematical details of how these deviations are measured are beyond the scope of this book. In the next exercise, we're going to learn how to calculate the Gap statistic with the help of the `factoviz` library.

Here is a reference dataset:

Figure 1.33: The reference dataset

The following is the observed dataset:

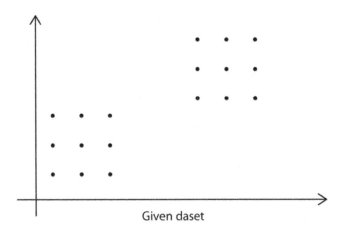

Given daset

Figure 1.34: The observed dataset

Exercise 9: Calculating the Ideal Number of Clusters with the Gap Statistic

In this exercise, we will calculate the ideal number of clusters using the Gap statistic:

1. Put the first two columns, sepal length and sepal width, of the Iris data set in the **iris_data** variable as follows:

    ```
    iris_data<-iris[,1:2]
    ```

2. Import the **factoextra** library as follows:

    ```
    library("factoextra")
    ```

3. Plot the graph of Gap statistics versus number of clusters (up to 20):

```
fviz_nbclust(iris_data, kmeans, method = "gap_stat",k.max=20)
```

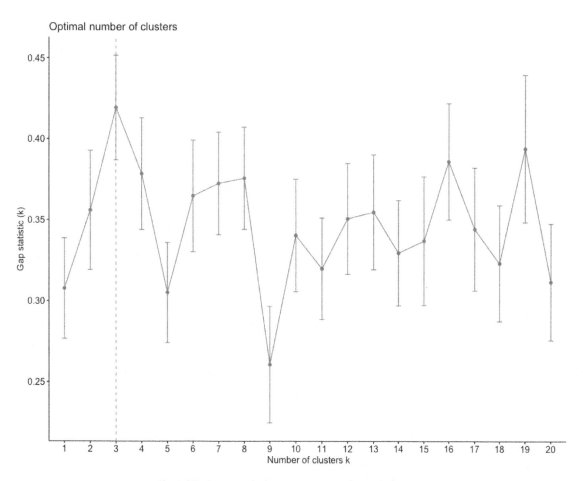

Fig 1.35: Gap statistics versus number of clusters

As we can see in the preceding graph, the highest value of the Gap statistic is for k=3. Hence, the ideal number of clusters in the iris dataset is three. Three is also the number of species in the dataset, indicating that the gap statistic has enabled us to reach a correct conclusion.

Activity 4: Finding the Ideal Number of Market Segments

Find the optimal number of clusters in the wholesale customers dataset with all three of the preceding methods:

> **Note**
>
> This dataset is taken from the UCI Machine Learning Repository. You can find the dataset at https://archive.ics.uci.edu/ml/machine-learning-databases/00292/. We have downloaded the file and saved it at https://github.com/TrainingByPackt/Applied-Unsupervised-Learning-with-R/tree/master/Lesson01/Activity04/wholesale_customers_data.csv.

1. Load columns 5 to 6 of the wholesale customers dataset in a variable.

2. Calculate the optimal number of clusters for k-means clustering with the silhouette score.

3. Calculate the optimal number of clusters for k-means clustering with the WSS score.

4. Calculate the optimal number of clusters for k-means clustering with the Gap statistic.

The outcome will be three graphs representing the optimal number of clusters with the silhouette score, with the WSS score, and with the Gap statistic.

> **Note**
>
> The solution for this activity can be found on page 208.

As we have seen, each method will give a different value for the optimal number of clusters. Sometimes, the results won't make sense, as you saw in the case of the Gap statistic, which gave the optimal number of clusters as one, which would mean that clustering shouldn't be done on this dataset and all data points should be in a single cluster.

All the points in a given cluster will have similar properties. Interpretation of those properties is left to domain experts. And there's almost never a right answer for the right number of clusters in unsupervised learning.

Summary

Congratulations! You have completed the first chapter of this book. If you've understood everything we've studied until now, you now know more about unsupervised learning than most people who claim to know data science. The k-means clustering algorithm is so fundamental to unsupervised learning that many people equate k-means clustering with unsupervised learning.

In this chapter, you not only learned about k-means clustering and its uses, but also k-medoids clustering, along with various clustering metrics and their uses. So, now you have a top-tier understanding of k-means and k-medoid clustering algorithms.

In the next chapter, we're going to have a look at some of the lesser-known clustering algorithms and their uses.

Advanced Clustering Methods

Learning Objectives

By the end of this chapter, you will be able to:

- Perform k-modes clustering
- Implement DBSCAN clustering
- Perform hierarchical clustering and record clusters in a dendrogram
- Perform divisive and agglomerative clustering

In this chapter, we will have a look at some advanced clustering methods and how to record clusters in a dendrogram.

Introduction

So far, we've learned about some of the most basic algorithms of unsupervised learning: k-means clustering and k-medoids clustering. These are not only important for practical use, but are also important for understanding clustering itself.

In this chapter, we're going to study some other advanced clustering algorithms. We aren't calling them advanced because they are difficult to understand, but because, before using them, a data scientist should have insights into why he or she is using these algorithms instead of the general clustering algorithms we studied in the last chapter. k-means is a general-purpose clustering algorithm that is sufficient for most cases, but in some special cases, depending on the type of data, advanced clustering algorithms can produce better results.

Introduction to k-modes Clustering

All the types of clustering that we have studied so far are based on a distance metric. But what if we get a dataset in which it's not possible to measure the distance between variables in a traditional sense, as in the case of categorical variables? In such cases, we use k-modes clustering.

k-modes clustering is an extension of k-means clustering, dealing with modes instead of means. One of the major applications of k-modes clustering is analyzing categorical data such as survey results.

Steps for k-Modes Clustering

In statistics, mode is defined as the most frequently occurring value. So, for k-modes clustering, we're going to calculate the mode of categorical values to choose centers. So, the steps to perform k-modes clustering are as follows:

1. Choose any k number of random points as cluster centers.

2. Find the Hamming distance (discussed in *Chapter 1, Introduction to Clustering Methods*) of each point from the center.

3. Assign each point to a cluster whose center it is closest to according to the Hamming distance.

4. Choose new cluster centers in each cluster by finding the mode of all data points in that cluster.

5. Repeat this from *Step 2* until the cluster centers stop changing.

You might have noticed that these steps are very similar to those for k-means clustering. Only the type of distance metric is changed here. So, if you understand k-means clustering, it will be very easy for you to understand k-modes clustering as well.

Exercise 10: Implementing k-modes Clustering

> **Note**
>
> For all the exercises and activities where we are importing external CSV's or images, go to **RStudio**-> **Session**-> **Set Working Directory**-> **To Source File Location**. You can see in the console that the path is set automatically.

The data for this exercise can be downloaded from here: https://github.com/TrainingByPackt/Applied-Unsupervised-Learning-with-R/tree/master/Lesson02/Exercise10/breast_cancer.csv. This is a categorical dataset that includes nine variables, some categorical and some nominal, describing different breast cancer cases. After saving this data in a file called **breast_cancer.csv**, we'll do the following:

> **Note**
>
> This dataset is taken from the UCI Machine Learning Repository. You can find the dataset at https://archive.ics.uci.edu/ml/machine-learning-databases/breast-cancer/breast-cancer.data. This breast cancer domain was obtained from the University Medical Centre, Institute of Oncology, Ljubljana, Yugoslavia. Thanks go to M. Zwitter and M. Soklic for providing the data. We have downloaded the file and saved it at https://github.com/TrainingByPackt/Applied-Unsupervised-Learning-with-R/tree/master/Lesson02/Exercise10/breast_cancer.csv.

1. Read the dataset and store it in a variable:

   ```
   bc_data<-read.csv('breast_cancer.csv',header = FALSE)
   ```

2. Store all of the columns from the second column to the end in a new variable:

   ```
   k_bc_data<-bc_data[,2:10]
   ```

3. View the first six rows of the **k_bc_data** variable:

```
head(k_bc_data)
```

The output contains the six rows with values for different attributes describing the patient, their symptoms, and their treatment:

```
     V2       V3    V4    V5  V6 V7   V8       V9      V10
1 30-39 premeno 30-34 0-2 no  3  left  left_low  no
2 40-49 premeno 20-24 0-2 no  2 right  right_up  no
3 40-49 premeno 20-24 0-2 no  2  left  left_low  no
4 60-69    ge40 15-19 0-2 no  2 right   left_up  no
5 40-49 premeno   0-4 0-2 no  2 right right_low  no
6 60-69    ge40 15-19 0-2 no  2  left  left_low  no
```

4. Import the **klaR** library, which has the **kmodes** function. **klaR** is an R library that is used for classification and visualization:

```
install.packages("klaR")
library(klaR)
```

5. Predict and store the final cluster centers in a variable. In this step, we enter the dataset and the number of clusters (that is, **k** and the maximum amount of iterations to find the number of clusters):

```
k.centers<-kmodes(k_bc_data,2,iter.max = 100)
```

6. View the cluster centers:

```
k.centers
```

The output is as follows:

```
> k.centers
K-modes clustering with 2 clusters of sizes 185, 101

Cluster modes:
     V2       V3    V4  V5 V6 V7   V8      V9 V10
1 40-49 premeno 25-29 0-2 no  2  left left_low  no
2 50-59    ge40 30-34 0-2 no  1 right  left_up  no

Clustering vector:
  [1] 1 1 1 2 1 1 1 1 1 1 1 1 1 1 1 1 1 1 1 1 1 1 2 1 1 1 1 2 1 1 1 2 1 1 1 2 1 1 1 2 2 1 1 1 2 1 1 1 2 1 2 1 2 1 2 2 2 1 2 1 1 1 1 1 2 2 2 2 2
 [59] 2 2 1 1 2 1 1 2 1 2 1 1 1 1 1 1 1 1 2 1 1 1 1 2 2 1 2 1 2 1 2 2 2 1 2 2 2 1 1 2 2 1 1 1 2 1 1 1 2 1 1 1 2 1 2 1 2 1 2 1 2
[117] 1 1 1 2 1 2 2 2 2 1 1 1 1 1 1 1 1 2 1 1 1 1 1 1 1 1 1 2 1 1 1 2 1 1 2 2 1 1 2 2 2 2 2 2 1 1 1 2 2 1 1 2 2 1 1 2 1 1 1 2 2
[175] 1 1 1 1 1 1 1 1 1 1 2 2 1 2 1 1 2 1 1 1 1 1 2 2 1 1 1 1 1 1 1 1 2 1 1 2 1 2 1 2 1 2 2 1 2 1 1 1 2 1 2 1 1 1 1 2 2 2 2 1
[233] 2 1 2 1 1 1 1 1 1 1 1 1 2 1 2 1 2 1 1 1 1 1 1 2 1 2 1 1 2 2 1 1 1 2 1 1 1 1 1 1 2 1 1 2 1 2 1 1 1 1 2 2 1 1 1 1 2 1 2

within cluster simple-matching distance by cluster:
[1] 671 335

Available components:
[1] "cluster"    "size"        "modes"      "withindiff" "iterations" "weighted"
```

Figure 2.1: Screenshot of the cluster centers

The clustering algorithm has grouped all of the breast cancer cases into two clusters, with each cluster containing cases that are similar to each other. In the output, there are two main components: the cluster modes and the clustering vector. The cluster modes section is telling us the modes or coordinates of the centers for cluster 1 and cluster 2. Below that, the clustering vector contains the cluster number of each data point in the index sequence.

> **Note**
>
> You could get different results every time you run the algorithm because of the random starting positions of the centers.

As it is a multi-dimensional categorical dataset, there's no easy way to visualize the results other than printing the data to the R console.

Activity 5: Implementing k-modes Clustering on the Mushroom Dataset

> **Note**
>
> This dataset is taken from the UCI Machine Learning Repository. You can find the dataset at https://archive.ics.uci.edu/ml/datasets/Mushroom. We have downloaded the file, cleaned the data, and saved it at https://github.com/TrainingByPackt/Applied-Unsupervised-Learning-with-R/tree/master/Lesson02/Activity05.

In this activity, we will perform k-modes clustering on the mushroom dataset. This dataset lists the attributes of 23 different species of mushrooms. Each species is classified as being either edible (e) or poisonous (p). We will see how well unsupervised learning can classify poisonous and edible mushrooms by grouping the data into two clusters. These steps will help you complete the activity:

1. Download **mushrooms.csv** from https://github.com/TrainingByPackt/Applied-Unsupervised-Learning-with-R/tree/master/Lesson02/Activity05.

2. Read the **mushroom.csv** file into a variable.

3. Import the **klaR** library.

4. Calculate the clusters according to k-modes clustering.

5. Check the results of clustering by forming a matrix of data labels versus the cluster assigned.

> **Note**
>
> The solution for this activity can be found on page 212.

The output will be a table of true labels and cluster labels, as follows:

```
       1    2
e     80 4128
p   3052  864
```

Introduction to Density-Based Clustering (DBSCAN)

Density-based clustering or DBSCAN is one of the most intuitive forms of clustering. It is very easy to find naturally occurring clusters and outliers in data with this type of clustering. Also, it doesn't require you to define a number of clusters. For example, consider the following figure:

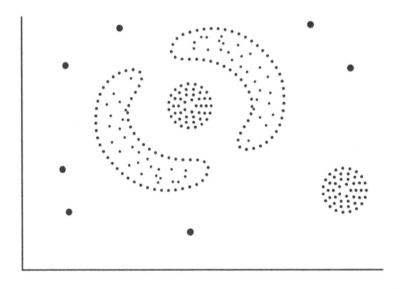

Figure 2.2: A sample scatter plot

There are four natural clusters in this dataset and a few outliers. So, DBSCAN will segregate the clusters and outliers, as depicted in the following figure, without you having to tell it how many clusters to identify in the dataset:

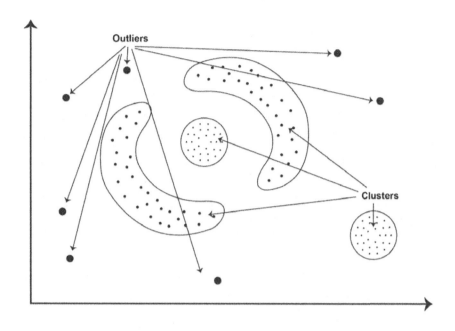

Figure 2.3: Clusters and outliers classified by DBSCAN

So, DBSCAN can find regions of high density separated by regions of low density in a scatter plot.

Steps for DBSCAN

As mentioned before, DBSCAN doesn't require you to choose a number of clusters, but you have to choose the other two parameters to perform DBSCAN. The first parameter is commonly denoted by ε (epsilon), which denotes the maximum distance between two points in the same cluster. Another parameter is the minimum number of points in a cluster, which is usually denoted by `minPts`. Now we'll look at the DBSCAN clustering algorithm step by step:

1. Select any point, **R**, in the dataset.
2. Find all the points within distance epsilon from point **R**.

3. If the total number of points within distance epsilon from point **R** is greater than `minPts`, then it is a cluster and **R** is the core point.

4. If the total number of points within distance epsilon from point p is less than `minPts`, all the points within distance epsilon will be classified as noise. We then start the process again from step 2 after selecting a new point, **R**, that has neither been classified as noise nor as part of the cluster.

5. Repeat the process for other points in the cluster to find points within distance epsilon that are not already in the cluster. Those new points will also be classified in the same cluster.

6. Once these steps have been performed for all points in the cluster, repeat the same process by selecting a new random point, **R**, that has neither been classified in a cluster nor as noise.

So, to illustrate of the preceding algorithm, let's take an example with epsilon as **x** and the minimum number of points in a cluster as 4. Look at the following figure:

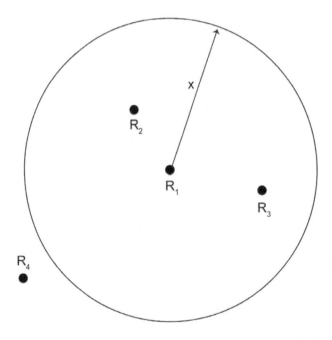

Figure 2.4: Only 2 points lie within x distance of point R1

Only three points lie within **x** distance of point **R1** and our threshold for the minimum number of points within **x** radius is four. So, these four points will be classified as outliers or noise. But if there were one more point, **R5**, somewhere between **R1** and **R4**, all of these four points would belong to a cluster as in the following figure:

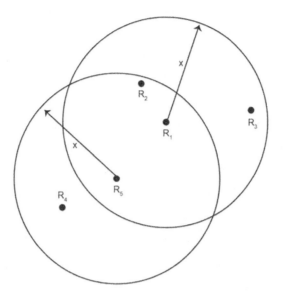

Figure 2.5: All of these four points belong to a cluster

In the preceding figure, points **R1** and **R5** are core points, as they have four points each within **x** distance from them. And points **R4**, **R2**, and **R3** are not core points, as illustrated in the following figure:

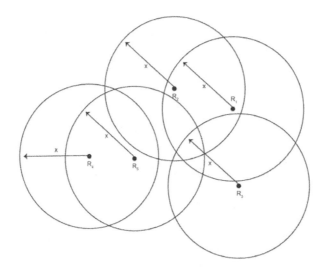

Figure 2.6: Core versus non-core points

Any point outside of any of these circles would be classified as a noise point like, **R6** in the following figure:

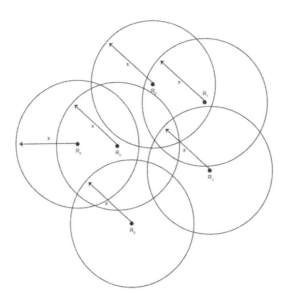

Figure 2.7: Noise point R6

Exercise 11: Implementing DBSCAN

In this exercise, we will have a look at the implementation of DBSCAN using the Iris dataset. To perform DBSCAN, we will execute the following steps:

1. Store the first two columns of the Iris dataset in **iris_data**:

    ```
    iris_data<-iris[,1:2]
    ```

2. Import the **dbscan** library, which contains the implementation of various DBSCAN algorithms:

    ```
    install.packages("dbscan")
    library(dbscan)
    ```

3. Calculate and store clusters in the **clus** variable. In this step, you also have to choose the values of epsilon and **minPts**:

    ```
    clus<-dbscan(iris_data,eps=.3,minPts = 5)
    ```

    > **Note**
    >
    > You can experiment with the values of epsilon. To get the desired output, we have set the value as 0.3.

4. Import the **factoextra** library for visualizing clusters:

    ```
    install.packages("factoextra") #use it only the first time if library is
    not installed already
    library(factoextra)
    ```

5. Plot the cluster centers. You need to enter the variable in which you stored the results of DBSCAN as the first parameter of the **plot** function. As the second parameter, you need to enter a dataset. In our case, it's **iris_data**. The **geom** variable in the function is used to define the geometry of the graph. We will only use **point**. Now, **ggtheme** is used to select a theme for the plot. **palette** is used to select the geometry of the points. The **ellipse** value is set to false so that the function does not draw an outline of the clusters.:

    ```
    fviz_cluster(clus,data=iris_data,geom =
    "point",palette="set2",ggtheme=theme_minimal(),ellipse=FALSE)
    ```

Here is the output:

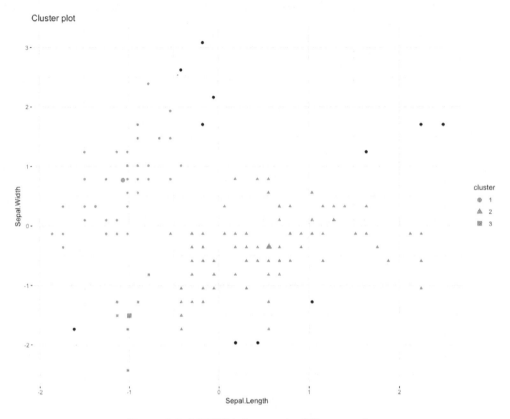

Figure 2.8: DBSCAN clusters in different colors

In Figure 2.8, there are three clusters in orange, blue, and green. The points in black are noise or outliers. Points in orange here belong to one species, but points in green belong to two different species.

> **Note**
>
> You can make a quick comparison of this scatter plot with Figure 1.18 of *Chapter 1, Introduction to Clustering Methods*.

DBSCAN is different from all the clustering we've studied so far and is one of the most common and one of the most frequently cited types of clustering methods in scientific literature. There are a few advantages that DBSCAN has over other clustering methods:

- You don't need to select the number of clusters initially.

- It does not produce different results every time you run it, unlike k-means or other "k-type" clustering methods, where starting points can have an effect on the end results. So, results are reproducible.

- It can discover clusters of any shape in data.

But there are also a few disadvantages of DBSCAN:

- The correct set of parameters, that is, epsilon and `minPts`, are hard to determine for the proper clustering of data.

- DBSCAN cannot differentiate between clusters based on density. If a dataset has large variations in density, it may not perform as well.

Uses of DBSCAN

As DBSCAN is one of the most frequently cited clustering methods, it has many practical uses. Some of the practical real-life uses of DBSCAN clustering are the following:

- DBSCAN can be used in urban planning in many ways. For example, given data about crime incidents with locations, DBSCAN can be used to identify crime-ridden areas in a city. This data can be used to plan police force deployment or even investigate potential gang activity.

- DBSCAN can be used to form strategies in games such as cricket and basketball. Given the data related to ball pitching on a cricket pitch, you can identify the strengths and weaknesses of batsmen and bowlers. Or if we have data on a batsman hitting the ball, data gained from DBSCAN can be used to adjust fielding accordingly.

- During natural disasters or the spread of viral diseases, the geolocation of tweets can be used to identify highly affected areas with DBSCAN.

Activity 6: Implementing DBSCAN and Visualizing the Results

In this activity, we will perform DBSCAN and compare the results with k-means clustering. To do this, we are going to use the **multishapes** dataset, which contains simulated data that represents different shapes.

These steps will help you complete the activity:

1. Generate and store the **multishapes** dataset in the **factoextra** library.

2. Plot the first two columns of the **multishapes** dataset.

3. Perform k-means clustering on the dataset and visualize.

4. Perform DBSCAN on the dataset and visualize the data to compare the results with k-means clustering.

> **Note**
>
> The solution for this activity can be found on page 213.

The plot of DBSCAN clustering will look as follows:

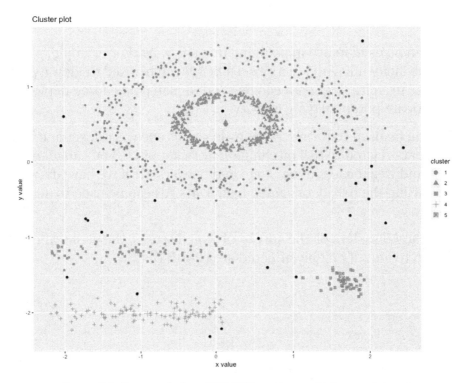

Figure 2.9: Expected plot of DBCAN on the multishapes dataset

Here, all the points in black are anomalies and are not classified in any cluster, and the clusters formed in DBSCAN cannot be obtained with any other type of clustering method. These clusters have taken several types of shapes and sizes, whereas, in k-means, all clusters are of approximately spherical shape.

Introduction to Hierarchical Clustering

The last type of clustering that we're going to study is hierarchical clustering. A hierarchy is defined as "a system in which people or things are placed in a series of levels with different importance or status." Hierarchical clustering merges clusters sequentially. This sequence of merged clusters is called a hierarchy. We can see that more clearly with the help of the output of a hierarchical clustering algorithm called a **dendrogram**.

Hierarchical clustering comes in two types:

- Agglomerative

- Divisive

Since both types of hierarchical clustering are similar, it makes sense to study both of them together.

Agglomerative clustering is also known as the bottom-up approach to hierarchical clustering. In this method, each data point is assumed to be a single cluster at the outset. From there, we start merging the most similar clusters according to a similarity or distance metric until all the data points are merged in a single cluster.

In divisive clustering, we do exactly the opposite. It is a top-down approach to hierarchical clustering. In this method, all the data points are assumed to be in a single cluster initially. From there on, we start splitting the cluster into multiple clusters until each data point is a cluster on its own. Differences and similarities between the two clustering types will become clear in further sections. But first, we should try to understand why we need this other type of clustering and the special purpose it serves that other types of clustering don't serve. Hierarchical clustering is used mainly for the following reasons:

- Just like DBSCAN, we don't have to choose a number of clusters initially.

- The final output of hierarchical clustering, dendrograms, can help us visualize the clustering results in a way that means we don't need to re-run the algorithm to see a different number of clusters in the results.

- Unlike k-means, any type of distance metric can be used in hierarchical clustering.

- It can find complex-shaped clusters, unlike other clustering algorithms, such as k-means, which only finds approximately spherical clusters.

The combination of all the preceding factors make hierarchical clustering an important clustering method in unsupervised learning.

Types of Similarity Metrics

As described previously, agglomerative hierarchical clustering is a bottom-up approach to hierarchical clustering. We merge the most similar clusters one by one based on a similarity metric. This similarity metric can be chosen from one of several different types:

- **Single link**: In single-link similarity, we measure the distance or similarity between the two most similar points of two clusters:

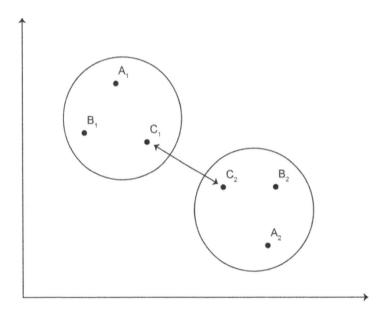

Figure 2.10: Demonstration of the single-link metric

- **Complete link**: In this type of metric, we measure the distance or similarity between the two most distant points of a cluster:

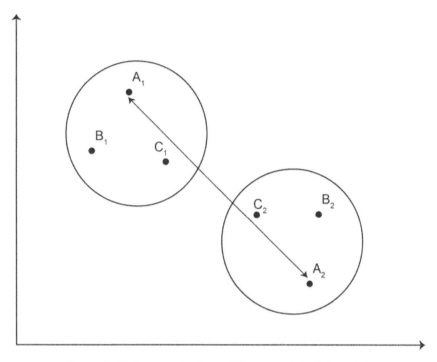

Figure 2.11: Demonstration of the complete-link metric

- **Group average**: In this metric, we measure the average distance between all members of one cluster and any members of a second cluster:

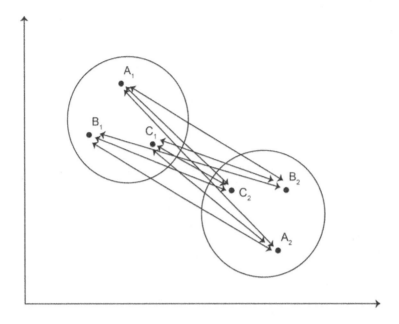

Figure 2.12: Demonstration of the group-average metric

Note

The distance between members of the same cluster is not measured in these similarity metrics.

- **Centroid similarity**: In this type of similarity, the similarity between two clusters is defined as the similarity between the centroids of both clusters:

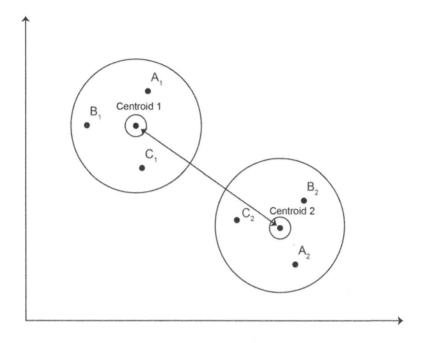

Figure 2.13: Demonstration of centroid similarity

Steps to Perform Agglomerative Hierarchical Clustering

With the knowledge of these similarity metrics, we can now understand the algorithm to perform agglomerative hierarchical clustering:

1. Initialize each point as a single cluster.

2. Calculate the similarity metric between every pair of clusters. The similarity metric can be any of the four metrics we just read about.

3. Merge the two most similar clusters according to the similarity metric selected in step 2.

4. Repeat the process from step 2 until we have only one cluster left.

This whole process will produce a graph called a dendrogram. This graph records the clusters formed at each step. A simple dendrogram with very few elements would look as follows:

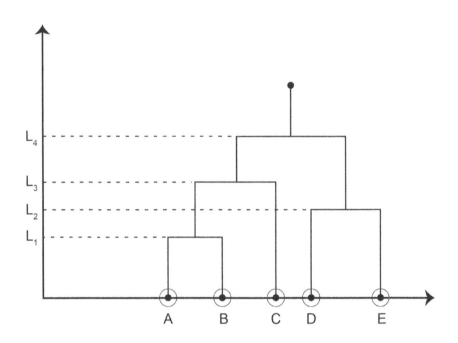

Figure 2.14: A sample dendrogram

In the preceding dendogram, suppose that point A and point B are the closest among all points on the similarity measure that we are using. Their closeness is used to determine the height of the joining line, which is at **L1** in the case of point **A** and point **B**. So, point **A** and point **B** are clustered first. After that, at **L2**, point **D** and point **E** are clustered, then, at **L3**, points **A**, **B**, and **C** are clustered. At this point, we have two clusters that are joined together to form one cluster at **L4**.

Now, to get clusters from this dendrogram, we make horizontal cuts. For example, if we make a cut between L4 and L3, we will get two clusters:

- Cluster 1 – A, B, and C

- Cluster 2 – D and E

The clusters will look as follows:

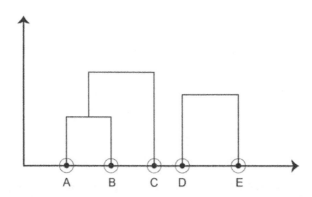

Figure 2.15: Clusters represented in the dendrogram

Similarly, if we make a horizontal cut in the dendrogram between L3 and L2, we will get three clusters:

- Cluster 1 – A and B

- Cluster 2 – C

- Cluster 3 – D and E

The clusters will look as follows:

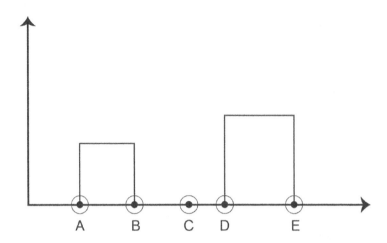

Figure 2.16: Representation of clusters in a dendrogram

So, to get a different number of clusters, we didn't need to rerun the process. With this method, we can get any number of clusters possible in the data without executing the whole process again.

Exercise 12: Agglomerative Clustering with Different Similarity Measures

In this exercise, we're going to perform agglomerative hierarchical clustering with different similarity measures and compare the results:

1. Let's enter the last three columns of the **iris_flowers** dataset, which are petal length, petal width, and species, in the **iris_data** variable, as follows:

    ```
    iris_data<-iris[,3:5]
    install.packages('cluster')
    library(cluster)
    ```

2. In this step, we use the **hclust** function to get hierarchical clustering. In the **hclust** function, we need to enter the pair-wise distance of all the points with each other, for which we use the **dist()** function. The second parameter, **method**, is used to define the similarity measure for the hierarchical clustering:

    ```
    h.clus<-hclust(dist(iris_data),method="complete")
    ```

3. Now, let's plot the results of the hierarchical clustering in a dendrogram, as follows:

```
plot(h.clus)
```

The output is as follows:

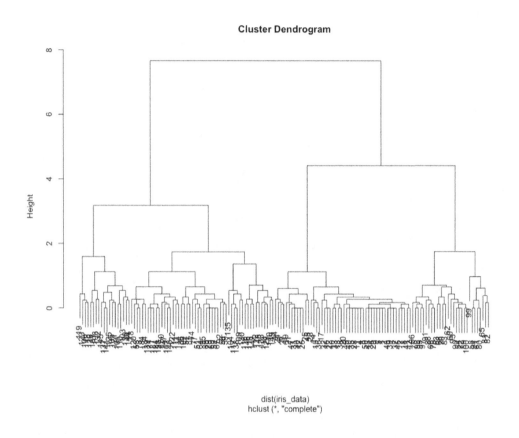

Figure 2.17: Dendrogram derived from the complete similarity metric

4. To select a number of clusters from the preceding dendrogram, we can use an R function called **cutree**. We feed the results of **hclust** along with the number of clusters to this function:

```
clusterCut <- cutree(h.clus, 3)
table(clusterCut, iris_data$Species)
```

The output table is as follows:

```
clusterCut setosa versicolor virginica
         1     50          0         0
         2      0         21        50
         3      0         29         0
```

Figure 2.18: Table displaying the distribution of clusters

The setosa and virginica species get classified accurately with this clustering method.

5. Use **single** as a similarity metric as follows:.

```
h.clus<-hclust(dist(iris_data),method = "single")
plot(h.clus)
```

The output is as follows:

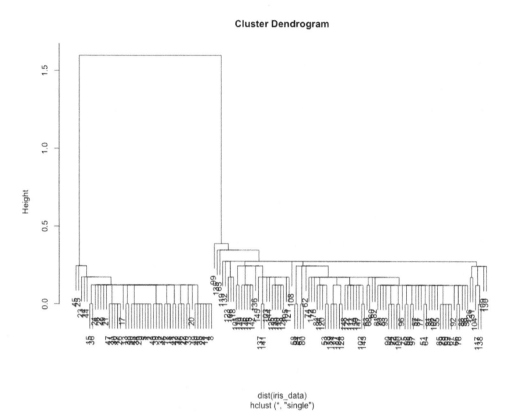

Figure 2.19: Dendrogram derived from the single similarity metric

Notice how this dendrogram is different from the dendrogram created with the **complete** similarity metric.

6. Divide this dataset into three clusters:

```
clusterCut <- cutree(h.clus, 3)
table(clusterCut, iris_data$Species)
```

The output is as follows:

```
clusterCut setosa versicolor virginica
         1     50          0         0
         2      0         49        50
         3      0          1         0
```

Figure 2.20: Table displaying the distribution of clusters

Here, our clustering method is successfully able to separate only one class from the other two.

7. Now let's perform hierarchical clustering with the **average** similarity metric:

```
h.clus<-hclust(dist(iris_data),method = "average")
plot(h.clus)
```

The output is as follows:

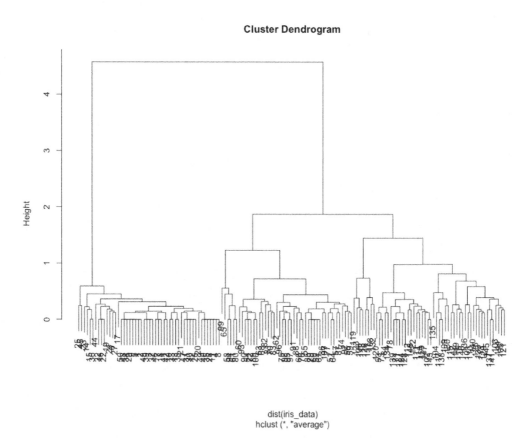

Figure 2.21: Dendrogram derived from the average similarity metric

8. Let's divide the preceding dendrogram into three clusters again and see the results:

```
clusterCut <- cutree(h.clus, 3)
table(clusterCut, iris_data$Species)
```

The output is as follows:

```
clusterCut setosa versicolor virginica
         1     50          0         0
         2      0         45         1
         3      0          5        49
```

Figure 2.22: Table displaying the distribution of clusters

Here, with the **average** similarity metric, we get almost completely correct classification results.

9. Now let's try creating a dendrogram with the last similarity metric, **centroid**:

```
h.clus<-hclust(dist(iris_data),method = "centroid")
plot(h.clus)
```

The output is as follows:

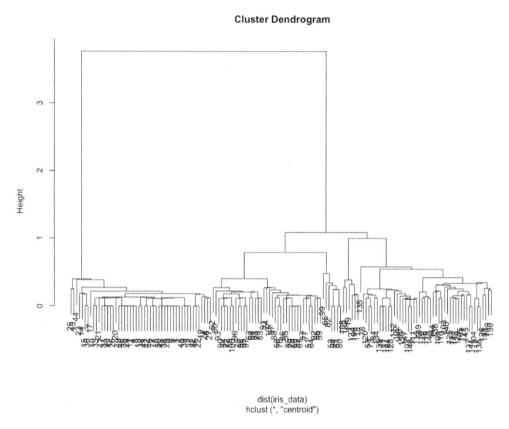

Figure 2.23: Dendrogram derived from the centroid similarity metric

10. Now, let's divide the preceding dendrogram into three clusters and see the results:

```
clusterCut <- cutree(h.clus, 3)
table(clusterCut, iris_data$Species)
```

The output is as follows:

```
clusterCut setosa versicolor virginica
         1     50          0         0
         2      0         45         1
         3      0          5        49
```

Figure 2.24: Table displaying the distribution of clusters

Although dendrograms of clusters with the **average** and **centroid** similarity metrics look different, they have the same number of elements in each cluster when we cut the dendrogram at three clusters.

Divisive Clustering

Divisive clustering is the opposite of agglomerative clustering. In agglomerative clustering, we start with each point as its own cluster, while in divisive clustering, we start with the whole dataset as one cluster and from there, we start dividing it into more clusters:

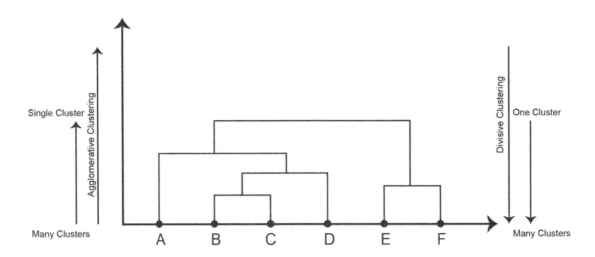

Figure 2.25: Representation of agglomerative and divisive clustering

So, the divisive clustering process can be summarized in one figure as follows:

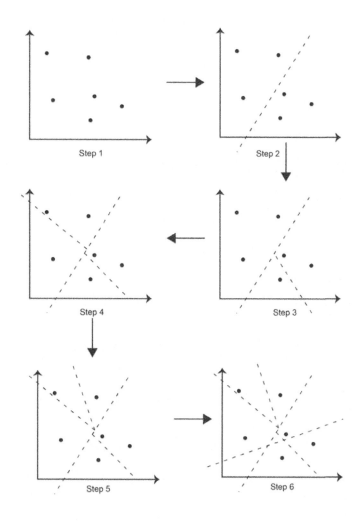

Figure 2.26: Representation of the divisive clustering process

Steps to Perform Divisive Clustering

From step 1 to step 6, the divisive clustering process keeps on dividing points into further clusters until each point is a cluster on its own. Figure 2.26 shows the first 6 steps of the divisive clustering process, but to correctly run the complete process, we will need to execute as many steps as there are points in the dataset.

So, for divisive clustering, we will use the DIANA algorithm – DIANA stands for Divisive Analysis. For this, we need to carry out the following steps:

1. Start with all the points in the dataset in one single cluster.

2. Choose two of the most dissimilar clusters of all the possible clusters in the dataset according to any distance metric you like.

3. Repeat step 2 until all the points in the dataset are clustered on their own.

We're going to use the **cluster** library in R to perform DIANA clustering.

Exercise 13: Performing DIANA Clustering

In this exercise, we will perform DIANA clustering:

1. Put the petal length, petal width and species name in the **iris_data** variable:

   ```
   iris_data<-iris[,3:5]
   ```

2. Import the **cluster** library:

   ```
   install.packages("cluster")
   library("cluster")
   ```

3. Pass the **iris_data** dataset and the metric by which to measure dissimilarity to the **diana()** function:

   ```
   h.clus<-diana(iris_data, metric="euclidean")
   ```

4. Plot the dendrogram with the **pltree()** function. To plot the dendrogram, pass the results of the **diana** function and the title of the graph to the **pltree()** function:

   ```
   pltree(h.clus, cex = 0.6, main = "Dendrogram of divisive clustering")
   ```

The dendrogram of the divisive clustering results appears as follows:

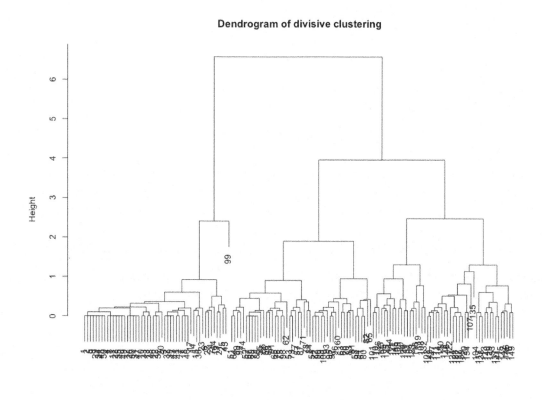

Figure 2.27: Dendrogram of divisive clustering

5. If we divide the preceding dendrogram into three clusters, we'll see that this clustering method is also able to identify different species of flowers on its own:

```
clusterCut <- cutree(h.clus, 3)
table(clusterCut, iris_data$Species)
```

The output is as follows:

```
clusterCut setosa versicolor virginica
         1     50          1         0
         2      0         49         0
         3      0          0        50
```

In the preceding output, only one flower is misclassified into another category. This is the best performance of all the clustering algorithms we have encountered in this book when it comes to classifying flower species without knowing anything about them.

Activity 7: Performing Hierarchical Cluster Analysis on the Seeds Dataset

In this activity, we will perform hierarchical cluster analysis on the seeds dataset. We will see what the results of the clustering are when classifying three types of seeds.

> **Note**
>
> This dataset is taken from the UCI Machine Learning Repository. You can find the dataset at http://archive.ics.uci.edu/ml/machine-learning-databases/00236/. We have downloaded the file, cleaned it, and saved it at https://github.com/TrainingByPackt/Applied-Unsupervised-Learning-with-R/tree/master/Lesson02/Activity07/seeds_data.txt.

These steps will help you complete the activity:

1. Download the seeds dataset from https://github.com/TrainingByPackt/Applied-Unsupervised-Learning-with-R/tree/master/Lesson02/Activity07/seeds_data.txt.

2. Perform agglomerative hierarchical clustering of the dataset and plot the dendrogram.

3. Make a cut at **k=3** and check the results of the clustering by forming a table with original labels.

4. Perform divisive clustering on the dataset and plot the dendrogram.

5. Make cut at **k=3** and check the results of the clustering by forming a table with original labels.

> **Note**
>
> The solution for this activity can be found on page 215.

The output of this activity will be a table that shows how the results of the clustering have performed at classifying the three types of seeds. It will look as follows:

```
         memb
         1   2   3
  1  65   3   1
  2   6   0  64
  3   9  61   0
```

Figure 2.28: Expected table classifying the three types of seeds

Summary

Congratulations on completing the second chapter on clustering techniques! With this, we've covered all the major clustering techniques, including k-modes, DBSCAN, and both types of hierarchical clustering, and we've also looked at what connects them. We can apply these techniques to any type of dataset we may encounter. These new methods, at times, also produced better results on the same dataset that we used in the first chapter. In the next chapter, we're going to study probability distributions and their uses in exploratory data analysis.

3

Probability Distributions

Learning Objectives

By the end of this chapter, you will be able to:

- Generate different distributions in R

- Estimate probability distribution functions for new datasets in R

- Compare the closeness of two different samples of the same distribution or different distributions

In this chapter, we will learn how to use probability distributions as a form of unsupervised learning.

Introduction

In this chapter, we're going to study another aspect of unsupervised learning, called **probability distributions**. Probability distributions are part of classical statistics covered in many mathematical textbooks and courses. With the advent of big data, we've started using probability distributions in exploratory data analysis and other modeling applications as well. So, in this chapter, we're going to study how to use probability distributions in unsupervised learning.

Basic Terminology of Probability Distributions

There are two families of methods in statistics: parametric and non-parametric methods. Non-parametric methods are meant to deal with data that could take any shape. Parametric methods, by contrast, make assumptions about the particular shape that data takes on. These assumptions are often encoded as parameters. The following are the two main parameters that you should be aware of:

- **Mean**: This is the average of all values in the distribution.

- **Standard Deviation**: This is the measure of the spread of values around the mean of a distribution.

Most of the parametric methods in statistics depend in some way on those two parameters. The parametric distributions that we're going to study in this chapter are these:

- Uniform distributions

- Normal distributions

- Log-normal distributions.

- Binomial distributions

- Poisson distributions

- Pareto distributions

Uniform Distribution

In the uniform distribution, all values between an interval, let's say [a,b], are equiprobable. Mathematically, it's defined as follows:

$$f(x) = \begin{cases} \frac{1}{b-a} & \text{for } a \leq x \leq b, \\ 0 & \text{for } x < a \text{ or } x > b \end{cases}$$

Figure 3.1: Mathematical formula for a uniform distribution

It can be plotted on a graph as follows:

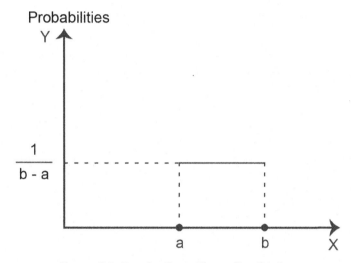

Figure 3.2: Graph of a uniform distribution

The uniform distribution is the simplest of the parametric distributions. There are many processes in the real world that follow uniform sampling:

- If it's raining in a very large area, the distribution of where raindrops will fall can be assumed to be uniform in a small area.

- The last digit of a social security number should follow a uniform distribution for any subset of people, such as for all the CEOs of start-ups in California.

- Uniform random sampling is very important for generating data for experiments and running controlled trials.

Exercise 14: Generating and Plotting Uniform Samples in R

In this exercise, we will generate uniform samples and plot them. To do this, perform the following steps:

1. Use the built-in **runif** R function to generate uniform samples. Firstly, enter the number of samples you want to generate. Here we're generating 1,000 samples. Then, enter the **min** value and **max** value:

    ```
    uni<-runif(1000, min=0, max=100)
    ```

2. After storing the generated random numbers in the **uni** variable, we'll plot their values versus their index:

    ```
    plot(uni)
    ```

    The output is as follows:

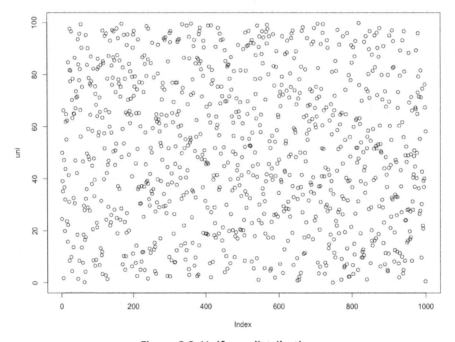

Figure 3.3: Uniform distribution

As you can see, the points are scattered everywhere almost equally. We can also plot a histogram of this to get a clearer picture of the distribution.

3. We'll use the **hist()** function of R to plot a histogram of the generated sample:

    ```
    hist(uni)
    ```

    The output is as follows:

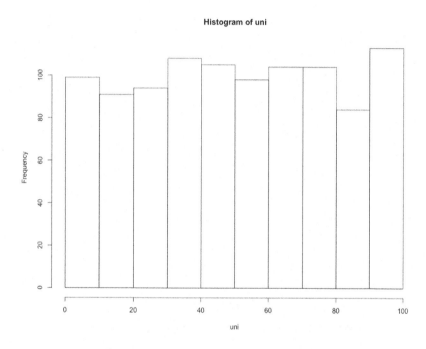

Figure 3.4: Histogram of the distribution

As you can see, it's not exactly flat, as we envisioned it previously. It's more or less uniform, but not exactly uniform, because it was randomly generated. Each time we generate a new sample, it will resemble this histogram, and most probably won't be exactly flat, because of the noise that comes with all random sampling methods.

Normal Distribution

The normal distribution is a type of parametric distribution that is governed by two parameters: mean and standard deviation from the mean. It's symmetric about the mean, and most values are near the mean. Its curve is also known as a bell curve:

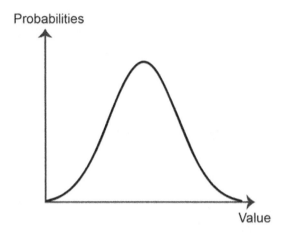

Figure 3.5: Approximate representation of a bell curve, typical with normally distributed data

The normal distribution is defined by the following equation:

$$P(x) = \frac{1}{\sigma\sqrt{2\pi}} e^{-(x-\mu)^2/(2\sigma^2)}$$

Figure 3.6: Equation for the normal distribution

Here, μ is the mean and σ is the standard deviation.

The normal distribution is a very common type of distribution in the real world. The following are some examples of the normal distribution:

- The height of NBA players is approximately normally distributed.

- The scores of students in a class could have a distribution that is very close to the normal distribution.

- The Nile's yearly flow volume is normally distributed.

Now we're going to generate and plot a normal distribution in R.

Exercise 15: Generating and Plotting a Normal Distribution in R

In this exercise, we will generate a normal distribution to model the test scores (out of 100) of 1,000 school pupils and plot them. To do this, perform the following steps:

1. Generate a normal distribution by entering the number of samples, the mean, and the standard deviation in the **rnorm** function in R:

    ```
    nor<-rnorm(1000,mean=50, sd= 15)
    ```

2. Plot the generated numbers against their index:

    ```
    plot(nor)
    ```

    The output is as follows:

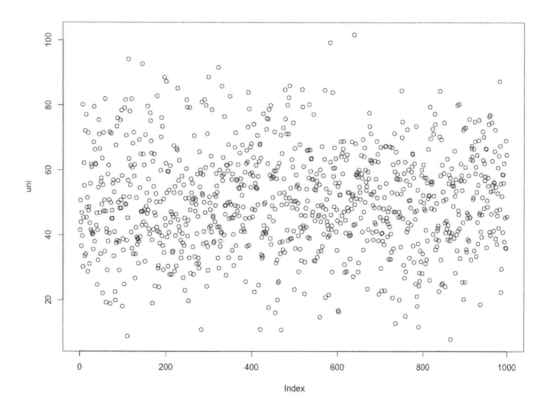

Figure 3.7: Normal distribution

As you can see here, most values are around the mean of 50, and as we move away from 50, the number of points starts decreasing. This distribution will be clarified by with a histogram in the next step.

3. Plot a histogram of the normal distribution with the **hist()** function:

```
hist(nor)
```

The output is as follows:

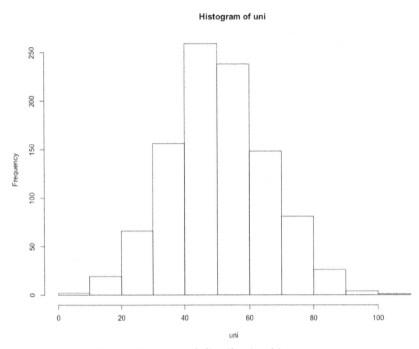

Figure 3.8: Normal distribution histogram

You can see that this shape very much resembles the bell curve of the normal distribution.

Skew and Kurtosis

As we have seen, many of the distributions you'll see in practice are assumed to be normal distributions. But not every distribution is a normal distribution. To measure the degree to which a distribution deviates from a standard normal distribution, we use two parameters:

- Skew
- Kurtosis

The **Skew** of a distribution is the measure its asymmetry compared to the standard normal distribution. In a dataset with high skew, the mean and mode will differ from each other. The skew can be of two types: positive and negative:

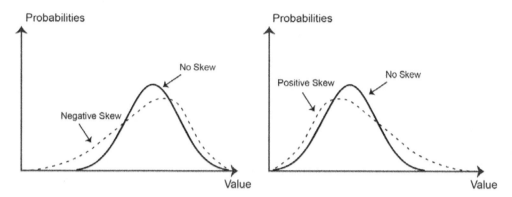

Figure 3.9: Negative skew and positive skew

Negative skew is when there is a long tail of values on the left-hand side of the mean, and positive skew is when there is a long tail of values on the right-hand side of the mean. Skewness can also be expressed with the following formula:

$$Skewness = \frac{E[(X - \mu)^3]}{\sigma^3}$$

Figure 3.10: Mathematical formula for skewness

Here, $E[(X - \mu)^3]$ is the expected value or the mean of $(X - \mu)^3$, where μ and σ are the mean and standard deviation of the distribution respectively.

Kurtosis is a measure of the fatness of tails of a distribution compared to the normal distribution. Kurtosis doesn't introduce asymmetry in a distribution, unlike skewness. An illustration of this is provided here:

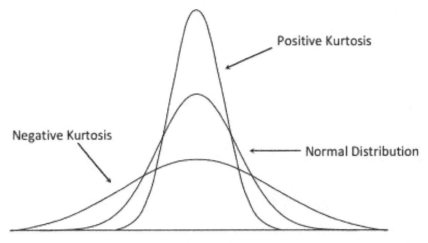

Figure 3.11: Kurtosis demonstration

Kurtosis can also be expressed with the following formula:

$$K = \frac{E[(X - \mu)^4]}{\sigma^4}$$

Figure 3.12: Mathematical formula for Kurtosis

Here, $E[(X - \mu)^4]$ is the expected or average value of $(X - \mu)^4$, where μ and σ are the mean and standard deviation of the distribution respectively. A standard normal distribution has a skew of 0 and a kurtosis measure equal to 3. Because normal distributions are very common, we sometimes just measure excess kurtosis, which is this:

```
Kexcess = K - 3
```

So, a normal distribution has excess kurtosis equal to 0.

Log-Normal Distributions

Log-normal distributions are distributions of values whose logarithm is distributed normally. If we show a log-normal distribution on a log scale, it is perfectly identical to a normal distribution, but if we show it on a standard distribution scale, it acquires very high positive skewness:

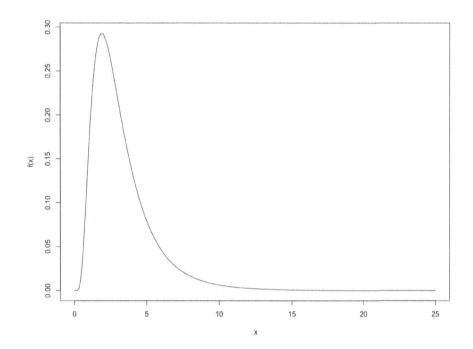

Figure 3.13: Log-normal distribution

To show that the log-normal distribution is a normal distribution on log scale, we're going to do an exercise.

Log-normal distributions are used in the field of financial risk management to model stock prices. As the growth factor is assumed to be normally distributed, the prices of stock can be modeled log-normally. This distribution is also used in calculations related to option pricing, including value at risk (VaR).

Exercise 16: Generating a Log-Normal Distribution from a Normal Distribution

In this exercise, we will generate a log-normal distribution from a normal distribution. To do this, perform the following steps:

1. Generate a normal distribution and store the values in a variable:

   ```
   nor<-rnorm(1000,mean=5, sd= 1)
   ```

2. Plot a histogram of the normal distribution with 100 different bins:

   ```
   hist(nor,breaks = 100)
   ```

   The output is as follows:

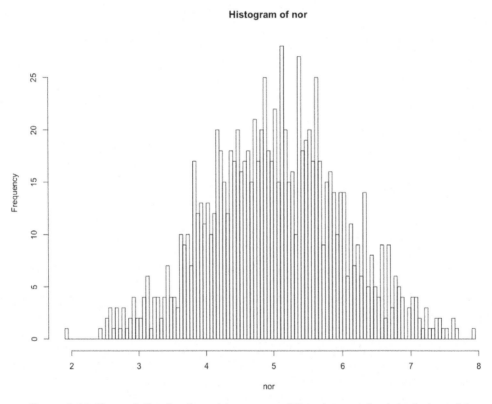

Figure 3.14: Normal distribution with a mean of 5 and a standard deviation of 1

3. Create a vector that will store 1,000 values for a log-normal distribution:

   ```
   lnor <- vector("list", 1000)
   ```

4. Enter exponential values into the **lnor** vector. The exponent function is the inverse function of the log function:

```
for (x in 1:1000){
   lnor[x]=exp(nor[x])
}
```

5. Plot a histogram of **lnor**:

```
hist(as.integer(lnor), breaks = 200)
```

The output is as follows:

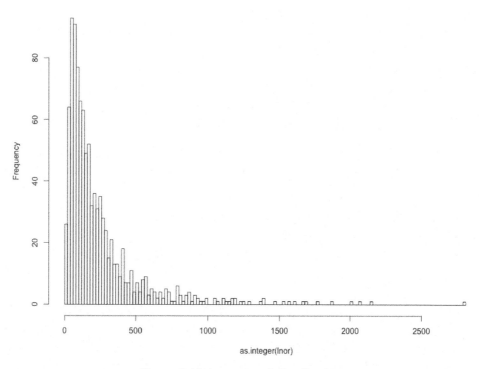

Figure 3.15: Log-normal distribution

Notice how the preceding figure looks like a log-normal distribution plot and that this

plot is generated from a normal distribution. If we plot a new graph after taking the log of values in the preceding graph, then it'll be a normal distribution again.

The Binomial Distribution

The binomial distribution is a discrete distribution, as opposed to normal or uniform distribution, which are continuous in nature. The binomial distribution is used to model the probability of multiple events occurring together where there are two possibilities for each event. One example where the binomial distribution can be applied is in finding out the probability of heads coming up for all three coins when we toss three coins together.

The mean and variance of a binomial distribution are n*p and n*p(1-p) respectively, where p is the probability of success and n is the number of trials. The binomial distribution is symmetric when p= 0.5. When p is less than 0.5, it's skewed more toward the right, and is skewed more toward the left when p is greater than 0.5.

The formula for the binomial distribution is as follows:

```
P(x) = n!/((n-x)!x!)*(p^x)*((1-p)^x)
```

Here, n is the total number of trials, x is the focal number of trials, and p is the probability of success.

Exercise 17: Generating a Binomial Distribution

In this exercise, we will generate a binomial distribution to model the number of times that heads will come up when tossing a coin 50 times. To do this, perform the following steps:

1. To generate a binomial distribution, we'll first need a sequence of 50 digits as an index, which will act as the number of successes we are interested in modeling. This would be x in the formula in the previous section:

   ```
   s <- seq(0,50,by = 1)
   ```

2. Now we will pass **s** as a parameter to the **dbinom()** function in R, which will calculate probabilities for every value in the **s** variable and store them in a new **probs** variable. Firstly, in the function, we enter the sequence that will encode the range of the number of successes. Then, we enter the length of the sequence, and then we enter the probability of success:

   ```
   probs <- dbinom(s,50,0.5)
   ```

3. In the final step, we plot **s** and **probs** together:

```
plot(s,probs)
```

The output is as follows:

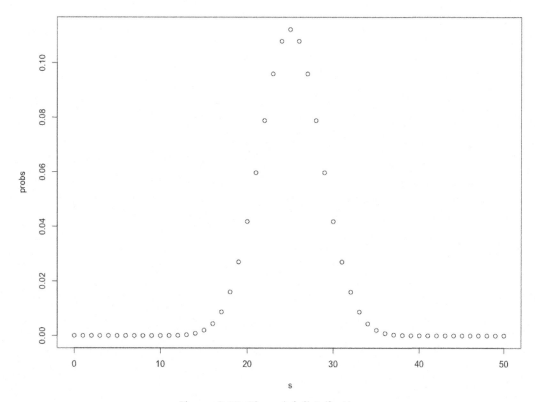

Figure 3.16: Binomial distribution

Here, the x axis shows a number of heads we are interested in, and the y axis shows the probability of getting exactly that number of heads in 50 trials. When we toss a coin 50 times, the most probable outcome is that we will get 25 heads and 25 tails, but the probability of getting all 50 heads or tails is very low. This is explained very well by the preceding graph.

The Poisson Distribution

The Poisson distribution is another type of discrete distribution that is used to model occurrences of an event in a given time period given the mean number of occurrences of that event in a particular time period.

It's formulated by the following equation:

$$P(X = x) = \frac{\lambda^x e^{-\lambda}}{x!}$$

Figure 3.17: Formula for poisson distribution

Here, lambda is the mean number of occurrences in a given time period, **e** is Euler's constant, and **x** is the number of events for which you want to find the probability. Given the number of new people that have been observed coming to an event every minute so far, the, Poisson distribution can be used to calculate the probability of any number of people coming to that event in the next minute.

A Poisson distribution plot looks like this:

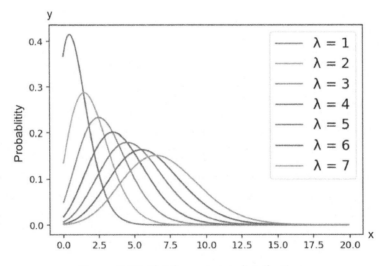

Figure 3.18: Plot for poisson distribution

Here, we can see probabilities of the different values of **x** vary with respect to lambda.

The Pareto Distribution

The pareto distribution is an exponent-based probability distribution. This distribution was invented to model the 80:20 rule that is observed in many real-world situations. Some fascinating situations that follow the 80:20 rule are listed here:

- Approximately 80% of the world's wealth is owned by 20% of people.

- In business management, it was found that for most companies, 80% of their revenue was generated by 20% of their customers.

- It is said that 20% of all drivers cause 80% of all accidents.

There are many other real-world observations that can be modeled by the Pareto distribution. The mathematical formula of the Pareto distribution is as follows:

$$F(x) = \begin{cases} \dfrac{\alpha x_m^{\alpha}}{x_m^{\alpha+1}} & x \geq x_m, \\ 0 & x < x_m. \end{cases}$$

Figure 3.19: Mathematical formula of the Pareto distribution

Introduction to Kernel Density Estimation

So far, we've studied parametric distributions in this chapter, but in real life, all distributions are either approximations of parametric distributions or don't resemble any parametric distributions at all. In such cases, we use a technique called **Kernel Density Estimation**, or **KDE**, to estimate their probability distributions.

KDE is used to estimate the probability density function of distributions or random variables with given finite points of that distribution using something called a kernel. This will be more clear to you after you continue further in the chapter.

KDE Algorithm

Contrary to what it might seem like given the heavy name, KDE is a very simple two-step process:

1. Choosing a kernel

2. Placing the kernel on data points and taking the sum of kernels

A kernel is a non-negative symmetric function that is used to model distributions. For example, in KDE, a normal distribution function is the most commonly used kernel function. Kernel functions can be of different types. They are very much related to the distributions we studied earlier in the chapter. Some of the types are summarized here:

- In a uniform kernel, all values in a range are given equal weightage. This is represented as follows:

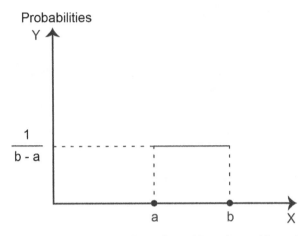

Figure 3.20: Representation of a uniform kernel function

- In a triangular kernel, weightage increases linearly as values move toward the middle of the range. This is represented as follows:

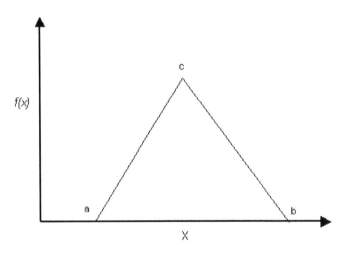

Figure 3.21: Representation of a triangular kernel function

- In a Gaussian kernel, weightage is distributed normally. This is represented as follows:

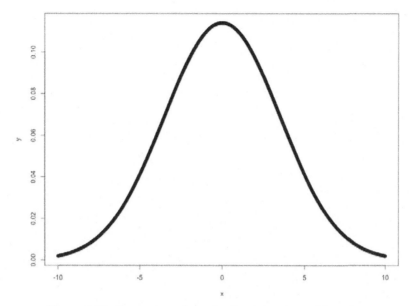

Figure 3.22: Representation of a Gaussian kernel function

Along with the kernel, in the first step, we have to choose another parameter called the bandwidth of the kernel. Bandwidth is the parameter that affects the smoothness of the kernel. Choosing the right bandwidth is very important, even more important than choosing the right kernel. We'll look at an example here.

Exercise 18: Visualizing and Understanding KDE

Let's suppose we have a distribution of five different points (1, 2, 3, 4, and 5). Let's visualize and understand KDE using this example:

1. Store the vector of the five points in a variable:

```
x<- c(1,2,3,4,5)
```

2. Plot the points:

```
y<-c(0,0,0,0,0)
plot(x,y)
```

The output is as follows:

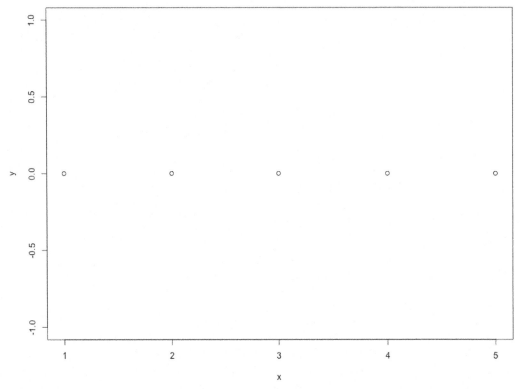

Figure 3.23: Plot of the five points

3. Install the **kdensity** package, if you don't have it already, and import it:

```
install.packages("kdensity")
library('kdensity')
```

4. Compute the kernel density with the **kdensity()** function. Enter the distribution, **x**, and the bandwidth parameter as **.35**. The kernel is **gaussian** by default:

```
dist <- kdensity(x, bw=.35)
```

5. Plot the KDE as follows:

```
plot(dist)
```

The output is as follows:

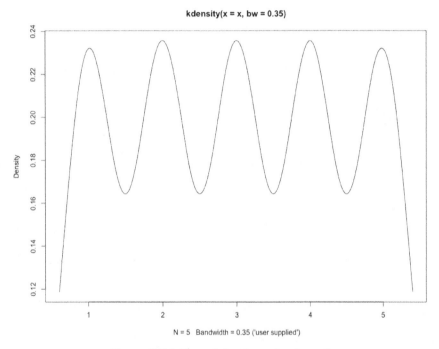

Figure 3.24: Plot of the Gaussian kernel

This is the final output of KDE. In this next step, it assumed that there was a Gaussian kernel centered on every point (1, 2, 3, 4, and 5) and summed them together to get this plot. The following figure will make it clearer:

Note

This graph is for illustration purposes rather than for generation in R.

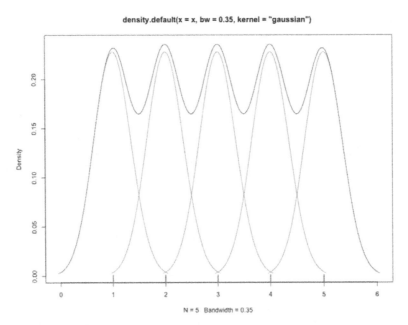

Figure 3.25: Gaussian kernel plotted on each point

As you can see in the preceding figure, a Gaussian kernel was plotted on each one of the points and then all the kernels were summed to get the final curve.

Now, what if we were to change the bandwidth to 0.5 instead of 0.35?

6. Change the bandwidth to 0.5 in the **kdensity()** function and plot the **kdensity** plot again:

```
dist <- kdensity(x, bw=.5)
plot(dist)
```

The output is as follows:

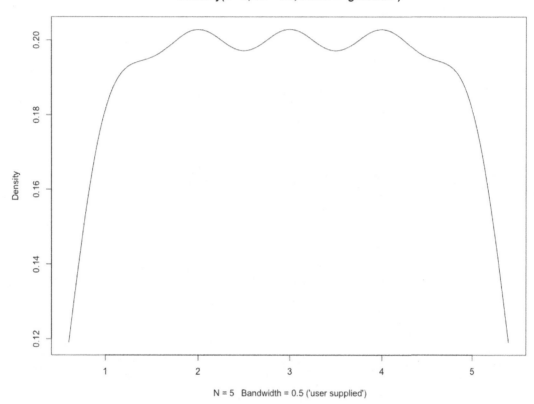

Figure 3.26: Plot of the Gaussian kernel with a bandwidth of .5

You can see that the kernel is much smoother now. The following kernels were used:

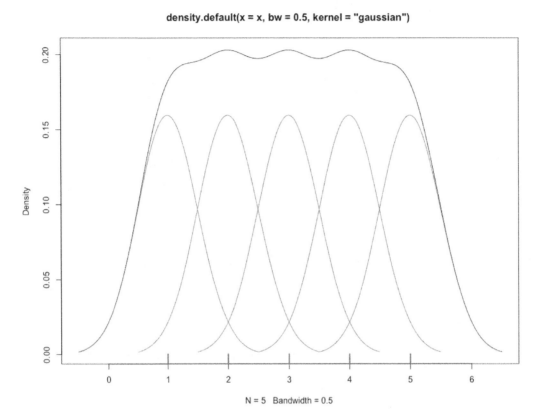

Figure 3.27: Gaussian kernel plotted on each point

> **Note**
>
> The graph is for illustration purposes rather than for generation in R.

This time, the kernels are much wider.

If we were given a sufficient amount of points for estimation, the choice of kernel wouldn't change the shape of the final KDE as much as the choice of bandwidth parameter. So, choosing the ideal bandwidth parameter is an important step. There are many techniques that are used to select the ideal bandwidth parameter. Studying them is beyond the scope of this book, but the R libraries can take care of selecting the ideal parameter on their own. We'll study this in the next exercise.

Exercise 19: Studying the Effect of Changing Kernels on a Distribution

In this exercise, we'll generate two normal distributions with different standard deviations and means, and combine them both to generate their combined KDE:

1. Generate two different normal distributions and store them in two variables:

```
y1 <- rnorm(100,mean = 0, sd = 1)
y2<-rnorm(100, mean = 3, sd=.2)
```

2. Combine the generated distributions and plot them:

```
y3<-c(y1,y2)
plot(y3)
```

The output is as follows:

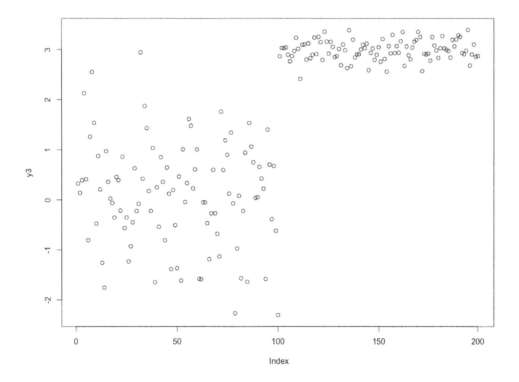

Figure 3.28: Plot of combined distributions

You can see there are two different distributions with different means and spreads (standard deviations).

3. Plot a histogram of **y3** for reference:

```
hist(y3)
```

The output is as follows:

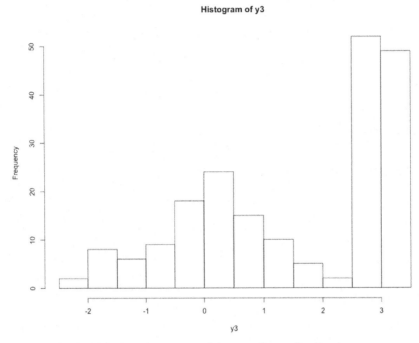

Figure 3.29: Histogram of the resultant distribution

4. Generate and plot the KDE of **y3** with a **gaussian** kernel:

```
dist<-kdensity(y3,kernel = "gaussian")
plot(dist)
```

The output is as follows:

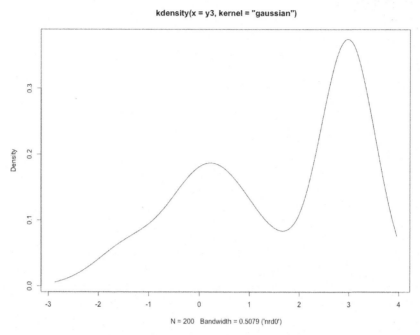

Figure 3.30: Plot of Gaussian kernel density

In the preceding plot, we used a Gaussian kernel and the bandwidth was selected by the function automatically. In this distribution, we have 200 points, which should be enough for generating a robust KDE plot such that changing the kernel type won't produce a significant difference in the final KDE plot. In the next step, let's try and change the kernel and look at the final plot.

5. Generate and plot the KDE with the **triangular** kernel:

```
dist<-kdensity(y3,kernel = "triangular")
plot(dist)
```

The output is as follows:

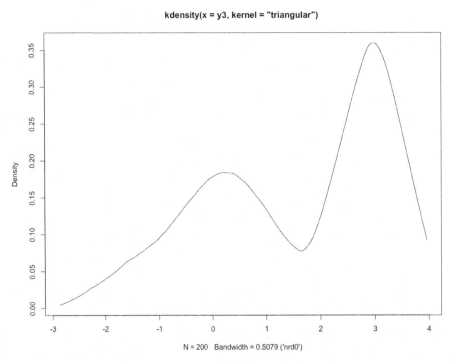

Figure 3.31: KDE with triangular kernel

Both plots with different kernels look almost identical. So, the choice of bandwidth is much more important than the choice of kernel. In this exercise, the bandwidth was chosen automatically by the **kdensity** library of R.

Activity 8: Finding the Standard Distribution Closest to the Distribution of Variables of the Iris Dataset

In this activity, we will find the standard distribution closest to the distribution of variables of the Iris dataset for the setosa species. These steps will help you complete the activity:

1. Load the Iris dataset.

2. Select rows corresponding to the setosa species only.

3. Plot the distribution generated by the **kdensity** function for sepal length and sepal width.

> **Note**
>
> The solution for this activity can be found on page 218.

The final outcome of this activity will be a plot of KDE for sepal width, as follows:

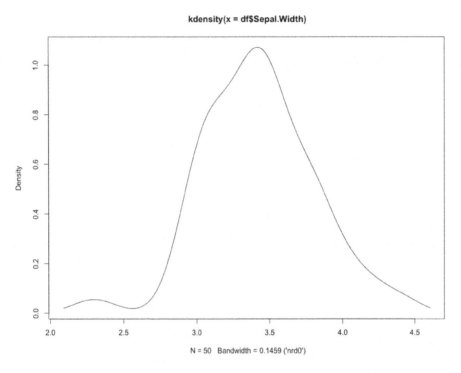

Figure 3.32: Expected plot of the KDE for sepal width

Introduction to the Kolmogorov-Smirnov Test

Now that we've learned how to generate the probability density functions of datasets that don't closely resemble standard distributions, we'll learn how to perform some tests to distinguish these nonstandard distributions from each other.

Sometimes, we're given multiple observed samples of data and we want to find out whether those samples belong to the same distribution or not. In the case of standard distributions, we have multiple tests, such as Student's t-test and z-test, to determine this. For non-standard distributions, or where we don't know the type of distribution, we use the Kolmogorov-Smirnov test. To understand the Kolmogorov-Smirnov test, you first need to understand a few terms:

- **Cumulative Distribution Function (CDF)**: This is a function whose value gives the probability of a random variable being less than or equal to the argument of the function.

- **Null Hypothesis**: In hypothesis testing, a null hypothesis means there is no significant difference between the observed samples. In hypothesis testing, our aim is to falsify the null hypothesis.

The Kolmogorov-Smirnov Test Algorithm

In a Kolmogorov-Smirnov test, we perform the following steps:

1. Generate a CDF for both functions.

2. Specify one of the distributions as the parent distribution.

3. Plot the CDF of the two functions together in the same plot.

4. Find the greatest vertical difference between the points in both CDFs.

5. Calculate the test statistic from the distance measured in the previous step.

6. Find the critical values in the Kolmogorov-Smirnov table.

In R, these steps are automated, so we don't have to do each one of them individually.

Exercise 20: Performing the Kolmogorov-Smirnov Test on Two Samples

To perform the Kolmogorov-Smirnov test on two samples, execute the following steps:

1. Generate two independent distributions for comparison:

```
x_norm<-rnorm(100, mean = 100, sd=5)
y_unif<-runif(100,min=75,max=125)
```

2. Plot the **CDF** of **x_norm** as follows:

```
plot(ecdf(x_norm))
```

The output is as follows:

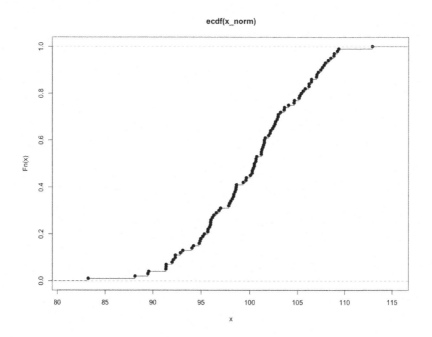

Figure 3.33: Plot of ecdf(x_norm)

To plot **ecdf(y_unif)**, execute the following:

```
plot(ecdf(y_unif),add=TRUE)
```

The output is as follows:

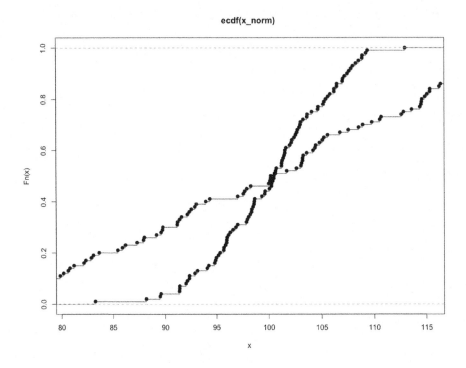

Figure 3.34: Plot of ecdf(y_unif)

As you can see, the CDF of the functions look completely different, so the Kolmogorov-Smirnov test will return p values that are very small.

3. Run the Kolmogorov-Smirnov test with the **ks.test()** function in R:

```
ks.test(x_norm,y_unif)
```

The output is as follows:

```
Two-sample Kolmogorov-Smirnov test

data:  x_norm and y_unif
D = 0.29, p-value = 0.0004453
alternative hypothesis: two-sided
```

> **Note**
>
> This exercise depends on randomly generated data. So, when you run this code, some of the numbers might be different. In hypothesis testing, there are two hypotheses: the null hypothesis, and the test hypothesis. The goal of hypothesis testing is to determine whether we have strong enough evidence to reject the null hypothesis. In this case, the null hypothesis is that the two samples were generated by the same distribution, and the test hypothesis is that the two samples were not generated by the same distribution. The p-value represents the probability, assuming the null hypothesis is true, of observing differences as extreme or more extreme than what is observed. When the p-value is very close to zero, we take that as evidence that the null hypothesis is false and vice versa.

As you can see, **ks.test()** returns two values, **D** and p-value. The **D** value is the absolute maximum distance between two points in the CDF of both distributions. The closer it is to zero, the greater the chance that both samples belong to the same distribution. The p-value has the same interpretation as in any other case.

In our case, **D** is **0.29** and the p-value is very low, near zero. So, we reject the null hypothesis that both samples belong to the same distribution. Now, in the next step, let's generate a new normal distribution and see its effect on the p-value and **D**.

4. Generate a new normal distribution with the same **mean** and **sd** as **xnorm**:

    ```
    x_norm2<-rnorm(100,mean=100,sd=5)
    ```

5. Plot the combined CDF of **x_norm** and **x_norm2**:

    ```
    plot(ecdf(x_norm))
    plot(ecdf(x_norm2),add=TRUE)
    ```

    The output is as follows:

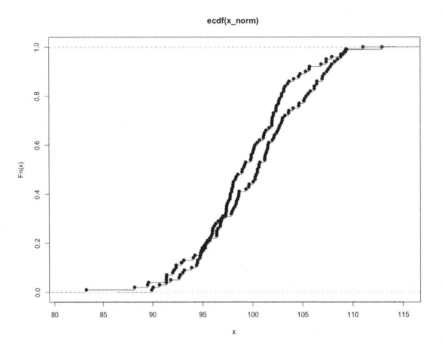

Figure 3.35 Plot of combined cdf

6. Run **ks.test()** on **x_norm** and **x_norm2**:

    ```
    ks.test(x_norm,x_norm2)
    ```

    The output is as follows:

    ```
            Two-sample Kolmogorov-Smirnov test

    data:  x_norm and x_norm2
    D = 0.15, p-value = 0.2106
    alternative hypothesis: two-sided
    ```

As you can see, the p-value is much higher this time and **D** is much lower. So, according to the p-value, we are less justified in rejecting the null hypothesis that both samples belong to the same distribution.

Activity 9: Calculating the CDF and Performing the Kolmogorov-Smirnov Test with the Normal Distribution

With the help of randomly generated distributions, calculate what standard distribution the sample of sepal length and width is closest to:

1. Load the Iris dataset into a variable.

2. Keep rows with the setosa species only.

3. Calculate the mean and standard deviation of sepal length.

4. Generate a new normal distribution with the mean and standard deviation of the sepal length column.

5. Plot the CDF of both functions.

6. Generate the results of the Kolmogorov-Smirnov test and check whether the distribution is a normal distribution.

7. Repeat steps 3, 4, 5, and 6 for the sepal width column.

> **Note**
>
> The solution for this activity can be found on page 219.

The final outcome of this activity will be as follows:

```
Two-sample Kolmogorov-Smirnov test
```

```
data: xnorm and df$Sepal.Width
D = 0.12, p-value = 0.7232
alternative hypothesis: two-sided
```

Summary

Congratulations on completing the third chapter of the book! In this chapter, we learned the types of standard probability distribution, as well as when and how to generate them in R. We also learned how to find PDFs and CDFs of unknown distributions with KDE. In the final section, we learned how to compare two samples and determine whether they belong to the same distribution in R. In further chapters, we will learn about other types of unsupervised learning techniques that will help not only in exploratory data analysis but also give us other useful insights into data as well.

Dimension Reduction

Learning Objectives

By the end of this chapter, you will be able to:

- Apply different dimension reduction techniques
- Execute market basket analysis using the Apriori algorithm
- Perform principal component analysis on a dataset

In this chapter, we will have a look at different dimension reduction techniques.

Introduction

This chapter presents techniques for unsupervised learning that accomplish something called **dimension reduction**. First, we will discuss what a dimension is, why we want to avoid having too many dimensions, and the basic idea of dimension reduction. The chapter then covers two dimension reduction techniques in detail: market basket analysis and **Principal Component Analysis (PCA)**. Market basket analysis is a technique for generating associative rules in datasets. The chapter will contain a walk-through of detailed R code that accomplishes this. PCA, a very common dimension reduction technique, comes from theoretical linear algebra. The chapter will also show a detailed walk-through of how to accomplish PCA with R.

The Idea of Dimension Reduction

The **dimensions** of a dataset are nothing more than the collection of distinct numbers that are required to describe observations in it. For example, consider the position of Pac-Man in the game named after him. Pac-Man is a game that was popular in the 20th century in America. It is an extremely simple game: Pac-Man is a little circular creature on a screen who likes to eat little dots and fruits. He lives in a maze that he has to navigate with only two sets of directions to move in: up/down and left/right. There are some monsters who try to chase Pac-Man and kill him. You can see in the following illustration what a Pac-Man game looks like, and what the world that he inhabits and has to move in looks like:

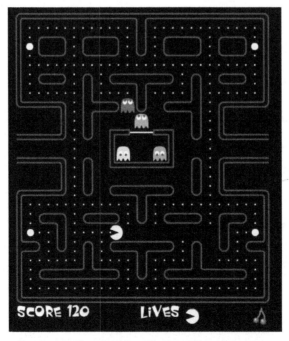

Figure 4.1: Illustration of a Pac-Man-style game

As you can see, Pac-Man's position can be fully described by two numbers: how far he is from the left side of the screen and how far he is from the top of the screen. If we know those two numeric measurements, then there is only one unique place on the screen where he could be. So, if we wanted to collect data on where Pac-Man was over time, we would be able to collect a two-dimensional dataset that consisted of those two numbers measured repeatedly. We would feel completely confident that each observation, consisting of two numbers, fully described everything that could be known about where Pac-Man was located at the time of the observation.

It is not only location data or geometric data that can be described as two-dimensional. Any dataset that contains two different measurements can be described as two-dimensional. For example, if we measured individuals' heights and weights, we could create a two-dimensional dataset that consisted of their height and weight measurements. If we recorded height, weight, and shoe size, then we would have a three-dimensional dataset. There is no limit to the number of dimensions that can be contained in a dataset.

Dimension reduction is the process of finding a lower-dimensional dataset that approximates a higher-dimensional dataset. Consider an example related to Pac-Man. Imagine that we have a three-dimensional dataset that describes Pac-Man's location. Suppose that the dimensions of this dataset are (1) how far Pac-Man is from the left side of the screen, (2) how far Pac-Man is from the top of the screen, and (3) how far Pac-Man is from the blue monster that is chasing him. This is a three-dimensional dataset; however, we can have complete knowledge of Pac-Man's location with only the information contained in the first two dimensions. The simplest way we could perform effective dimension reduction here would be to discard the third dimension, since it would not help us locate Pac-Man any better than we would be able to with only the first two dimensions. So, the two-dimensional dataset consisting of the dataset's first two dimensions would be a good approximation of the three-dimensional dataset that we started with.

In most real-life scenarios, dimension reduction is not as easy as discarding dimensions. Typically, we will attempt to use data from all dimensions to create a completely new dataset whose dimensions have different meanings from the dimensions in the original dataset. The exercises in the rest of the chapter will illustrate this process.

In the following exercise, we will look at a dataset that contains multiple dimensions. We will create plots that illustrate dimension reduction and how it can help us.

Exercise 21: Examining a Dataset that Contains the Chemical Attributes of Different Wines

Prerequisites:

To download the data, go to https://github.com/TrainingByPackt/Applied-Unsupervised-Learning-with-R/tree/master/Lesson04/Exercise21/wine.csv.

> ### Note
>
> This dataset is taken from the UCI Machine Learning Repository. You can find the dataset at http://archive.ics.uci.edu/ml/datasets/Wine. We have downloaded the file and saved it at https://github.com/TrainingByPackt/Applied-Unsupervised-Learning-with-R/tree/master/Lesson04/Exercise21/wine.csv.

Download this data and store it on your computer in a file called `wine.csv`.

> ### Note
>
> For all the exercises and activities where we are importing external csv or images, Go to **R Studio**-> **Session**-> **Set Working Directory**-> **To Source File Location**. You can see in the console that the path is set automatically.

This data contains information about the chemical measurements of 13 different attributes of 178 different samples of wine. Altogether, this is a 13-dimensional dataset. If we consider a subset of the data consisting of only 2 of the 13 attributes, we will have a 2-dimensional dataset comparable to our hypothetical Pac-Man data. With 2-dimensional data, we can always plot it on a 2-dimensional scatterplot.

In this dataset, the first column records the class of the wine, or, in other words, what type of wine it is. Every other column records a measurement related to the chemical makeup of the wine. One wonderful thing about machine learning is that even without knowing anything about the chemistry of wine, we can use pure data analysis tools to find patterns and draw conclusions that may be unnoticed even by chemistry experts.

Here are the steps for completion:

1. Open the R console and make sure you have saved the data file (**wine.csv**) in a location that R can access. You can use the **setwd()** command to make sure your file is accessible. For example, if your **wine.csv** file is located in the **C:/Users/me/datasets** folder, then you can run the **setwd('C:/Users/me/datasets')** command in the R console. Then, you will be able to open the wine data file in R as follows:

   ```
   wine<-read.csv('wine.csv')
   ```

2. Consider the following scatterplot of the two-dimensional data created by the **flavanoids** and **total phenols** attributes:

   ```
   plot(wine$flavanoid,wine$phenol)
   ```

   The output is as follows:

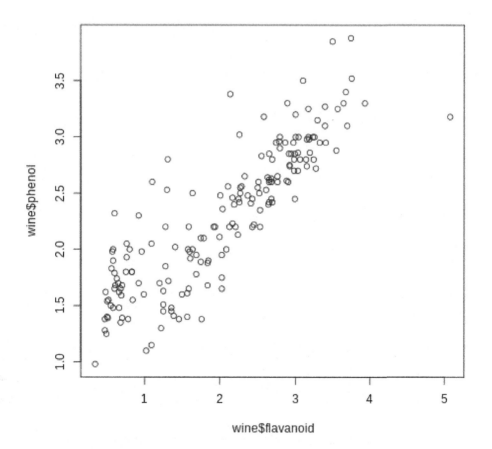

Figure 4.2: Scatterplot of two-dimensional data of flavanoids and phenol

3. After plotting the data, we observe that there appears to be a strong correlation between the **flavanoid** and **phenol** measurements. We can draw a line on the plot that represents this correlation. For now, don't worry about where we found the coefficients labeled **a** and **b** in the following commands:

```
plot(wine$flavanoid,wine$phenol)
abline(a=1.1954,b=.54171,col='red',lwd=5)
```

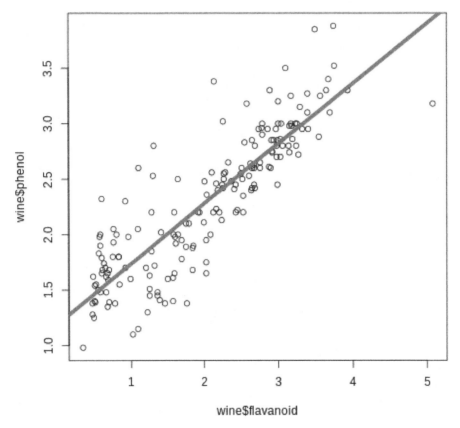

Figure 4.3: Scatterplot with a line representing correlation between flavanoids and phenol

As you can see, the red line follows the geometric shape of our data quite closely. The majority of the points in the data are quite close to the red line. If we wanted a concise way to describe the points, we could simply say what point on the red line they are closest to. This would not be a perfect description of the data, since some points would map to the same point on the red line even though they have different **flavanoid** and **phenol** levels. However, describing this data using only the red line is a reasonable approximation to the actual data.

If we describe each observation using the point on the red line that it is closest to, then what we have accomplished is dimension reduction. We started with a dataset that requires two measurements to describe each observation and found a way to describe each observation using only one point. This is the basic idea of every dimension reduction strategy, and this chapter contains several practical strategies to accomplish it.

Importance of Dimension Reduction

Why is dimension reduction something that we are interested in doing? Here are a couple of reasons:

- One reason may be for the sake of compressing data. If a dataset is particularly large, and if the R instance running on your laptop takes too long to do simple calculations on it, it may be useful to reduce the dimensions of the data so that it can more easily fit into your computer's memory.

- A more interesting reason for dimension reduction is that it provides insights into the underlying structure of our data and the ways that different attributes relate to each other. In the preceding exercise, even if we don't have advanced training in chemistry, we can use what we have learned from our simple dimension reduction exercise to understand wine chemistry better.

> **Note**
>
> If we read a little more about phenols and flavanoids (for example, at this website: https://www.researchgate.net/post/What_is_the_relation_between_total_Phenol_total_Flavonoids), we can learn that phenols and flavanoids both possess antioxidant activity. So, it could be that the red line on the chart represents the level of antioxidant activity of a particular wine, and that flavanoid and phenol measurements are both just capturing a noisy measurement of this one thing. So, dimension reduction has enabled us to generate a hypothesis about the chemical makeup of wine, even without advanced domain knowledge.

Market Basket Analysis

Market basket analysis is a method that allows us to take high-dimensional data and reduce it to something that is simple and manageable without losing too much information along the way. In market basket analysis, our goal is to generate rules that govern the data.

Market basket analysis is also called **affinity analysis**. It is named after the example of a grocery store trying to do analysis on its customers' transactions – analysis of the products each customer puts in his or her basket. A large grocery store may have something like 5,000 items for sale at any given time. They may have thousands of customers per day. For each customer, the grocery store can keep a record of those customers' transactions. One way to do this would be to use binary encodings, as shown in the following example:

Customer 1's transactions on Day 1:

Peanut Butter: No

Jelly: Yes

Bread: No

Milk: No

...

Customer 2's transactions on Day 1:

Peanut Butter: Yes

Jelly: Yes

Bread: No

Milk: No

...

These transactions could be stored in a table that had 5,000 columns – one for each item for sale in the store – and one row for every recorded transaction. And instead of storing "Yes" and "No" values for every item, they could store 1s and 0s, where 1 denotes "Yes" and 0 denotes "No", in a table that looks something like the following:

	Peanut Butter	Jelly	Bread	Milk
Transaction 1	0	1	0	0
Transaction 2	1	1	0	0
Transaction 3	0	0	0	1
Transaction 4	1	1	1	1
Transaction 5	1	0	0	0

Figure 4.4: Table demonstrating transactions of the customers

The preceding table shows only four columns and five rows, but in practice, the table would be much, much larger.

The simplest use case for market basket analysis is to answer a simple question: what items are usually bought together? A grocery store owner may be interested in this purely out of curiosity. But, in fact, there are some compelling business reasons why they would want to know about their customers' most common baskets.

So far, this problem seems quite simple. Our binary data is as simple as it could be, consisting only of 0s and 1s. Our problem is merely to find what items tend to be purchased together. The complexity lies not in these simple ideas, but rather in their practical implementation.

Consider the **brute-force** approach to finding items that tend to be bought together. If we consider every possible basket of items, which is every possible combination of 0s and 1s in the preceding data, we find that there are 2^{5000} possible baskets. This is much more than the estimated number of particles in the known universe, and it would not be computationally feasible to check each possible basket in a reasonable amount of time, or to store findings about each possible basket.

If we cannot check each possible basket, how can we find baskets that are bought together with any confidence that we are doing a comprehensive check? The answer is to apply an algorithmic solution. The **Apriori** algorithm is the most popular method to do thorough market basket analysis given time and space constraints. It was invented by Agrawal and Srikant, who published a paper about it in 1994. It proceeds sequentially through increasing market basket sizes.

The Apriori algorithm consists of several steps. In the first few steps, we will **pass** through our data set to find the most common baskets. In our first pass, we will find the most common baskets that have exactly one item in them. In our second pass, we will find the most common baskets that have exactly two items in them. We will continue these passes until we have found the most common baskets of every size that interests us. In the example of a grocery store, maybe the most common two-item basket is "peanut butter, jelly" and the most common three-item basket is "peanut butter, jelly, bread."

After finding the most common baskets, we will generate **associative rules** for these baskets. These rules will express relationships between items in the most common baskets. For example, an associative rule for a grocery store might be something such as, "if peanut butter and jelly are both in a basket, then it is likely that bread is also in the basket." These types of rules enable us to find associations between different individual items that could be useful for us. For example, after knowing that peanut butter and jelly are often accompanied by bread, the grocery store owner might be interested in rearranging the displays of these items so that they are closer together in the store and easier for shoppers to put into their baskets with minimal effort.

> **Note**
>
> The rule "If peanut butter and jelly are present [in a basket], then bread is likely to be present [in that basket]" is a simple associative rule. Associative rules are sometimes drawn with an arrow pointing from X to Y, indicating the idea that X "implies" Y, although associative rules are not necessarily causal.

Many Americans have grown up eating peanut butter and jelly sandwiches, so it may seem obvious to them that peanut butter, jelly, and bread are likely to be bought together. Market basket analysis may generate some seemingly obvious associative rules like these. However, in practice, market basket analysis is likely to generate associative rules that are surprising and unexpected. This is another example where without being an expert in grocery shopping or retail, we can use machine learning to find patterns and insights that are surprising even to experts.

In the next exercise, we will be applying market basket analysis to census survey data. The data in the dataset looks as follows:

```
40, Private,121772, Assoc-voc,11, Married-civ-spouse, Craft-repair, Husband, Male,0,0,40, ?, >50K
34, Private,245487, 7th-8th,4, Married-civ-spouse, Transport-moving, Husband, Male,0,0,45, Mexico, <=50K
25, Self-emp-not-inc,176756, HS-grad,9, Never-married, Farming-fishing, Own-child, Male,0,0,35, United-States, <=50K
32, Private,186824, HS-grad,9, Never-married, Machine-op-inspct, Unmarried, Male,0,0,40, United-States, <=50K
38, Private,28887, 11th,7, Married-civ-spouse, Sales, Husband, Male,0,0,50, United-States, <=50K
43, Self-emp-not-inc,292175, Masters,14, Divorced, Exec-managerial, Unmarried, Female,0,0,45, United-States, >50K
40, Private,193524, Doctorate,16, Married-civ-spouse, Prof-specialty, Husband, Male,0,0,60, United-States, >50K
54, Private,302146, HS-grad,9, Separated, Other-service, Unmarried, Female,0,0,20, United-States, <=50K
35, Federal-gov,76845, 9th,5, Married-civ-spouse, Farming-fishing, Husband, Male,0,0,40, United-States, <=50K
43, Private,117037, 11th,7, Married-civ-spouse, Transport-moving, Husband, Male,0,2042,40, United-States, <=50K
59, Private,109015, HS-grad,9, Divorced, Tech-support, Unmarried, Female,0,0,40, United-States, <=50K
56, Local-gov,216851, Bachelors,13, Married-civ-spouse, Tech-support, Husband, Male,0,0,40, United-States, >50K
19, Private,168294, HS-grad,9, Never-married, Craft-repair, Own-child, Male,0,0,40, United-States, <=50K
54, ?,180211, Some-college,10, Married-civ-spouse, ?, Husband, Male,0,0,60, South, >50K
39, Private,367260, HS-grad,9, Divorced, Exec-managerial, Not-in-family, Male,0,0,80, United-States, <=50K
49, Private,193366, HS-grad,9, Married-civ-spouse, Craft-repair, Husband, Male,0,0,40, United-States, <=50K
23, Local-gov,190709, Assoc-acdm,12, Never-married, Protective-serv, Not-in-family, Male,0,0,52, United-States, <=50K
20, Private,266015, Some-college,10, Never-married, Sales, Own-child, Male,0,0,44, United-States, <=50K
45, Private,386940, Bachelors,13, Divorced, Exec-managerial, Own-child, Male,0,1408,40, United-States, <=50K
30, Federal-gov,59951, Some-college,10, Married-civ-spouse, Adm-clerical, Own-child, Male,0,0,40, United-States, <=50K
22, State-gov,311512, Some-college,10, Married-civ-spouse, Other-service, Husband, Male,0,0,15, United-States, <=50K
48, Private,242406, 11th,7, Never-married, Machine-op-inspct, Unmarried, Male,0,0,40, Puerto-Rico, <=50K
21, Private,197200, Some-college,10, Never-married, Machine-op-inspct, Own-child, Male,0,0,40, United-States, <=50K
19, Private,544091, HS-grad,9, Married-AF-spouse, Adm-clerical, Wife, Female,0,0,25, United-States, <=50K
31, Private,84154, Some-college,10, Married-civ-spouse, Sales, Husband, Male,0,0,38, ?, >50K
48, Self-emp-not-inc,265477, Assoc-acdm,12, Married-civ-spouse, Prof-specialty, Husband, Male,0,0,40, United-States, <=50K
31, Private,507875, 9th,5, Married-civ-spouse, Machine-op-inspct, Husband, Male,0,0,43, United-States, <=50K
53, Self-emp-not-inc,88506, Bachelors,13, Married-civ-spouse, Prof-specialty, Husband, Male,0,0,40, United-States, <=50K
24, Private,172987, Bachelors,13, Married-civ-spouse, Tech-support, Husband, Male,0,0,50, United-States, <=50K
49, Private,94638, HS-grad,9, Separated, Adm-clerical, Unmarried, Female,0,0,40, United-States, <=50K
25, Private,289980, HS-grad,9, Never-married, Handlers-cleaners, Not-in-family, Male,0,0,35, United-States, <=50K
57, Federal-gov,337895, Bachelors,13, Married-civ-spouse, Prof-specialty, Husband, Male,0,0,40, United-States, >50K
53, Private,144361, HS-grad,9, Married-civ-spouse, Machine-op-inspct, Husband, Male,0,0,38, United-States, <=50K
44, Private,128354, Masters,14, Divorced, Exec-managerial, Unmarried, Female,0,0,40, United-States, <=50K
41, State-gov,101603, Assoc-voc,11, Married-civ-spouse, Craft-repair, Husband, Male,0,0,40, United-States, <=50K
29, Private,271466, Assoc-voc,11, Never-married, Prof-specialty, Not-in-family, Male,0,0,43, United-States, <=50K
```

Figure 4.5: Screenshot of the dataset

Note

This dataset is taken from the UCI Machine Learning Repository. You can find the dataset at http://archive.ics.uci.edu/ml/datasets/Adult. We have downloaded the file and saved it at https://github.com/TrainingByPackt/Applied-Unsupervised-Learning-with-R/tree/master/Lesson04/Exercise22-Exercise25/.

This data is different from the hypothetical grocery basket data we described previously as its columns are not 0-1 binary encodings, but rather can take in multiple values. Since the Apriori algorithm is designed for 0-1 data, we will do **re-coding** of the data. Here, re-coding means that we will create new variables that are simpler and easier to work with than the original variables, but nevertheless convey the same information. The re-coding that we will perform here will transform the data so that it consists of 0-1 encodings. Another term for what we will do here is creating dummy variables. A dummy variable is a variable that only takes on the values 0 and 1. For each of the columns in the dataset, we can refer to the data at http://archive.ics.uci.edu/ml/datasets/Adult to find information about the column, and then use that information for our re-coding. We can do analogous transformations to all of the variables.

For categorical variables such as employment status, we make new 0-1 variables for each possible response. For ordinal variables such as age, we make two new variables, indicating whether the value is high or low.

We will draw conclusions about what survey answers tend to be answered in the same way. Market basket analysis can be used for a wide variety of datasets outside of just grocery data. No matter what dataset is used, market basket analysis will generate associative rules and tell us which attributes of the data tend to take the same values.

Exercise 22: Data Preparation for the Apriori Algorithm

> **Note**
>
> Exercise 22-25 should be executed together.

In this exercise, we will use data that is freely available at https://github.com/TrainingByPackt/Applied-Unsupervised-Learning-with-R/tree/master/Lesson04/Exercise22-Exercise25/census.csv. This is survey data. To use this data, you should first download it to your computer – save it to a file called **census.csv**. You will not need to load any special packages in order to run this data or complete any prerequisites:

1. Use the **setwd()** function in R to read data. After you have set the working directory, you can read it into R as follows:

```
filepath='census.csv'
mkt<-read.csv(filepath,stringsAsFactors=FALSE,header=FALSE,sep=',')
```

2. Examine the data:

```
head(mkt)
```

```
    V1                   V2      V3              V4 V5                        V6
1 39            State-gov   77516    Bachelors 13            Never-married
2 50    Self-emp-not-inc   83311    Bachelors 13   Married-civ-spouse
3 38             Private  215646      HS-grad  9                 Divorced
4 53             Private  234721         11th  7   Married-civ-spouse
5 28             Private  338409    Bachelors 13   Married-civ-spouse
6 37             Private  284582      Masters 14   Married-civ-spouse
                   V7                V8          V9  V10 V11 V12
1        Adm-clerical   Not-in-family      Male 2174    0  40
2     Exec-managerial         Husband      Male    0    0  13
3   Handlers-cleaners   Not-in-family      Male    0    0  40
4   Handlers-cleaners         Husband      Male    0    0  40
5       Prof-specialty            Wife    Female    0    0  40
6     Exec-managerial            Wife    Female    0    0  40
               V13       V14
1   United-States    <=50K
2   United-States    <=50K
3   United-States    <=50K
4   United-States    <=50K
5            Cuba    <=50K
6   United-States    <=50K
```

Figure 4.6: Screenshot of the data

One thing you will notice is that R has automatically assigned column names to the data, since the raw data file did not contain column names. By default, R assigns numbered column names beginning with **V**, since each column can be thought of as a vector.

3. Create dummy variables.

We can see from the data's website that the first variable, which R has called **V1**, is a measurement of age in years. For this variable, we recode it as a 0-1 binary variable based on whether its value is above the median age value or below the median age value. We can calculate the median age value with "**median(mkt$V1)**":

```
mkt$old<-1*(mkt$V1>median(mkt$V1))
mkt$young<-1*(mkt$V1<=median(mkt$V1))
```

4. Similarly, we can see on the website that the second column, which R has labeled **V2**, refers to employment status. For employment, we can create several new variables, one for each class of employment:

```
mkt$government_employee<-1*(mkt$V2 %in% c(" State-gov"," Local-gov","
Federal-gov"))
mkt$self_employed<-1*(mkt$V2 %in% c(" Self-emp-not-inc"," Self-emp-inc"))
mkt$never_worked<-1*(mkt$V2 %in% c(" Never-worked"))
mkt$private_employment<-1*(mkt$V2 %in% c(" Private"))
mkt$other_employment<-1*(mkt$V2 %in% c(" ?"," Without-pay" ))
```

5. Here we encode 0-1 variables for the education level of a respondent:

```
mkt$high_school_incomplete<-1*(mkt$V4 %in% c(" 1st-4th"," Preschool","
5th-6th"," 7th-8th"," 9th"," 10th"," 11th"," 12th"))
mkt$high_school_complete<-1*(mkt$V4 %in% c(" HS-grad"," Some-college","
Assoc-acdm"," Assoc-voc"))
mkt$bachelors<-1*(mkt$V4 %in% c(" Bachelors"))
mkt$post_bachelors<-1*(mkt$V4 %in% c(" Masters"," Prof-school","
Doctorate" ))
```

We use the **V4** column to encode education levels as the column labeled **V3** is not useful for our purposes. We will not use the **V5** column, which contains the same data expressed in a different way.

6. Here we encode 0-1 variables for a person's marital status:

```
mkt$married<-1*(mkt$V6 %in% c(" Married-civ-spouse"," Married-AF-spouse","
Married-spouse-absent"))
mkt$never_married<-1*(mkt$V6 %in% c(" Never-married"))
mkt$divorced_separated<-1*(mkt$V6 %in% c(" Divorced"," Separated"))
mkt$widowed<-1*(mkt$V6 %in% c( " Widowed"))
```

7. Here we encode 0-1 variables for a respondent's occupation:

```
mkt$clerical<-1*(mkt$V7 %in% c(" Adm-clerical"))
mkt$managerial<-1*(mkt$V7 %in% c(" Exec-managerial"))
mkt$moving<-1*(mkt$V7 %in% c(" Transport-moving"))
mkt$farming_fishing<-1*(mkt$V7 %in% c(" Farming-fishing"))
mkt$craft_repair<-1*(mkt$V7 %in% c(" Craft-repair" ))
mkt$sales<-1*(mkt$V7 %in% c(" Sales"))
mkt$tech_support<-1*(mkt$V7 %in% c(" Tech-support"))
```

```
mkt$service<-1*(mkt$V7 %in% c(" Protective-serv"," Priv-house-serv", "
Other-service"))
mkt$armed_forces<-1*(mkt$V7 %in% c(" Armed-Forces"))
mkt$other_occupation<-1*(mkt$V7 %in% c(" Handlers-cleaners"," ?"," 
Machine-op-inspct"," Prof-specialty"))
```

We will not use the **V8** column since it is recorded for census purposes and is not useful for our analysis.

8. Here we encode 0-1 variables for a respondent's self-reported sex:

```
mkt$male<-1*(mkt$V9 %in% c(" Male"))
mkt$female<-1*(mkt$V9 %in% c(" Female"))
```

The **V10** and **V11** columns are not very informative, so we will not use them in our analysis.

9. Here we encode 0-1 variables for the self-reported number of work hours of each respondent:

```
mkt$high_hours<-1*(mkt$V12 > median(mkt$V12))
mkt$low_hours<-1*(mkt$V12 <= median(mkt$V12))
```

10. Here we encode 0-1 variables for whether a respondent reports that their native country is the United States:

```
mkt$usa<-1*(mkt$V13==" United-States")
mkt$not_usa<-1*(mkt$V13!=" United-States")
```

11. Here we encode 0-1 variables for whether a respondent reports an income above or below $50,000:

```
mkt$low_income<-1*(mkt$V14==" <=50K")
mkt$high_income<-1*(mkt$V14==" >50K")
```

12. Now, we have added 33 new variables that are 0-1 encodings. Since we will be performing market basket analysis only on the 0-1 encodings, we can remove the initial 14 variables that we started with to create a dummy-only dataset as follows:

```
mktdummies<-mkt[,15:ncol(mkt)]
mktdummies
```

13. We can see the mean values of each of our variables by running the following code:

```
print(colMeans(mktdummies,na.rm=TRUE))
```

The mean of a dummy variable is equal to the percentage of the time that it is equal to 1. So, when we see that the mean of the **married** variable is 0.473, we know that about 47.3% of survey respondents were married.

After completing this exercise, your data will have 33 columns, each of which is a **dummy variable** instance that takes only the values 0 and 1. If you print the top 6 rows by running **print(head(mktdummies))** in the console, then you can see that the resulting dataset looks as follows:

```
             old               young    government_employee   self_employed       never_worked   private_employment
      0.4877000092        0.5122999908           0.1041429932    0.0780381438       0.0002149811         0.6970301895
other_employment high_school_incomplete   high_school_complete       bachelors      post_bachelors              married
      0.0568164368        0.1203894229           0.5888639784    0.1644605510       0.0832898253         0.4599367341
    never_married       divorced_separated              widowed        clerical          managerial               moving
      0.3280918891        0.1679309604           0.0304966064    0.1157826848       0.1248733147         0.0490464052
  farming_fishing          craft_repair                sales    tech_support             service         armed_forces
      0.0305273180        0.1258867971           0.1120972943    0.0285003532       0.0245078468         0.0002764043
 other_occupation                  male               female      high_hours           low_hours                  usa
      0.2873069009        0.6692054912           0.3307945088    0.2942477197       0.7057522803         0.8958570068
          not_usa            low_income          high_income
      0.1041429932        0.7591904426           0.2408095574
```

Figure 4.7: Section of resulting dataset of dummy variables

Now that we have completed the exercise, we have a dummy-only dataset that consists of 0-1 variables that give true/false information about each of the original variables in the dataset.

Finally, we are ready to actually perform the Apriori algorithm. In the following exercise, we will begin to "take passes" through our data. In each pass, we will find the most common baskets that have a particular size.

Before we begin to pass through our data, we will need to specify something called **support**. Support is a name for one of the parameters of the Apriori algorithm. Here, support refers to the percentage of baskets that contain a particular combination of items. If we find that 40% of survey takers in the marketing data are both high income and female, then we will say that high-income, female "baskets" have 40% support in our data.

We need to make a decision about the minimum support we are interested in. If we set the minimum support threshold too high, we will not find any baskets that meet the threshold. If we set the minimum support threshold too low, we will find so many baskets that it will be difficult to look at all of them to find an interesting one. Also, since we want to find rules that will be practically useful, we want to find baskets that are relatively common, because more common baskets are more likely to have practical use for us.

Exercise 23: Passing through the Data to Find the Most Common Baskets

Now our data is prepared for the main steps of market basket analysis. Before going further, we have to make decisions about the parameters we will use in our algorithm:

1. The first parameter we will work with is support, as explained previously. In this case, we can start by setting the minimum support threshold at 10%.

   ```
   support_thresh<-0.1
   ```

2. First, we will find all one-item baskets that match our support threshold as follows:

   ```
   firstpass<-unname(which(colMeans(mktdummies,na.rm=TRUE)>support_thresh))
   ```

   This shows the collection of all survey items that were answered in the same way by at least 10% of respondents.

3. To take the second pass through the data, we will define all possible candidates for two-item baskets that might have more than 10% support as follows:

   ```
   secondcand<-t(combn(firstpass,2))
   secondpass<-NULL
   ```

   Note

   If less than 10% of baskets contain a particular item, then it is impossible that more than 10% of baskets contain that item plus a different item. So, the candidates for two-item baskets that have more than 10% support will be combinations of items that survived the first pass through the data.

   We have defined **secondcand**, which is the set of candidates for our second pass, and **secondpass**, which we will use to store the results of the second pass. The **secondpass** variable starts with a **NULL** value because we have not yet begun the second pass.

If we look at **secondcand**, we can see that it consists of pairs of numbers. Each number refers to a column in the `mktdummies` data. For example, the fourth row of **secondcand** refers to a potential basket consisting of people who responded that they are older than the median age and also privately employed. In the second pass through the data, we will check each two-item candidate in **secondcand**, and if it has greater than 10% support, it will survive the second pass through the data.

4. In order to check the support of the fourth row of our candidates in **secondcand**, we can do the following calculation:

```
k<-4
support<-mean(mktdummies[,secondcand[k,1]]*mktdummies[,secondcand[k,2]]
,na.rm=TRUE)
print(support)
```

The output is as follows:

```
0.05515801
```

5. We need to do this same calculation for every candidate basket, which we can do by putting this calculation in a loop. This loop will save the final two-item baskets that reach the support threshold in the **secondpass** variable:

```
k<-1
while(k<=nrow(secondcand)){
support<-mean(mktdummies[,secondcand[k,1]]*mktdummies[,secondcand[k,2]]
,na.rm=TRUE)
if(support>support_thresh){
secondpass<-rbind(secondpass,secondcand[k,])
}
k<-k+1
}
```

6. The important outcome variable of this exercise is the variable called **secondpass**. This variable contains all two-item baskets that reach the support threshold (10%) that we have specified. Look at the top six rows of this variable by running the following in the console:

```
print(head(secondpass))
```

The output is as follows:

```
        [,1] [,2]
  [1,]    1    6
  [2,]    1    9
  [3,]    1   12
  [4,]    1   14
  [5,]    1   25
  [6,]    1   26
```

Here, each row contains two numbers, and each refers to a column number in the original dataset. For example, the first row indicates that the first column and the sixth column of the `mktdummies` dataset together constitute a two-item basket that has greater than 10% support. Since the first column of our dataset is called `old` and the sixth column in our dataset is called `private_employment`, then we conclude that survey respondents who are both old and employed privately constitute more than 10% of all survey respondents.

After this, we have finalized the second pass through the data. By completing the second pass, we now have a list of all of the most common baskets that have size two.

The point of the Apriori algorithm is that we can use the two-item baskets and one-item baskets to narrow down the three-item candidate baskets that we look at, which makes our search much faster.

To get a full sense of how the Apriori algorithm works, we should pass through the data at least one more time, which is covered in the following exercise.

Exercise 24: More Passes through the Data

In the following exercise, we will take more passes through the data. Recall that each time we pass through the data, we are looking for baskets that meet our support threshold. In each pass, we seek baskets that have more items than we sought in previous passes. So, in the first pass, we sought one-item baskets that met our support threshold. In the second pass, we sought two-item baskets that met our support threshold. In the following exercise, we will illustrate how to take more passes through the data, including a third pass, in which we will seek baskets with three items that meet our support threshold, and a fourth pass, in which we will seek baskets with four items that meet our support threshold.

Being able to take many passes through the data will be important to us if we are interested in complex rules that govern many items:

1. In the third pass through the data, we will look for three-item baskets that have at least 10% support. The third pass through the data will start with a **product** variable equal to 1. This **product** variable will give us the product of different columns of our data, and the mean of the **product** variable will give us the support of different baskets, as follows:

   ```
   product<-1
   n<-1
   ```

2. This **product** variable will be multiplied by the observations related to a two-item basket that survived the second pass:

   ```
   thirdpass<-NULL
   k<-1
   while(k<=nrow(secondpass)){
   j<-1
   while(j<=length(firstpass)){
   n<-1
   product<-1
   while(n<=ncol(secondpass)){
   product<-product*mktdummies[,secondpass[k,n]]
   n<-n+1
   }
   ```

3. Finally, each **product** variable will be multiplied by the observations of a one-item basket that survived the first pass:

   ```
   if(!(firstpass[j] %in% secondpass[k,])){
   product<-product*mktdummies[,firstpass[j]]
   ```

4. We take the mean of our product to find the support of the basket we have specified:

   ```
   support<-mean(product,na.rm=TRUE)
   ```

5. If the support of the resulting three-item basket is higher than our specified support threshold, then we save it to our final **thirdpass** variable:

   ```
   if(support>support_thresh){
   thirdpass<-rbind(thirdpass,c(secondpass[k,],firstpass[j]))
   }
   }
   j<-j+1
   }
   ```

```
k<-k+1
}
```

> **Note**
>
> Steps 2-5 should be executed together.

Now we have a list of all baskets of size three that are common in the data.

6. After going through several passes through the data, we can start to see the general form of the steps taken in the Apriori algorithm. In general, to find the baskets that survive pass **n**, we need to take the baskets that survived pass **n-1**, add an item to them that survived pass 1, and see whether the resulting combination has support greater than our chosen threshold:

```
fourthpass<-NULL
k<-1
while(k<=nrow(thirdpass)){
j<-1
while(j<=length(firstpass)){
n<-1
product<-1
while(n<=ncol(thirdpass)){
product<-product*mktdummies[,thirdpass[k,n]]
n<-n+1
}
if(!(firstpass[j] %in% thirdpass[k,])){
product<-product*mktdummies[,firstpass[j]]
support<-mean(product,na.rm=TRUE)
if(support>support_thresh){
fourthpass<-rbind(fourthpass,c(thirdpass[k,],firstpass[j]))
}
}
j<-j+1
}
k<-k+1
}
```

We can continue in this way indefinitely and create baskets of any size that meet our support threshold. For our purpose here, we will stop after four passes through the data, and we will examine the results of our third pass.

7. The final important outcomes of this exercise are the `thirdpass` and `fourthpass` variables. These variables contain information about the three-item and four-item baskets that have met our support threshold. You can interpret each row of these variables in the same way you interpreted each row of **secondpass**. Each row represents one basket that meets our support threshold, and each number in each row refers to a column number in our dataset.

You can verify what the top six rows of `thirdpass` look like by executing the following:

```
print(head(thirdpass))
```

The output is as follows:

```
      [,1] [,2] [,3]
[1,]    1    6    9
[2,]    1    6   12
[3,]    1    6   26
[4,]    1    6   29
[5,]    1    6   30
[6,]    1    6   32
```

We can interpret row 2 as indicating that the basket containing item 1, item 6, and item 12 meets our support threshold.

8. You can verify the top six rows of **fourthpass** as follows:

```
print(head(fourthpass))
```

The output is as follows:

```
      [,1] [,2] [,3] [,4]
[1,]    1    6    9   26
[2,]    1    6    9   29
[3,]    1    6    9   30
[4,]    1    6    9   32
[5,]    1    6   12   26
[6,]    1    6   12   29
```

We can interpret row 5 as telling us that the basket containing items 1, 6, 12, and 26 meets our support threshold.

In the previous exercises, we have found the baskets that interest us. In this exercise, we will obtain the final product of market basket analysis. The final product we are interested in will be coherent **associative rules**. In other words, we are not only interested in the fact that a basket containing "old", "private_employment", and "low_hours" is common. We are also interested in generating a rule that relates these three items. One such rule might be "people who are older than the median survey respondent and who are privately employed are highly likely to work fewer hours than the median respondent". Market basket analysis thus goes further than other distribution analyses and clustering methods that only find groups in data. Market basket analysis not only finds groups but also groups them in coherent, meaningful rules.

In order to generate these rules, we will need to specify more parameters, similar to the support threshold we specified earlier.

One of these parameters is called **confidence**. Confidence is merely a conditional likelihood. Given that a person is both female and low-income, what is the likelihood that she is also divorced? What we have determined so far is support, which may tell us that the three-item basket consisting of female, low income, and divorced makes up more than 10% of all survey takers. Confidence tells us more – it tells us whether "divorced" is only a common basket item, or whether it is especially common conditional on the presence of "female" and "low income."

The final parameter we will have to specify is called **lift**. Lift is the confidence divided by the overall prevalence of the item predicted by the rule. In this case, suppose that if a person is female and low income, she has a 90% likelihood of also being divorced. Then 90% is the confidence of this rule, which seems quite high. However, this confidence will not seem impressive if 89% of all people are divorced anyway. If so, then knowing the presence of "female" and "low income" in the basket only improves our predictive capabilities very slightly, by about 1%. The value of lift in this case will be 90%/89%, or about 1.011. That is just a hypothetical – we will have to check the actual data to see what the actual value of lift is.

Together, confidence and lift provide measurements that help us decide whether an associative rule is useful or not. In a complex situation such as the many-question survey we are looking at here, we specify minimum thresholds for confidence and lift that filter out associative rules that are not sufficiently useful, so that we finish the Apriori algorithm with a small number of very useful rules.

Exercise 25: Generating Associative Rules as the Final Step of the Apriori Algorithm

In this exercise, we will complete the final steps of the Apriori algorithm. Any of the baskets that have survived our passes through the data so far can be considered candidate rules. In the final steps of market basket analysis, we will reduce the candidate rules further based on our final criteria – confidence and lift:

1. Examine baskets that have survived multiple passes through the data as follows:

    ```
    head(thirdpass)
    ```

    The output is as follows:

    ```
          [,1] [,2] [,3]
    [1,]    1    6    9
    [2,]    1    6   12
    [3,]    1    6   26
    [4,]    1    6   29
    [5,]    1    6   30
    [6,]    1    6   32
    ```

    You can see the number of three-item baskets that survived the third pass as follows:

    ```
    nrow(thirdpass)
    ```

    The output is as follows:

    ```
    [1] 549
    ```

    We see that there are 549 three-item baskets, that is, 549 candidate rules that have at least 10% support in our data. These baskets are not the final products of market basket analysis – associative rules are the final products we are looking for.

2. The formula for confidence for our three-item baskets is as follows: the support of the basket consisting of all three items, divided by the support of a basket consisting of only the first two items. We can calculate confidence as follows for the fifth row of our **thirdpass** three-item baskets:

```
k<-5
confidence<-mean(mktdummies[,thirdpass[k,1]]*mktdummies[,
thirdpass[k,2]]*mktdummies[,thirdpass[k,3]],na.rm=TRUE)/
mean(mktdummies[,thirdpass[k,1]]*mktdummies[,thirdpass[k,2]],na.rm=TRUE)
```

> **Note**
>
> This is just the support of the full three-item basket, divided by the support of the two-item basket not containing the third item.

3. Lift is the confidence divided by the overall prevalence of the item predicted by the rule. Lift can be calculated easily as follows for the fifth row of our third-pass candidates:

```
k<-5
lift<-confidence/mean(mktdummies[,thirdpass[k,3]],na.rm=TRUE)
```

4. To narrow down candidate rules to a final set of acceptable associative rules, we will specify minimum thresholds for confidence and lift, just like we did for support. Here, we have specified a lift threshold of 1.8 and a confidence threshold of 0.8:

> **Note**
>
> You can choose any values you prefer for those thresholds, but remember that lift thresholds should be higher than 1, and confidence thresholds should be between 0 and 1, and close to 1.

```
lift_thresh<-1.8
conf_thresh<-.8
```

5. We can calculate **lift** and **confidence** for each of our candidate rules by constructing a loop as follows:

```
thirdpass_conf<-NULL
k<-1
while(k<=nrow(thirdpass)){
   support<-mean(mktdummies[,thirdpass[k,1]]*mktdummies[,thirdpass[k,2]]*mk
tdummies[,thirdpass[k,3]],na.rm=TRUE)
   confidence<-mean(mktdummies[,thirdpass[k,1]]*mktdummies[,

thirdpass[k,2]]*mktdummies[,thirdpass[k,3]],na.rm=TRUE)/
      mean(mktdummies[,thirdpass[k,1]]*mktdummies[,thirdpass[k,2]],na.
rm=TRUE)
   lift<-confidence/mean(mktdummies[,thirdpass[k,3]],na.rm=TRUE)
   thirdpass_conf<-rbind(thirdpass_
conf,unname(c(thirdpass[k,],support,confidence,lift)))
   k<-k+1
}
```

This has generated a new variable called **thirdpass_conf**, which is a DataFrame that contains columns for the **support**, **confidence**, and **lift** for each candidate rule. Here, **conf** is used to be short for **confidence**, something we have added to the **thirdpass** data.

6. Finally, we can eliminate all candidate rules that do not meet the specified confidence and lift thresholds, as follows:

```
thirdpass_high<-thirdpass_conf[which(thirdpass_conf[,5]>conf_thresh &
thirdpass_conf[,6]>lift_thresh),]
```

7. Now we have **thirdpass_high**, which is a set of associative three-item rules that have high confidence and high lift in our data. We can browse through some of them by printing the DataFrame to the console as follows:

```
head(thirdpass_high)
```

```
     [,1] [,2] [,3]       [,4]        [,5]       [,6]
[1,]    1   33   12 0.1481834 0.8645404 1.879694
[2,]    6   33   12 0.1296029 0.8502922 1.848715
[3,]   26   33   12 0.1823654 0.8913239 1.937927
[4,]   29   33   12 0.1069992 0.8742785 1.900867
[5,]   30   33   12 0.1878628 0.8530191 1.854644
```

Figure 4.8: Output of thirdpass_high

Altogether, the steps we have followed in market basket analysis can be summarized as follows:

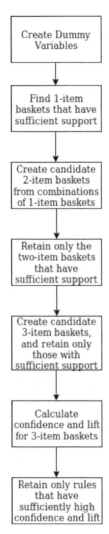

Figure 4.9: Flowchart of steps followed in market basket analysis

> **Note**
>
> Remember, these refer to the dummy variables we created in *Exercise 22, Data Preparation for the Apriori Algorithm*, where we created a dummy variable called **old** that was 1 for individuals in the higher age ranges and 0 otherwise. We also created a dummy variable for high income where 1 was used to indicate annual income greater than $50,000, and 0 was used otherwise.

The interpretation of the rule on the first row of `thirdpass_high` is that people who are older than median, and also have high income, are likely (with high confidence and high lift) to also be married. This makes intuitive sense: marriage and high income can both take many years to achieve, so it makes sense that there are not many young, married, high income individuals. We find that this has confidence of about 87% and lift of about 1.84.

In this case, the firm that conducted the survey could use this data to create advertising campaigns – either creating a campaign that targeted older married people for homeownership because that is a proven high-income demographic, or targeting younger married people for homeownership because that could be an underserved demographic that would constitute a business opportunity. Each of the seven three-item rules we found could provide insights into population patterns and business opportunities, together with quantified measurements of what these rules tell us and what certainty they provide.

There are some different choices we could make in our market basket analysis process that could change our results. If we change the thresholds we specified, we could potentially get more rules, or more useful rules. For example, if we set a 9% instead of a 10% support threshold, fewer rules would be filtered out, and we might have ended with a rule such as "young students who live in condominiums are likely to be Asian-Americans," a rule referring to a group that constitutes only about 9% of survey respondents.

We have focused only on three-item baskets and rules that relate elements of these baskets. By allowing more or fewer items into the baskets we are using to search for rules, we could find more interesting rules that could lead to solid business insights. All of this has been done with relatively few lines of code in a relatively short amount of time. This indicates the usefulness and potential of market basket analysis for solving data problems and business problems.

Market basket analysis has taken a high-dimensional problem (the problem of finding patterns in a large dataset) and given us a low-dimensional solution (six simple, high-confidence rules) without too much effort, computational power, or time.

Principal Component Analysis

The next type of dimension reduction method we will cover is called PCA. This is a very common technique used by researchers in a wide variety of fields.

Linear Algebra Refresher

This short section will not contain an exhaustive review of linear algebra, but merely a reminder of some of its main points.

> **Note**
>
> http://joshua.smcvt.edu/linearalgebra/#current_version covers some basics, including matrices, covariance matrices, eigenvectors, and eigenvalues. You can feel free to skip the linear algebra refresher if you are already familiar with these terms.

Matrices

Linear algebra is largely concerned with the analysis of matrices. A matrix can be thought of as just a collection of numbers in a rectangular format. We can create a matrix in R as follows:

```
matrix1<-matrix(c(1,2,3,4,5,6),nrow=2)
```

Here we have created a matrix with two rows and three columns, with six entries total. We describe entries in a matrix according to the row and column in which they appear. In our "**matrix1**" that we have just created, the number 3 is in the "1-2" position, because it is in the first row and the second column. We can access that particular position in R by calling **matrix1[1,2]**.

Variance

In general, the variance of a variable gives us an idea of how widely that variable is spread out.

Covariance

Covariance is variance that is measured for two different variables together. It measures the extent to which their dispersion matches. In other words, it measures the extent to which if one is high, the other is also high, and how high each of them is expected to be.

Exercise 26: Examining Variance and Covariance on the Wine Dataset

Execute all the steps that are to be followed in *Exercise 21, Examining a Dataset that Contains Chemical Attributes of Different Wines*. Then calculate variance and covariance for the same dataset: *Pg 128*

1. The alcohol measurements are all between 11.03 and 14.83, which you can see by running the following:

    ```
    range(wine$alcohol)
    ```

    The output is as follows:

    ```
    [1] 11.03 14.83
    ```

2. We can calculate variance by using R's **var** command. For the wine's alcohol measurement, we find **var(wine$alcohol)** is about 0.66. By contrast, we find that the magnesium measurements in our dataset are more widely dispersed by executing the following:

    ```
    range(wine$magnesium)
    ```

    The output is as follows:

    ```
    [1] 70 162
    ```

3. This shows that the variable ranges from 70 to 162. Since it is more widely dispersed, we should expect a higher variance, which we indeed find by executing the following:

    ```
    var(wine$magnesium)
    ```

    The output is as follows:

    ```
    [1] 203.9893
    ```

4. To calculate covariance, execute the following code:

    ```
    cov(wine$alcohol,wine$magnesium)
    ```

    The output is as follows:

    ```
    [1] 3.139878
    ```

5. In *Step 4*, we found that the covariance of the alcohol and magnesium variables is about 3.14. Please note that covariance is symmetric, so the covariance of X with Y is the same as the covariance of Y with X. You can check this by trying the following:

    ```
    cov(wine$magnesium,wine$alcohol)
    ```

The output is as follows:

```
[1] 3.139878
```

You will note that it yields the same value.

6. Variance of a variable is just the covariance of that variable with itself. You can see this by running the following code:

```
var(wine$magnesium)
```

The output is as follows:

```
[1] 203.9893
```

You will yield the same output by executing the following code:

```
cov(wine$magnesium,wine$magnesium)
```

The output is as follows:

```
[1] 203.9893
```

The covariance matrix is a square matrix where every entry is a variance or a covariance. To construct a covariance matrix, first we must number each of the variables in our dataset. In the wine dataset, we can give each variable a number according to its order in the list of columns. So, alcohol would be variable 1, malic would be variable 2, and so on.

> **Note**
>
> Remember that you can see the list of variables at the data's source website at https://archive.ics.uci.edu/ml/datasets/wine.

After ordering the variables, we can create the covariance matrix. In this matrix, what we say is, "the i-j entry is the covariance of variable i and variable j." So, the item in the first row, second column is the 1-2 entry, and it will be equal to the covariance of the first variable (alcohol) with the second variable (malic). Since covariance is a symmetric operation, the 2-1 entry will be the same as the 1-2 entry. This means that the matrix itself will be symmetrical – every entry is the same as the entry on the mirror image other side of the main diagonal.

The entries on the main diagonal of the covariance matrix will be variances rather than covariances. For example, the entry in the 3-3 position of the matrix will be the covariance of variable 3 with variable 3 – this is the covariance of a variable with itself, which is another way of saying it is the variable's variance.

Eigenvectors and Eigenvalues

When we have a square matrix such as a covariance matrix, there are certain special vectors we can calculate called **eigenvectors**. Each eigenvector has a value associated with it called an **eigenvalue**. A discussion about eigenvectors and eigenvalues could easily fill a whole book. For our purposes, the most important thing to know about eigenvectors is that they express the directions of maximum variance in our data. The most important thing to know about eigenvalues is that they indicate which eigenvectors are the most important.

The Idea of PCA

PCA is a powerful dimension reduction technique that is based on the linear algebra topics described in the preceding refresher.

To accomplish PCA, we will take the covariance matrix of our data, and then find its eigenvectors. The eigenvectors of the covariance matrix are called **principal components**. The principal components enable us to re-express the data in different terms and different numbers of dimensions.

We will use the dataset related to wine that we explored at the beginning of the chapter. Recall that the wine dataset had 13 dimensions that measured a particular chemical attribute of a particular wine. One observation in that dataset consists of 13 numbers – one for each of the dimensions of the data.

One of the things that PCA enables is re-expressing data in different terms. The covariance matrix of the wine dataset will have 13 eigenvectors. We can interpret those eigenvectors as a set of 13 new dimensions – we will see how to do this in the following exercise. Essentially, we will be able to fully describe each observation in terms of a new set of dimensions that we discovered with PCA.

More importantly, PCA enables us to do dimension reduction. Instead of re-expressing the data in terms of 13 new dimensions defined by the eigenvectors, we can select only the 12 most important of these new dimensions, and express the data in terms of those 12 dimensions instead of the original 13. PCA makes it easy to select which dimensions are the most important, because the importance of each eigenvector is measured by its corresponding eigenvalue. The following exercise will illustrate how to do this more thoroughly.

There is a new type of plot that we will create as part of PCA, called a **scree plot**. A scree plot is a simple line segment plot that shows the eigenvalues of a matrix represented in order from highest to lowest, in order to indicate the relative importance of their associated eigenvectors.

A scree plot shows the values of the eigenvalues of a matrix, plotted in order from largest to smallest. We will use the scree plot to decide which eigenvectors (that is, which dimensions) are the most important.

PCA may sound difficult, and it is based on some terms and ideas that may be new to you, but actually it is relatively simple to implement in R.

Exercise 27: Performing PCA

If we have a covariance matrix, we are ready to perform PCA. In this case, we will use the wine dataset that we explored earlier in this chapter. Our goal is to perform dimension reduction – to express the wine dataset in fewer dimensions than it originally possessed. This exercise is built on top of *Exercise 26, Examining Variance and Covariance on the Wine Dataset*:

1. To begin, load the same **wine** dataset that we used earlier in the chapter. As a first step, we will remove the **class** column from our wine dataset. We are doing this because **class** is not a chemical attribute of the wine, but rather a label, and we are interested in studying the chemical attributes of wine. We can remove this column as follows:

    ```
    wine_attributes<-wine[,2:14]
    ```

2. We can get the covariance matrix of this smaller matrix as follows:

    ```
    wine_cov<-cov(wine_attributes)
    ```

3. Next, we will use a function in R called **eigen**. This function calculates the special vectors called **eigenvectors**, and the special values called **eigenvalues**. We can apply it to our covariance matrix as follows:

    ```
    wine_eigen<-eigen(wine_cov)
    ```

4. Now we can look at the eigenvectors we have found:

    ```
    print(wine_eigen$vectors)
    ```

    The output is as follows:

    ```
                [,1]          [,2]          [,3]          [,4]          [,5]          [,6]          [,7]          [,8]          [,9]          [,10]
    [1,]  -0.0016592647 -1.203406e-03  0.016873809 -0.141446778  0.020336977 -0.194120104  0.923280337 -2.848207e-01  8.660061e-02 -2.245000e-03
    [2,]   0.0006810156 -2.154982e-03  0.122003373 -0.160389543 -0.612883454 -0.742472963 -0.150109941  6.467447e-02  1.566214e-02 -1.850935e-02
    [3,]  -0.0001949057 -4.593693e-03  0.051987430  0.009772810  0.020175575 -0.041752912  0.045009549  1.493395e-01  7.364985e-02 -8.679965e-02
    [4,]   0.0046713006 -2.645039e-02  0.938593003  0.330965260  0.064352340  0.024065303  0.031526583 -1.515391e-02  2.044578e-03  3.554028e-03
    [5,]  -0.0178680075 -9.993442e-01 -0.029780248  0.005393756 -0.006149345  0.001923782  0.001797363  3.552212e-03 -1.963668e-03 -4.051542e-05
    [6,]  -0.0009898297 -8.779622e-04 -0.040484644  0.074584656  0.315245063 -0.278716809 -0.020185710  1.772379e-01  2.556729e-01  8.471951e-01
    [7,]  -0.0015672883  5.185073e-05 -0.085443339  0.169086724  0.524761088 -0.433597955 -0.038868518  2.481166e-01  3.783067e-01 -5.201384e-01
    [8,]   0.0001230867  1.354479e-03  0.013510780 -0.010805561 -0.029647512  0.021952834 -0.004665483 -6.497968e-03  3.675204e-02  3.771319e-02
    [9,]  -0.0006006078 -5.004400e-03 -0.024659382  0.050120952  0.251182529 -0.241884488 -0.309799487 -8.704332e-01 -5.152017e-02  9.722752e-03
    [10,] -0.0023271432 -1.510035e-02  0.291398464 -0.878893693  0.331747051 -0.002739609 -0.112836514  8.128692e-02 -9.902908e-02 -2.314712e-02
    [11,] -0.0001713800  7.626731e-04 -0.025977662  0.060034945  0.051524077  0.023776167  0.030819813  2.951904e-03  3.306512e-02 -3.846983e-02
    [12,] -0.0007049316  3.495364e-03 -0.070323969  0.178200254  0.260639176 -0.288912753  0.101973518  1.867145e-01 -8.737465e-01  1.701708e-02
    [13,] -0.9998229365  1.777381e-02  0.004528682  0.003112916 -0.002298569  0.001212255 -0.001076189 -1.034095e-05 -7.255852e-05  4.926638e-05
                [,11]         [,12]         [,13]
    [1,]  -0.0149715080  1.565141e-02  8.029245e-03
    [2,]  -0.0231876506 -6.729555e-02 -1.109039e-02
    [3,]   0.9540106426  1.320630e-01 -1.736857e-01
    [4,]  -0.0528216953 -5.393806e-03  1.939563e-03
    [5,]  -0.0030248882 -6.208885e-04  2.284536e-03
    [6,]   0.0088016070 -3.882903e-03 -2.669144e-02
    [7,]  -0.1332046120  3.748803e-02  6.959853e-02
    [8,]   0.1991789841 -1.475524e-01  9.664662e-01
    [9,]   0.1356214601  1.311883e-02 -1.760357e-02
    [10,] -0.0098196717 -5.035557e-02 -4.632943e-03
    [11,]  0.0975106606 -9.755619e-01 -1.665508e-01
    [12,]  0.0284851062 -1.163025e-02  4.419224e-02
    [13,] -0.0002404522  9.999951e-05  3.626701e-05
    ```

    Figure 4.10: Eigenvectors of wine

5. R has compiled the eigenvectors into a square matrix the same size as our original covariance matrix. Each column of this new matrix is one of the eigenvectors of the covariance matrix. If we look at the eigenvalues we have found, we can see the relative importance of each of these eigenvectors. Execute the following to look at the eigenvalues:

    ```
    print(wine_eigen$values)
    ```

    The output is as follows:

    ```
     [1] 9.920179e+04 1.725353e+02 9.438114e+00 4.991179e+00 1.228845e+00 8.410639e-01 2.789735e-01 1.513813e-01 1.120968e-01 7.170260e-02 3.757598e-02
    [12] 2.107237e-02 8.203703e-03
    ```

    Figure 4.11: Eigenvalues of wine

6. We are essentially finished with our PCA. The eigenvectors of the covariance matrix are called the principal components of the data. Let's look at the first one:

    ```
    print(wine_eigen$vectors[,1])
    ```

    The output is as follows:

    ```
     [1] -0.0016592647  0.0006810156 -0.0001949057  0.0046713006 -0.0178680075 -0.0009898297 -0.0015672883  0.0001230867 -0.0006006078 -0.0023271432
    [11] -0.0001713800 -0.0007049316 -0.9998229365
    ```

    Figure 4.12: This first eigenvector expresses a linear combination of our original dimensions.

We can understand our first principal component as follows:

Principal Component 1 = -0.0016592647 * alcohol + 0.0006810156 * malic -0.0001949057 * ash + 0.0046713006 * alcalinity -0.0178680075 * magnesium - 0.0009898297 * phenol -0.0015672883 * flavanoid +0.0001230867 * nonfphenol -0.0006006078 * proanthocyanin -0.0023271432 * color -0.0001713800 * hue -0.0007049316 * od280 -0.9998229365 * proline

So, each element of the eigenvector is a coefficient in this equation to generate a new principal component. The principal component is a linear combination of the original dimensions. We can use each of the principal components as new dimensions. So, instead of describing an observation by saying "it has a 14.23 measurement for alcohol, a 1.71 measurement for malic...." and so on, we can describe it by saying something like "it has a 5.62 measurement for principal component 1, a 9.19 measurement for principal component 2...." and so on.

The most important outcomes for this exercise are the **wine_eigen$vectors** and **wine_eigen$values** objects.

Any dimension reduction technique will mean that we have to lose some of the information encoded in the dataset. This is inevitable: one number can never completely express everything that is expressed in 13 numbers. The benefit of PCA is that it guarantees that it is the most efficient way to do dimension reduction – that by expressing data in terms of the principal components, we have lost the least possible amount of what is encoded in the original data.

In the following exercise, we will discuss how to transform the data to accomplish dimension reduction.

Exercise 28: Performing Dimension Reduction with PCA

This exercise is a continuation of the previous exercise – it will use the same data and the same matrices and eigenvectors that we calculated there:

1. Remember, each of the eigenvectors of our covariance matrix tells us a linear combination of the 13 wine attributes that can be used to summarize the data. In this case, the first eigenvector is telling us that we can make transformation of the data as follows:

```
neigen<-1
transformed<-t(t(as.matrix(wine_eigen$vectors[,1:neigen])) %*% t(as.
matrix(wine_attributes)))
```

Here, we have specified a number of eigenvectors (1), and we have multiplied our original dataset by this number of eigenvectors, creating a transformed dataset that is expressed in terms of this eigenvector or our first principal component.

2. We can look at part of our transformed dataset as follows:

    ```
    print(head(transformed))
    ```

    This will give us the following output:

    ```
                  [,1]
    [1,] -1067.0557
    [2,] -1051.5901
    [3,] -1186.5538
    [4,] -1481.7328
    [5,]  -736.9213
    [6,] -1451.7239
    ```

    Figure 4.13: Transformed dataset

    Here, we have a one-dimensional dataset that describes each observation with only one number. So, we are saying that the first observed wine has a score of -1067.0557 on principal component 1. We have accomplished dimension reduction.

3. We can do a partial restoration of the dataset with the following multiplication:

    ```
    restored<- t(as.matrix(wine_eigen$vectors[,1:neigen]) %*% t(as.
    matrix(transformed)))
    ```

    This should approximately restore our original dataset.

    > **Note**
    >
    > Since dimension reduction always loses some of the original information encoded in data, it will not be a perfect restoration.

4. We can test whether our transformation has led to an accurate reconstruction of the data as follows:

    ```
    print(mean(abs(wine_attributes[,13]-restored[,13])))
    ```

    The output is as follows:

    ```
    [1] 1.466919
    ```

In this case, the error is quite small, indicating that we have been fairly successful in restoring our data.

5. We can do dimension reduction using any number of dimensions. In general, we can determine how many dimensions we should use in transformations by generating a scree plot, as follows:

```
plot(wine_eigen$values,type='o')
```

In this case, our scree plot appears as follows:

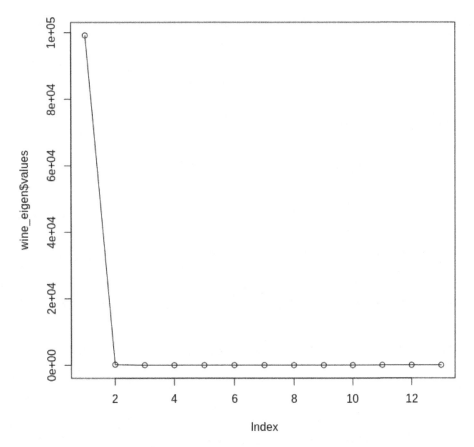

Figure 4.14: Scree plot showing the eigenvalues of a covariance matrix

To decide how many dimensions to use for dimension reduction, we can look at this scree plot and choose a number of dimensions corresponding to the number of eigenvalues that are relatively high compared to the rest.

We can see that the first eigenvalue is by far the highest, so therefore the first eigenvector is by far the most important one, telling us that the first principal component is the most important dimension. In this case, reduction to a one-dimensional dataset is quite appropriate.

You have just performed PCA on a covariance matrix.

Activity 10: Performing PCA and Market Basket Analysis on a New Dataset

In the following activity, you will load a new dataset, and then you will perform PCA and market basket analysis on it. The activity will go through each of the major steps of both of those procedures, including the required data preparation. The dataset we will use comes from a study that was done of neighborhoods in the area around Boston, Massachusetts, and it contains features of many neighborhoods, including tax rates, property values, and demographics of the local populations.

For this activity, use the "**Boston**" dataset, which can be obtained by running the following code in R:

```
library(MASS)
```
```
data(Boston)
```

These steps will help you complete the activity:

1. Convert all variables into dummy variables by doing the following: for each variable, create a new variable that is equal to 1 if it is at or above that variable's median, and 0 if it is below that variable's median. Create another new variable that is the complement of this: where every 0 in the previously created dummy variable is a 1 and every 1 in the previously created dummy variable is a 0. Save all the dummy variables into a new dataset called **Bostondummy**.

2. Find all eigenvectors and eigenvalues of the original data

3. Create a scree plot of the eigenvalues of this data. How should this scree plot be interpreted?

4. Attempt to approximate this data using only a few of the principal components. How close is your approximation to the original data?

5. Using the dummy variables you created in *Step 1*, perform the first pass of market basket analysis by finding all of the variables whose value is 1 for more than 10% of rows.

6. Perform the second pass of market basket analysis by finding all combinations of variables in the data that have more than 10% support in the data.

7. Complete market basket analysis up to three-item baskets.

Expected output: The most important outputs for this activity are the principal components of the dataset, as well as the three-item rules obtained from market basket analysis. The principal components are obtained in the solution to the activity's second step, when we create `Boston_eigen`, and we can run the `print(Boston_eigen$vectors)` command to see the principal components as follows:

```
              [,1]         [,2]          [,3]          [,4]          [,5]
 [1,]  2.964674e-02 -0.015003651 -0.0268303390  0.3105083975  0.9159233539
 [2,] -4.492354e-02  0.631037941 -0.7639084529  0.0914984764 -0.0419675589
 [3,]  2.939532e-02 -0.088515154  0.0130376306  0.0541523272 -0.1258473131
 [4,] -5.070965e-05 -0.000906056 -0.0009292491 -0.0055661084  0.0009662470
 [5,]  4.615941e-04 -0.001817055 -0.0006921813  0.0002758662 -0.0003315697
 [6,] -1.225450e-03  0.005008013 -0.0063668357 -0.0463339423  0.0208901648
 [7,]  8.630861e-02 -0.752355714 -0.6397040816 -0.0812146848 -0.0035253723
 [8,] -6.760251e-03  0.044759063 -0.0017451705  0.0325596672 -0.0278668129
 [9,]  4.670538e-02  0.002571526  0.0181608586 -0.0234532588  0.2379011114
[10,]  9.926372e-01  0.101541990  0.0199846897 -0.0305981550 -0.0272793198
[11,]  5.910888e-03 -0.011370960  0.0329866611  0.0589679625 -0.0184675768
[12,]  2.321636e-02 -0.096883535 -0.0409221274  0.4586710733 -0.0858251068
[13,] -2.565800e-02  0.076330017 -0.0528757677 -0.8167640810  0.2778687767
              [,6]         [,7]          [,8]          [,9]         [,10]
 [1,] -0.155644295 -0.158326612  0.111224831  0.025486508 -0.0227333012
 [2,] -0.038206577 -0.006260425 -0.057018732  0.017656920  0.0318490448
 [3,] -0.860395716 -0.075885802 -0.465215293  0.009900762 -0.0977504102
 [4,] -0.006737114  0.005445449 -0.006327226 -0.009680569 -0.0052830397
 [5,] -0.004868223  0.001270763 -0.003446759 -0.015765167  0.0154002725
 [6,]  0.011854493 -0.009388874 -0.006015218 -0.009814883 -0.0007255794
 [7,]  0.078477626 -0.061457820 -0.007848599  0.009174481 -0.0238738299
 [8,]  0.110677220 -0.041812471  0.013583151  0.116127372 -0.9839320643
 [9,]  0.358117027  0.407606104 -0.793550182 -0.126111107 -0.0106763230
[10,]  0.003158506 -0.016277550  0.044752857  0.001579001 -0.0006268944
[11,]  0.088474600 -0.046285998 -0.146719744  0.973113016  0.1268199497
[12,] -0.170432847  0.807481699  0.287200268  0.071157157 -0.0279765721
[13,] -0.224240115  0.378038741  0.178558244  0.130435940 -0.0545477337
              [,11]        [,12]         [,13]
 [1,] -3.579451e-03 -1.386274e-03  7.168469e-04
 [2,] -2.722109e-03 -1.079790e-04  1.021309e-05
 [3,]  1.260538e-02  8.190011e-03 -4.138848e-03
 [4,] -2.085826e-02 -9.995483e-01 -1.406496e-02
 [5,] -3.828993e-04 -1.392499e-02  9.996394e-01
 [6,]  9.982814e-01 -2.054663e-02  2.645536e-05
 [7,] -5.357718e-03  1.068461e-03 -8.705608e-04
 [8,]  7.023865e-04  2.505075e-03  1.772891e-02
 [9,] -1.221601e-02  6.746324e-03 -3.164339e-03
[10,]  7.268209e-05 -4.231324e-04 -4.147717e-05
[11,]  1.046531e-02 -1.078571e-02  1.320768e-02
[12,]  3.536485e-02 -6.651794e-05  3.293986e-04
[13,] -3.579491e-02  6.976225e-03  2.455507e-03
```

Figure 4.15: Principal components of the original data

The three-item rules for market basket analysis are obtained in the solution to the activity's *Step 14*, and we can see the final results when we run `print(head(thirdpass_conf))` in the console:

```
     [,1] [,2] [,3]       [,4]       [,5]       [,6]
[1,]    1    3    6 0.2588933 0.9776119 1.917332
[2,]    1    3    8 0.2509881 0.9477612 1.018189
[3,]    1    3   10 0.2411067 0.9104478 1.693701
[4,]    1    3   14 0.2332016 0.8805970 1.761194
[5,]    1    3   15 0.2371542 0.8955224 1.791045
[6,]    1    3   18 0.2015810 0.7611940 1.254606
```

Figure 4.16: Three-item rules for market basket analysis

> **Note**
>
> The solution for this activity can be found on page 222.

Summary

In this chapter, we discussed the idea of the dimensionality of data. We went over why it could be useful to reduce the dimensionality of data and highlighted that the process of dimension reduction can reveal important truths about the underlying structure of data. We covered two important dimension reduction methods. The first method we discussed was market basket analysis. This method is useful for generating associative rules from complex data and can be used for the use case it was named after (analyzing baskets of groceries) or a wide variety of other applications (such as analyzing the clustering of survey responses). We also discussed PCA, a common way to describe data in terms of linear combinations of its dimensions. PCA is easy to perform with some linear algebra tools, and provides an easy way to approximate even very complex data.

In the next chapter, we will have a look at the different data comparison methods.

5

Data Comparison Methods

Learning Objectives

By the end of this chapter, you will be able to:

- Create hashes of data

- Create image signatures

- Compare image datasets

- Perform factor analysis to isolate latent variables

- Compare surveys and other datasets using factor analysis

In this chapter, we will have a look at different data comparison methods.

Introduction

Unsupervised learning is concerned with analyzing the structure of data to draw useful conclusions. In this chapter, we will examine methods that enable us to use the structure of data to compare datasets. The major methods we will look at are hash functions, analytic signatures, and latent variable models.

Hash Functions

Imagine that you want to send an R script to your friend. However, you and your friend have been having technical problems with your files – maybe your computers have been infected by malware, or maybe a hacker is tampering with your files. So, you need a way to ensure that your script is sent intact to your friend, without being corrupted or changed. One way to check that files are intact is to use **hash functions**.

A hash function can create something like a **fingerprint** for data. What we mean by a fingerprint is something that is small and easy to check that enables us to verify whether the data has the identity we think it should have. So, after you create the script you want to send, you apply your hash function to the script and get its fingerprint. Then, your friend can use the same hash function on the file after it is received and check to make sure the fingerprints match. If the fingerprint of the file that was sent matches the fingerprint of the file that was received, then the two files should be the same, meaning that the file was sent intact. The following exercise shows how to create and use a simple hash function.

Exercise 29: Creating and Using a Hash Function

In this exercise, we will create and use a hash function:

1. Specify the data on which you need to use the hash function. We have been exploring the scenario of an R script that you want to send. Here is an example of a simple R script:

   ```
   string_to_hash<-"print('Take the cake')"
   ```

   Here, we have a script that prints the string **Take the cake**. We have saved it as a variable called **string_to_hash**.

2. Specify the total number of possible hash values. Our goal is to create a fingerprint for our script. We need to specify the total number of possible fingerprints that we will allow to exist. We want to specify a number that is low enough to work with easily, but high enough that there is not much likelihood of different scripts having the same fingerprint by coincidence. Here, we will use 10,000:

```
total_possible_hashes<-10000
```

3. Convert the script (currently a string) to numeric values. Hash functions are usually arithmetic, so we will need to be working with numbers instead of strings. Luckily, R has a built-in function that can accomplish this for us:

```
numeric<-utf8ToInt(string_to_hash)
```

This has converted each of the characters in our script to an integer, based on each character's encoding in the UTF-8 encoding scheme. We can see the result by printing to the console:

```
print(numeric)
```

The output is as follows:

```
 [1] 112 114 105 110 116  40  39  84  97 107 101  32 116 104 101  32  99
97 107[20] 101  39  41
```

4. Apply our hashing function. We will use the following function to generate our final hash, or in other words, the fingerprint of the script:

```
hash<-sum((numeric+123)^2) %% total_possible_hashes
```

After running this line in R, we find that the final value of **hash** is 2702. Since we have used the modulo operator (**%%** in R), the value of **hash** will always be between 0 and 10,000.

The simple function we used to convert a numeric vector to a final hash value is not the only possible hash function. Experts have designed many such functions with varying levels of sophistication. There is a long list of properties that good hash functions are supposed to have. One of the most important of these properties is **collision resistance**, which means that it is difficult to find two datasets that yield the same hash.

Exercise 30: Verifying Our Hash Function

In this exercise, we will verify that our hash function enables us to effectively compare different data by checking that different messages produce different hashes. The outcome of this exercise will be hash functions of different messages that we will compare to verify that different messages produce different hashes:

1. Create a function that performs hashing for us. We will put the code that we introduced in the preceding exercise together into one function:

   ```
   get_hash<-function(string_to_hash, total_possible_hashes){
   numeric<-utf8ToInt(string_to_hash)
   hash<-sum((numeric+123)^2) %% total_possible_hashes
   return(hash)
   }
   ```

   This function takes the string we want to hash and the total number of possible hashes, then applies the same hashing calculation we used in the previous exercise to calculate a hash, and then returns that hash value.

2. Compare hashes of different inputs. We can compare the hashes that are returned from different inputs as follows:

   ```
   script_1<-"print('Take the cake')"
   script_2<-"print('Make the cake')"
   script_3<-"print('Take the rake')"
   script_4<-"print('Take the towel')"
   ```

   Here, we have four different strings, expressing different messages. We can see the value of their hashes as follows:

   ```
   print(get_hash(script_1,10000))
   print(get_hash(script_2,10000))
   print(get_hash(script_3,10000))
   print(get_hash(script_4,10000))
   ```

   The first script returns the hash 2702, as we found in the preceding exercise. The second script, even though it is only differs from the first script by one character, returns the hash 9853, and the third script, also differing by only one character from the first script, returns the hash 9587. The final script returns the hash 5920. Though these four scripts have substantial similarities, they have different fingerprints that we can use to compare them and distinguish them.

These hashes are useful for you and the recipient of your message to verify that your script was sent intact without tampering. When you send the script, you can tell your friend to make sure that the hash of the script is 2702. If the hash of the script your friend receives is not 2702, then your friend can conclude that the script was tampered with between being sent and being received. If your friend can reliably detect whether a file was corrupted, then you can avoid spreading malware or arguing with your friend over miscommunication.

Software that is distributed online is sometimes distributed with a hash value that users can use to check for file corruption. For this purpose, professionals use hash functions that are more advanced than the simple function presented in the preceding exercises. One of the hash functions that professionals use is called MD5, which can be applied very easily in R using the **digest** package:

```
install.packages('digest')

library(digest)

print(digest(string_to_hash,algo='md5'))
```

The output is as follows:

```
[1] "a3d9d1d7037a02d01526bfe25d1b7126"
```

Here, we can see the MD5 hash of our simple R script. You can feel free to try out MD5 hashes of other data as well to compare the results.

Analytic Signatures

In *Chapter 4*, *Dimension Reduction*, we discussed dimension reduction – methods that enable us to express data succinctly in ways that give us insights into the data. A hash function, discussed previously, is yet another way to accomplish dimension reduction. Hash functions are effective for many purposes, including the file verification use case we discussed. In that scenario, we were interested in determining whether two scripts were exactly the same or not. Even a slight difference in data, such as changing the word "take" to "make," had the potential to completely corrupt the intended message, so exactness was required.

In other cases, we may want to make meaningful comparisons between different datasets without requiring the exact identity of the two datasets being compared. Consider the case of detecting copyright violations. Suppose that a website hosts images from its users. It wants to ensure that users are not submitting images that are protected by copyright. So, every time it receives an upload, it wants to check whether that upload is the same as any of the images in a large database of copyrighted images.

It is not sufficient to check whether images are exactly the same, since unscrupulous uploaders may make slight alterations and attempt to upload anyway. For example, they might change the color of one pixel, or crop the image very slightly, or compress it to be larger or smaller than the original. Even with these slight alterations, the images would still violate copyright laws. A hash function that checked for exact identity would fail to recognize these copyright violations. So, the image hosting site will want to check whether there is any underlying structure in the data representing the two pictures that is substantially similar.

We mentioned that hash functions created something that's like a fingerprint for data. Fingerprints should be exactly the same each time they are observed, and even if two fingerprints are similar in most ways, we will not regard them as matching each other unless they match completely.

Instead of a fingerprint, in this case we need something more like a signature. Each time you sign your name, your signature should look more or less the same. But, there will be small differences in each signature, even when signed by the same person and even when attempting to match previous signatures. In order to verify whether a signature matches, we need to check for substantial similarity but not perfect identity. The code we present here will show how to encode any image of any size in a small and robust encoding that enables quick and accurate approximate comparisons between datasets. This method for encoding image data can be referred to as creating an **analytic signature**.

Our method for creating a signature for an image will proceed as follows. First, we will divide our image into a 10x10 grid. We will then measure the brightness of each section of this grid. After that, we will compare the brightness of each section to the brightness of its neighbors. The final signature will consist of a vector of comparisons between each grid section and each of its neighbors. This signature method was invented by Wong, Bern, and Goldberg, who published it in a paper called *An Image Signature for Any Kind of Image*.

Before we create an analytic signature, we will need to do some data preparation, as outlined in the next exercise.

Exercise 31: Perform the Data Preparation for Creating an Analytic Signature for an Image

In this exercise, we will perform the data preparation for creating an analytic signature for a photo of the Alamo.

> **Note**
>
> For all the exercises and activities where we are importing external CSV files or images, go to **RStudio**-> **Session**-> **Set Working Directory**-> **To Source File Location**. You can see in the console that the path is set automatically.

1. First, we will need to configure R to be able to read in and work with our image data. We will need to install the **imager** package. You can install this package by executing **install.packages('imager')** in the R console, and then you can load it by running **library('imager')** in the console.

2. Next, we will need to read in the data. We will be working with this photo of the Alamo in our example:

Figure 5.1: Alamo image

First, download this to your computer from https://github.com/TrainingByPackt/ Applied-Unsupervised-Learning-with-R/Lesson05/Exercise31/alamo.jpg and save it as **alamo.jpg**. Make sure that it is saved in R's working directory. If it is not in R's working directory, then change R's working directory using the **setwd()** function. Then, you can load this image into a variable called **im** (short for image) as follows:

```
filepath<-'alamo.jpg'
im <- imager::load.image(file =filepath)
```

The rest of the code we will explore will use this image called **im**. Here, we have loaded a photo of the Alamo into **im**. However, you can run the rest of the code on any image, simply by saving the image to your working directory and specifying its path in the **filepath** variable.

3. The signature we are developing is meant to be used for grayscale images. So, we will convert this image to grayscale by using functions in the **imager** package:

```
im<-imager::rm.alpha(im)
im<-imager::grayscale(im)
im<-imager::imsplit(im,axis = "x", nb = 10)
```

The second line of this code is the conversion to grayscale. The last line performs a split of the image into 10 equal sections.

4. The following code creates an empty matrix that we will fill with information about each section of our 10x10 grid:

```
matrix <- matrix(nrow = 10, ncol = 10)
```

Next, we will run the following loop. The first line of this loop uses the **imsplit** command. This command was also used earlier to split the x-axis into 10 equal parts. This time, for each of the 10 x-axis splits, we will do a split along the yaxis, also splitting it into 10 equal parts:

```
for (i in 1:10) {
  is <- imager::imsplit(im = im[[i]], axis = "y", nb = 10)
  for (j in 1:10) {
    matrix[j,i] <- mean(is[[j]])
  }
}
```

After splitting along the y axis, the matrix is updated with **mean(is[[j]])**. This is a measure of the mean brightness of the selected section.

The result of this code is a 10x10 matrix, where the **i-j** element contains the average brightness of the **i-j** section of the original photo.

If you print this matrix, you can see the brightness numbers for each section of the photo:

```
print(matrix)
```

The output should look like the following:

```
            [,1]       [,2]       [,3]       [,4]       [,5]       [,6]
 [1,]  0.8013922  0.8222856  0.8685930  0.8860392  0.8790931  0.8543929
 [2,]  0.7894936  0.8038676  0.8190953  0.8486792  0.8580144  0.8787474
 [3,]  0.8364491  0.8344346  0.8684280  0.8793931  0.8654631  0.8381220
 [4,]  0.8285232  0.8608995  0.8577416  0.8791815  0.8901511  0.8678896
 [5,]  0.7722914  0.7996539  0.7830312  0.7346689  0.7528258  0.8230921
 [6,]  0.5818810  0.6800845  0.7049547  0.6165779  0.5959824  0.6451469
 [7,]  0.3869945  0.5499423  0.5784381  0.5099081  0.5700767  0.5818399
 [8,]  0.1772511  0.4792003  0.4952705  0.3892928  0.4537441  0.5686928
 [9,]  0.1416325  0.2946302  0.3490931  0.2626835  0.3579248  0.4588876
[10,]  0.2487561  0.2265129  0.2497341  0.2668862  0.2668478  0.2782614
            [,7]       [,8]       [,9]      [,10]
 [1,]  0.8131941  0.8397566  0.7535993  0.5631498
 [2,]  0.8876371  0.8710443  0.6074711  0.3195716
 [3,]  0.8250339  0.7549411  0.5641089  0.3053245
 [4,]  0.8860902  0.7095673  0.3035896  0.2377038
 [5,]  0.8191305  0.7778448  0.4690702  0.1963085
 [6,]  0.6660920  0.6378310  0.5663493  0.2437251
 [7,]  0.4905826  0.4436965  0.2017358  0.1559014
 [8,]  0.5182057  0.4634460  0.1914863  0.1269013
 [9,]  0.4728699  0.4246325  0.1942542  0.1460421
[10,]  0.2671916  0.2420319  0.1878105  0.1782178
```

Figure 5.2: Screenshot of the output matrix

You can compare these brightness numbers to the appearance of the original photo.

We could stop here, since we have generated a compressed encoding of a complex dataset. However, we can take some further steps to make this encoding more useful.

One thing we can do is create a **brightnesscomparison** function. The purpose of this function is to compare the relative brightness of two different sections of an image. Eventually, we will compare all of the different sections of each image we analyze. Our final fingerprint will consist of many such brightness comparisons. The purpose of this exercise is to create the brightness comparison function that will eventually enable us to create the final fingerprint.

Please note, this exercise is built on top of the previous exercise, meaning that you should run all of the code in the previous exercise before you run the code in this exercise.

Exercise 32: Creating a Brightness Comparison Function

1. In this function, we pass two arguments, **x** and **y**: each argument represents the brightness of a particular section of the picture. If **x** and **y** are quite similar (less than 10% different), then we say that they are essentially the same and we return 0, indicating approximately 0 difference in brightness. If **x** is more than 10% greater than **y**, we return 1, indicating that **x** is brighter than **y**, and if **x** is more than 10% smaller than **y**, we return -1, indicating that **x** is less bright than **y**.

2. Create the brightness comparison function. The code for the **brightnesscomparison** function is as follows:

```
brightnesscomparison<-function(x,y){
compared<-0
if(abs(x/y-1)>0.1){

if(x>y){
compared<-1
}

if(x<y){
compared<-(-1)
}

}

return(compared)
}
```

3. We can use this function to compare two sections of the 10x10 grid we formed for our picture. For example, to find the brightness comparison of a section with the section that is directly to its left, we can execute the following code:

```
i<-5
j<-5
left<-brightnesscomparison(matrix[i,j-1],matrix[i,j])
```

Here, we looked at the 5th row and 5th column of our matrix. We compared this section to the section directly to the left of it – the 5th row and 4th column, which we accessed by specifying **j-1**.

4. Use the brightness comparison function to compare an image section to its neighbor above it. We could do an analogous operation to compare this section to the section above it:

```
i<-5
j<-5
top<-brightnesscomparison(matrix[i-1,j],matrix[i,j])
```

Here, **top** is a comparison of the brightness of section 5, 5 with the section immediately above it, which we accessed by specifying **i-1**.

The important outputs of this exercise are the values of **top** and **left**, which are both comparisons of an image section to other, neighboring sections. In this case, left is equal to zero, meaning that the image section we selected has about the same brightness as the image section to its left. Also, **top** is equal to 1, meaning that the section directly above the section we selected is brighter than the section we selected.

In the next exercise, we will create a **neighborcomparison** function. This function takes every section of our 10x10 grid and compares the brightness of that section to its neighbors. These neighbors include the left neighbor, whose brightness we compared a moment ago, and also the top neighbor. Altogether, there are eight neighbors for each section of our picture (top, bottom, left, right, top-left, top-right, bottom-left, and bottom-right). The reason we will want this neighbor comparison function is because it will make it very easy for us to get our final analytic signature.

Please note that this exercise builds on the previous exercises, and you should run all of the previous code before running this code.

Exercise 33: Creating a Function to Compare Image Sections to All of the Neighboring Sections

In this exercise, we will create a **neighborcomparison** function to compare image sections to all other neighboring sections. To do this, perform the following steps:

1. Create a function that compares an image section to its neighbor on the left. We did this in the previous exercise. For any image section, we can compare its

   brightness to the brightness of its neighbor on the left as follows:

```
i<-5
j<-5
left<-brightnesscomparison(matrix[i,j-1],matrix[i,j])
```

2. Create a function that compares an image section to its neighbor on top. We did this in the previous exercise. For any image section, we can compare its brightness to the brightness of its neighbor above it as follows:

```
i<-5
j<-5
top<-brightnesscomparison(matrix[i-1,j],matrix[i,j])
```

3. If you look at *Step 1* and *Step 2*, you can start to notice the pattern in these neighbor comparisons. To compare an image section to the section on its left, we need to access the part of the matrix at index **j-1**. To compare an image section to the section on its right, we need to access the part of the matrix at index **j+1**. To compare an image section to the section above it, we need to access the part of the matrix at index **i-1**. To compare an image section to the section below it, we need to access the part of the matrix at index **i+1**.

So, we will have comparisons of each image section to each of its neighbors, above, below, left, and right. The following code shows the comparisons we will make in addition to the top and left comparisons made in *Step 1* and *Step 2*:

```
i<-5
j<-5
top_left<-brightnesscomparison(matrix[i-1,j-1], matrix[i,j])
bottom_left<-brightnesscomparison(matrix[i+1,j-1],matrix[i,j])
top_right<-brightnesscomparison(matrix[i-1,j+1],matrix[i,j])
right<-brightnesscomparison(matrix[i,j+1],matrix[i,j])
bottom_right<-brightnesscomparison(matrix[i+1,j+1],matrix[i,j])
bottom<-brightnesscomparison(matrix[i+1,j],matrix[i,j])
```

4. Initialize a vector that will contain the final comparison of a section to each of its neighbors:

```
comparison<-NULL
```

We will use this **comparison** vector to store all of the neighbor comparisons that we eventually generate. It will consist of comparisons of an image section to each of its neighbors.

5. In steps 1-4, we have shown the individual parts of the neighbor comparison function. In this step, we will combine them. The neighbor comparison function that you can see takes an image matrix as an argument, and also **i** and **j** values, specifying which part of the image matrix we are focusing on. The function uses the code we wrote for the **top** and **left** comparisons, and also adds other comparisons for other neighbors, such as **top_left**, which compares an image brightness level with the image brightness of the section above and to the left. Altogether, each image section should have eight neighbors: top-left, top,

   top-right, left, right, bottom-left, bottom, and bottom-right. In this step, we will do each of these eight comparisons and store them in the **comparison** vector. Finally, there is a **return** statement that returns all of the comparisons together.

   Here is the function we can use to get all of the neighbor comparisons:

```
neighborcomparison<-function(mat,i,j){
comparison<-NULL

top_left<-0
if(i>1 & j>1){
top_left<-brightnesscomparison(mat[i-1,j-1],mat[i,j])
}

left<-0
if(j>1){
left<-brightnesscomparison(mat[i,j-1],mat[i,j])
}

bottom_left<-0
if(j>1 & i<nrow(mat)){
bottom_left<-brightnesscomparison(mat[i+1,j-1],mat[i,j])
}

top_right<-0
if(i>1 & j<nrow(mat)){
top_right<-brightnesscomparison(mat[i-1,j+1],mat[i,j])
}

right<-0
if(j<ncol(mat)){
right<-brightnesscomparison(mat[i,j+1],mat[i,j])
}
```

```
bottom_right<-0
if(i<nrow(mat) & j<ncol(mat)){
bottom_right<-brightnesscomparison(mat[i+1,j+1],mat[i,j])
}

top<-0
if(i>1){
top<-brightnesscomparison(mat[i-1,j],mat[i,j])
}

bottom<-0
if(i<nrow(mat)){
bottom<-brightnesscomparison(mat[i+1,j],mat[i,j])
}

comparison<-c(top_left,left,bottom_left,bottom,bottom_right,right,top_
right,top)

return(comparison)
}
```

This function returns a vector with eight elements: one for each of the neighbors of a particular section of our grid. You may have noticed that some sections of the 10x10 grid do not appear to have eight neighbors. For example, the 1-1 element of the 10x10 grid has a neighbor below it, but does not have a neighbor above it. For grid locations that do not have particular neighbors, we say that their brightness comparison is 0 for that neighbor. This decreases the level of complexity in creating and interpreting the brightness comparisons.

The final output is a vector called **comparison**, which contains comparisons of brightness levels between an image section and each of its eight neighbors.

In the next exercise, we will finish creating our analytic signature. The analytic signature for each image will consist of comparisons of each image section with each of its eight neighbors. We will use two nested **for** loops to iterate through every section of our 10x10 grid. The expected output of this exercise will be a function that generates an analytic signature for an image.

Exercise 34: Creating a Function that Generates an Analytic Signature for an Image

In this exercise, we will create a function that generates an analytic signature for an image. To do this, perform the following steps:

1. We begin by creating a **signature** variable and initializing it with a **NULL** value:

    ```
    signature<-NULL
    ```

    This **signature** variable will store the complete signature when we have finished.

2. Now we can loop through our grid. For each section of the grid, we add eight new elements to the signature. The elements we add are the outputs of the **neighborcomparison** function we introduced earlier:

    ```
    for (i in 1:nrow(matrix)){
    for (j in 1:ncol(matrix)){
    signature<-c(signature,neighborcomparison(matrix,i,j))
    }
    }
    ```

    We can see what our fingerprint looks like by running **print(signature)** in the console. It is a vector of 800 values, all of which are equal to either 0 (indicating similar brightness or no neighbor), 1 (indicating that a section is more bright than its neighbor), or -1 (indicating that a section is less bright than its neighbor).

3. Put *Step 1* and *Step 2* together in a function that can generate a signature for any

    image matrix:

    ```
    get_signature<-function(matrix){
    signature<-NULL
    for (i in 1:nrow(matrix)){
    for (j in 1:ncol(matrix)){
    signature<-c(signature,neighborcomparison(matrix,i,j))
    }
    }
    return(signature)
    }
    ```

    This code defines a function called **get_signature**, and it uses the code from *Step 1* and *Step 2* to get that signature. We can call this function using the image matrix we created earlier.

4. Since we are going to create more signatures later, we will save this signature to a variable that refers to what it is a signature of. In this case, we will call it **building_signature** since it is a signature of an image of a building. We can do this as follows:

```
building_signature<-get_signature(matrix)
building_signature
```

The output is as follows:

```
  [1]  0  0  0  0  0  0  0  0  0  0  0  0  0  0  0  0  0  0  0  0  0  0  0  0  0  0  0  0  0  0  0  0  0  0  0  0  0  0  0  0  0  0  0  0  0  0  0  0  0  0  0  0  0  0
  0  0  0  0  0  0
 [55]  0  0  0  0  0  0 -1 -1  0  0  0  1  1 -1 -1 -1 -1  0  0  0  1  0 -1  0  0  0  0  0  0  0  0  0  0  0  0  0  0  0  0  0  0  0  0  0  0  0  0  0  0  0  0  0  0  0
  0  0  0  0  0  0
[109]  0  0  0  0  0  0  0  0  0  0  0  0  0  0  0  0  0  0  0  0  0  0  0  0 -1  0  0  0  0  0  0 -1 -1 -1 -1  0  1  1  1  1  0 -1 -1  0  1  1  1  1  1  0
  0  0  0  1  0  0
[163]  0  0  0  0  0  0  0  0  0  0  0  0  0  0  0  0  0  0  0  0  0  0  0  0  0  0  0  0  0  0  0  0  0  0  0  0  0  0  0  0  0  0  0  0  0  0  0  0  0  0  0  0  0  0
  0  0 -1  0  0  0
[217]  1  0  1  0 -1 -1 -1  1  1  1  1  1 -1 -1 -1 -1 -1  0  1  1  0 -1  0  0  0  0  0  0  0  0  0  0  0  0  0 -1  0  0  0  0  0  0  0  0  0 -1  0  0  0
  0  0 -1 -1 -1  0
[271]  0  0  0  0 -1 -1  0  0  0  0  0  0 -1  0  0  0  0  0  0  0  0  0 -1 -1 -1  0  1  1  1  0 -1 -1 -1  0  1  1  1  1 -1 -1  0  1  1  1  1 -1  0  0
  0  1  0  0  0 -1
[325] -1  0  1  0  0  0 -1 -1 -1  0  0  0  0  0 -1  0 -1  0  1  0  1  0  0 -1 -1  0  1  1  1  0 -1 -1 -1  0  1  1  0  0 -1 -1 -1  0  0  0  0  0 -1 -1
  1  0 -1  0  1  0
[379] -1 -1 -1 -1 -1  0  1  1  1  1 -1 -1 -1 -1  1  1  1  1  0  0  0  1  0  0  0 -1  0  1  1  1  1 -1 -1 -1 -1  0  1  1  1  0 -1 -1 -1 -1  0  1  1  1
  0 -1  0  0  1  1
[433]  1  0 -1  0  0  0  1  1  1  0 -1  0 -1  0  1  1  1  0 -1 -1 -1  0  1  1  1  0 -1 -1 -1 -1 -1  1  1  1 -1 -1 -1 -1 -1 -1 -1  1  1 -1 -1  0  0  0 -1
  0  0  0 -1  1  1
[487]  1  1  0 -1 -1 -1  0  0  1  1  1  0 -1 -1 -1 -1  0  1  1  1  0 -1 -1  1  1  1  1  0 -1 -1 -1  0  0  1  0  0  0 -1  0 -1 -1  1  1  1  1  1  0  0  0
  1  1  1  1  1  0
[541] -1 -1  1  1  1  1  1  0 -1 -1  1  1  1  1  1 -1  0  0  0  1  0  0  0 -1  1  1  1  1 -1 -1 -1 -1 -1  0  1  1  1  0 -1 -1 -1 -1  0  1  1  1 -1 -1
  0  1  1  1  1 -1
[595] -1 -1  0  1  1  1  0 -1 -1 -1 -1  0 -1  0  1  0 -1  0 -1 -1 -1  0  0  1  0  0 -1 -1 -1  0  1  1  1  0 -1 -1 -1 -1  0  1  1  1  1  0  0  0  1  0  0
  0  1  1  1  1  1
[649] -1 -1 -1 -1 -1  1  1  1  1  1 -1 -1 -1 -1 -1  1  1  1  1  0  0  0  1  1  1  0 -1 -1 -1 -1  1  1  1  0 -1 -1 -1 -1  0  1  1  1  0 -1 -1 -1 -1  0  0
  1  1 -1 -1 -1 -1
[703] -1  0  1  1  1  0  0 -1 -1  0  1  1  1  1  0  0  0 -1  0  0  0  0  0  0  1 -1 -1  0  0  0  0  1  1  1  1  0  0  0  0  0  0  1  1  0  0  0  0  0
  1  0  0  0  0  0
[757]  0  0  1  1  1  0  0  0  0  0  1  1  1  0  0  0  0  0  1  1  1  1  0  0  0 -1 -1  1  1  1  0  0  0  0 -1  0  0  0  0  0  0  0  0  0  0 -1
```

Figure: 5.3: Matrix of building_signature

The vector stored in **building_signature** is the final output of this exercise, and it is the image signature we have been trying to develop throughout this chapter.

This signature is meant to be like a human's handwritten signature: small and apparently similar to other signatures, but sufficiently unique to enable us to distinguish it from millions of other existing signatures.

We can check the robustness of the signature solution we have found by reading in a completely different image and comparing the resulting signatures. This is the scenario for the following activity.

Activity 11: Creating an Image Signature for a Photograph of a Person

Let's try to create an image fingerprint for this image, a photograph of the great Jorge Luis Borges.

To accomplish this activity, you can follow all of the steps we have followed so far in this chapter. The following steps will outline this process for you. Remember that in our previous image signature exercise, we used a 10x10 matrix of brightness measurements. However, a 10x10 matrix may be inappropriate for some situations, for example, if the image we are working with is particularly small, or if we have data storage constraints, or if we expect higher accuracy with a different matrix size. So, in the following activity, we will also calculate a signature using a 9x9 matrix:

> **Note**
>
> This can be performed on any given matrix size. It could be a 5x5 matrix for data storage purposes or a 20x20 matrix for accurate signatures.

Figure 5.4: Jorge Luis Borges image

These steps will help us complete the activity:

1. Load the image into your R working directory. Save it to a variable called **im**.

2. Convert your image to grayscale and split it into 100 sections.

3. Create a matrix of brightness values.

4. Create a signature using the **get_signature** function we created earlier. Save the signature of the Borges image as **borges_signature**.

> **Note**
>
> The solution for this activity can be found on page 227.

The final output of this activity is the **borges_signature** variable, which is the analytic signature of the Borges photo. Additionally, we have created the **borges_signature_ninebynine** variable, which is also an analytic signature, but based on a 9x9 rather than a 10x10 matrix. We can use either of them in our analysis, but we will use the **borges_signature** variable. If you have completed all of the exercises and activities so far, then you should have two analytic signatures: one called **building_signature**, and one called **borges_signature**.

Comparison of Signatures

Next, we can compare these two signatures, to see whether they have mapped our different images to different signature values.

You can compare the signatures with one simple line of R code as follows:

```
comparison<-mean(abs(borges_signature-building_signature))
```

This comparison takes the absolute value of the difference between each element of the two signatures, and then calculates the mean of those values. If two signatures are identical, then this difference will be 0. The larger the value of **comparison**, the more different the two images are.

In this case, the value of **comparison** is 0.644, indicating that on average, the corresponding signature entries are about 0.644 apart. This difference is substantial for a dataset where the values only range between 1 and -1. So we see that our method for creating signatures has created very different signatures for very different images, as we would expect.

Now, we can calculate a signature for an image that is very similar to our original image, but not identical:

Figure 5.5: Alamo_marked image

To obtain this image, I started with the original Alamo image, and I added the word **watermark** in four places, simulating what someone might do to alter an image. Naive copyright detection software might be fooled by this watermark, since the image is now different from the original. Our analytic signature method should not be so naive. We will accomplish this in the following activity.

Activity 12: Creating an Image Signature for the Watermarked Image

In this activity, we will create an image signature for the watermarked image:

1. Load the image into your R working directory. Save it to a variable called **im**.

2. Convert your image to grayscale and split it into 100 sections.

3. Create a matrix of brightness values.

4. Create a signature using the **get_signature** function we created earlier. Save the signature of the Alamo image as **watermarked_signature**.

5. Compare the signature of the watermarked image to the signature of the original image to determine whether the signature method can tell the images apart.

The output will be as follows:

```
 [1] 0  0  0  0  0  0  0  0  0  0  0  0  0  0  0  0  0  0  0  0  0  0  0  0  0  0  0  0  0  0  0  0  0  0  0  0  0  0  0  0  0  0  0  0  0  0  0  0  0  0  0  0  0  0
 0  0  0  0  0  0
 [55] 0  0  0  0  0  0 -1 -1  0  0  0  1  1 -1 -1 -1 -1  0  0  0  1  0 -1  0  0  0  0  0  0  0  0  0  0  0  0  0  0  0  0  0  0  0  0  1  0  0  0  0  0  0  0  0  0  0
 1  0  0  0  0  0
 [109] 0  0  0  0  0  0  0  0  0  0  0  0  0  0  0  0  0  0  0  0  0  0  0  0 -1  0  0  0  0  0  0 -1 -1 -1 -1  0  1  1  1  0 -1 -1  0  1  1  1  1  0
 0  0  0  1  0  0
 [163] 0  0  0  0  0  0  0  0  0  0  0  0  0  0 -1  0  0  0  0  0  0  0  0  0  0  0  0  0  0  0  0  0  0  0  0  0  0  0  0  0  0  0  0  0  0  0  0  0
 0  0 -1  0  0  0
 [217] 1  0  1  0 -1 -1 -1  1  1  1  1 -1 -1 -1 -1  0  1  1  0 -1  0  0  0  0  0  0  0  0  0  0  0  0  0  0 -1  0  0  0  0  0  0  0  0  0 -1  0  0  0
 0  0 -1 -1 -1  0
 [271] 0  0  0  0 -1 -1  0  0  0  0  0  0 -1  0  0  0  0  0  0  0  0  0 -1 -1 -1  0  1  1  1  0 -1 -1 -1  0  1  1  1  1 -1 -1  0  1  1  1  1 -1  0  0
 0  1  0  0  0 -1
 [325] -1  0  1  0  0  0 -1 -1 -1  0  0  0  0  0 -1  0 -1  0  1  0  1  0  0 -1 -1  0  1  1  1  0 -1 -1 -1  0  1  1  0  0 -1 -1 -1  0  0  0  0  0 -1 -1 -
 1  0 -1  0  1  0
 [379] -1 -1 -1 -1 -1  0  1  1  1  1 -1 -1 -1 -1  1  1  1  1  0  0  0  1  0  0  0 -1  0  1  1  1  1 -1 -1 -1 -1  0  1  1  1  0 -1 -1 -1 -1  0  1  1  1
 0 -1  0  0  1  1
 [433] 1  0 -1  0  0  0  1  1  1  0 -1 -1 -1  0  1  1  1  0 -1 -1 -1  0  1  1  1  0 -1 -1 -1 -1 -1  1  1  1 -1 -1 -1 -1 -1 -1 -1  1  1 -1 -1  0  0  0 -1
 0  0  0 -1  1  1
 [487] 1  1  0 -1 -1 -1 -1  0  1  1  1  0 -1 -1 -1 -1  0  1  1  1  0 -1 -1  1  1  1  0 -1 -1 -1  0  0  1  0  0  0 -1  0 -1 -1  1  1  1  1  1  1  0  0  0
 1  1  1  1  0
 [541] -1 -1  1  1  1  1  1  0 -1 -1  1  1  1  1  1 -1  0  0  0  1  0  0  0 -1  1  1  1  1 -1 -1 -1 -1 -1  0  1  1  1  0 -1 -1 -1 -1  0  1  1  1 -1 -1
 0  1  1  1 -1
 [595] -1 -1  0  1  1  1  0 -1 -1 -1 -1 -1 -1  0  1  1  0  0 -1  0 -1  0  0  0  0  0 -1 -1 -1  0  1  1  1  0 -1 -1 -1  0  1  1  1  1  0  0  0  1  0  0
 0  1  1  1  1
 [649] -1 -1 -1 -1 -1  1  1  1  1 -1 -1 -1 -1 -1  1  1  1  1  0  0  0  1  1  1  0 -1 -1 -1 -1  1  1  1  0 -1 -1 -1 -1  0  0  1  1  0 -1 -1 -1 -1  0  0
 1  1 -1 -1 -1 -1
 [703] -1  0  1  1  1  0  0 -1 -1  0  1  1  1  1  0  0  0 -1  0  0  0  0  0  1 -1 -1  0  0  0  0  0  1  1  1  0  0  0  0  0  1  1  0  0  0  0  0
 1  0  0  0  0  0
 [757] 0  0  1  1  1  0  0  0  0  0  1  1  1  0  0  0  0  0  1  1  1  0  0  0 -1 -1  1  1  1  0  0  0  0 -1  0  0  0  0  0  0  0  0 -1
```

Figure 5.6: Expected signature of watermarked image

> **Note**
>
> The solution for this activity can be found on page 230.

In order to detect copyright violations, we can calculate signatures for every copyrighted image in a database. Then, for every newly uploaded image, we compare the signature of the newly uploaded image to the signatures in the database. If any of the copyrighted images have a signature that is identical to or substantially close to the signature of the new upload, we flag them as potential matches that need further investigation. Comparing signatures can be much faster than comparing original images, and it has the advantage of being robust to small changes such as watermarking.

The signature method we just performed is a way to encode data to enable comparisons between different datasets. There are many other encoding methods, including some that use neural networks. Each encoding method will have some of its own unique characteristics, but they will all share some common features: they will all try to return compressed data that enables easy and accurate comparison between datasets.

Applying Other Unsupervised Learning Methods to Analytic Signatures

So far, we have only used hashes and analytic signatures to compare two images or four short strings. However, there is no limit to the unsupervised learning methods that can be applied to hashes or analytic signatures. Creating analytic signatures for a set of images can be the first step of an in-depth analysis rather than the last step. After creating analytic signatures for a set of images, we can attempt the following unsupervised learning approaches:

- **Clustering**: We can apply any of the clustering methods discussed in the first two chapters to datasets consisting of analytic signatures. This could enable us to find groups of images that all tend to resemble each other, perhaps because they are photographs of the same type of object. Please see the first two chapters for more information about clustering methods.

- **Anomaly detection**: We can apply the anomaly detection methods described in *Chapter 6, Anomaly Detection*, to datasets that consist of analytic signatures. This will enable us to find images that are very different from the rest of the images in the dataset.

Latent Variable Models – Factor Analysis

This section will cover latent variable models. Latent variable models attempt to express data in terms of a small number of variables that are hidden or latent. By finding the latent variables that correspond to a dataset, we can better understand the data and potentially even understand where it came from or how it was generated.

Consider students receiving grades in a wide variety of classes, from math to music to foreign languages to chemistry. Psychologists or educators may be interested in using this data to better understand human intelligence. There are several different theories of intelligence that researchers might want to test in the data, for example:

- **Theory 1**: There are two different types of intelligence, and people who possess one type will excel in one set of classes, while people who possess the other type will excel in other classes.

- **Theory 2**: There is only one type of intelligence, and people who possess it will excel at all types of classes, and people who do not possess it will not.

- **Theory 3**: People may be highly intelligent when judged by the standards of one or a few of the classes they are taking, but not intelligent when judged by other standards, and every person will have a different set of classes at which they excel.

Each of these theories is expressing a notion of latent variables. The data only contains student grades, which could be a manifestation of intelligence but are not a direct measure of intelligence itself. The theories express ways that different kinds of intelligence affect grades in a latent way. Even though we do not know which theory is true, we can use tools of unsupervised learning to understand the structure of the data and which theory fits the data best.

Anyone who remembers being a student is probably fed up with people evaluating their intelligence. So, we will use a slightly different example. Instead of evaluating intelligence, we will evaluate personality. Instead of looking for a right brain and a left brain, we will look for different features of people's personalities. But we will take the same approach – using latent variables to identify whether complex data can be explained by some small number of factors.

In order to prepare for our analysis, we will need to install and load the right packages. The next exercise will cover how to load the packages that will be necessary for factor analysis.

Exercise 35: Preparing for Factor Analysis

In this exercise, we will prepare the data for factor analysis:

1. Install the necessary packages:

    ```
    install.packages('psych')
    install.packages('GPArotation')
    install.packages('qgraph')
    ```

2. Then, you can run the following lines to load them into your R workspace:

    ```
    library(psych)
    library(GPArotation)
    library(qgraph)
    ```

3. Next, load the data. The data we will use is a record of 500 responses to a personality test called the "Revised NEO Personality Inventory". The dataset is included in the R package called **qgraph**. To begin, read the data into your R workspace. This code will allow you to access it as a variable called **big5**:

    ```
    data(big5)
    ```

4. You can see the top section of the data by running the following line in the R console:

    ```
    print(head(big5))
    ```

The output is as follows:

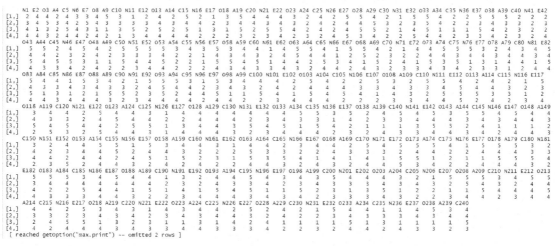

Figure 5.7: Top section of the data

5. You can see the number of rows and columns of your data as follows:

    ```
    print(nrow(big5))
    ```

    The output is as follows:

    ```
    500
    ```

    To check the columns, execute the following:

    ```
    print(ncol(big5))
    ```

    The output is as follows:

    ```
    240
    ```

    This data contains 500 rows and 240 columns. Each row is the complete record

related to one survey respondent. Each column records answers to one question. So, there are 500 survey respondents who have each answered 240 questions. Each of the answers are numerical, and you can see the range of responses as follows:

```
print(range(big5))
```

The output is as follows:

```
[1] 1 5
```

The answers range from 1 to 5.

The expected output of this exercise is an R workspace that has the `big5` data loaded. You can be sure that the data is loaded because when you run `print(range(big5))` in the console, you get `1 5` as output.

The questions are asked in this survey by showing survey respondents a question and asking them the degree to which they agree with the answer, where 5 represents strong agreement and 1 represents strong disagreement. The statements are statements about a person's particular characteristics, for example:

"I enjoy meeting new people."

"I sometimes make mistakes."

"I enjoy repairing things."

You can imagine that some of these questions will be measuring the same underlying "latent" personality trait. For example, we often describe people as curious, in the sense that they like to learn and try new things. Someone who strongly agrees with the statement "I enjoy meeting new people" might be likely to also agree with the statement "I enjoy repairing things" if both of those statements are measuring latent curiosity. Or, it could be that some people possess the personality trait of being interested in people, and others possess the personality trait of being interested in things. If so, people who agree with "I enjoy meeting new people" would not be expected to also agree with "I enjoy repairing things." The point of factor analysis here is to discover which of these questions correspond to one underlying idea, and to get an idea of what those underlying ideas are.

You can see that most of the columns begin with a letter of the alphabet as well as a number. For now, you can ignore these labels and just keep in mind that each question is slightly different, but many of them are similar to each other.

We are ready to begin our latent variable model. In this case, we will be performing factor analysis. Factor analysis is a powerful and very common method that can perform the type of latent variable analysis we discussed earlier. Factor analysis assumes that there are certain latent factors that govern a dataset, then shows us what those factors are and how they relate to our data.

To begin our factor analysis, we will need to specify how many factors we are looking for. There are several methods for deciding the number of factors we should seek. For now, we will start by looking at five factors since this data is called Big 5, and then we will check later whether another number of factors is better.

We will need to create a correlation matrix for our new data. A correlation matrix is a matrix where the **i-j** entry is the correlation between the variable stored in column **i** and the variable stored in column **j**. It is similar to the covariance matrices we discussed in *Chapter 4, Dimension Reduction*. You can create a correlation matrix for this data as follows:

```
big_cor <- cor(big5)
```

Now, the factor analysis itself is quite simple. We can perform it by using the **fa** command, which is part of the **psych** R package:

```
solution <- fa(r = big_cor, nfactors = 5, rotate = "oblimin", fm = "pa")
```

You will notice several arguments in this command. First, we specify **r=big_cor**. In this case, the authors of R's **psych** package decided to use a lowercase **r** to refer to the covariance matrix used for the factor analysis. The next argument is **nfactors=5**. This specifies the number of factors we will seek in our factor analysis. We have chosen five factors this time, but we will look at using more or fewer later.

The final two arguments are less important to our purposes here. The first says **rotate="oblimin"**. Factor analysis is doing what is called a rotation of our data behind the scenes before presenting its result to us. There are many techniques that can be used to accomplish this behind-the-scenes rotation, and **oblimin** is the default that has been chosen by the authors of the **fa** function. Feel free to experiment with other rotation methods, but they usually deliver substantially similar results. The last argument, just like the rotation argument, specifies a method that is used behind the scenes. Here, **fm** stands for factoring method and **pa** stands for principal. You can experiment with other factoring methods as well, but once again, they should deliver substantially similar results.

> **Note**
>
> You can use the **?** command in R to look up the documentation related to any other command. In this case, if you are curious about the **fa** command that we have just used, you can run **?fa** to load the documentation from your R console.

Now, we can look at the output of our factor analysis:

```
print(solution)
```

The output is as follows:

```
Factor Analysis using method =  pa
Call: fa(r = big_cor, nfactors = 5, rotate = "oblimin", fm = "pa")
Standardized loadings (pattern matrix) based upon correlation matrix
        PA1    PA4    PA2    PA3    PA5    h2    u2 com
N1     0.54 -0.03   0.07   0.04   0.09 0.304 0.70 1.1
E2    -0.15 -0.01   0.20   0.31  -0.04 0.173 0.83 2.3
O3     0.11 -0.10  -0.10   0.06   0.47 0.259 0.74 1.3
A4    -0.31  0.02   0.38   0.21  -0.05 0.312 0.69 2.6
C5    -0.15  0.39   0.09  -0.22   0.19 0.269 0.73 2.6
N6     0.45  0.00  -0.27  -0.08   0.01 0.296 0.70 1.7
E7    -0.24 -0.06   0.00   0.38  -0.12 0.225 0.78 2.0
O8     0.08  0.08   0.09   0.11   0.43 0.232 0.77 1.4
A9     0.04  0.10   0.45   0.16  -0.06 0.247 0.75 1.4
C10    0.26  0.31  -0.06  -0.18  -0.13 0.202 0.80 3.0
N11    0.62  0.04   0.00  -0.11   0.18 0.430 0.57 1.2
E12   -0.38  0.15  -0.44   0.21  -0.02 0.444 0.56 2.7
O13    0.12  0.02  -0.05   0.21   0.34 0.193 0.81 2.0
A14   -0.06  0.15   0.56   0.05   0.06 0.367 0.63 1.2
C15    0.03  0.33   0.22   0.05   0.05 0.178 0.82 1.9
N16    0.47 -0.01   0.00  -0.21  -0.03 0.307 0.69 1.4
E17    0.42 -0.01  -0.03  -0.10  -0.01 0.203 0.80 1.1
O18   -0.14 -0.23  -0.03  -0.01   0.16 0.087 0.91 2.5
A19   -0.05  0.01   0.39   0.26   0.05 0.237 0.76 1.8
C20   -0.23  0.37   0.00   0.19  -0.01 0.279 0.72 2.2
N21    0.02 -0.17  -0.15   0.26   0.08 0.133 0.87 2.6
E22    0.12 -0.16  -0.22   0.22   0.18 0.178 0.82 4.3
O23   -0.17 -0.13  -0.12  -0.23   0.52 0.323 0.68 1.9
A24    0.07  0.05   0.50  -0.01  -0.12 0.282 0.72 1.2
C25   -0.20  0.47  -0.06   0.06   0.10 0.326 0.67 1.5
N26    0.63 -0.03  -0.05   0.00  -0.04 0.418 0.58 1.0
E27   -0.06 -0.01   0.01   0.45   0.06 0.228 0.77 1.1
O28   -0.11  0.03   0.13   0.04   0.29 0.124 0.88 1.8
A29    0.12  0.07   0.16  -0.06   0.11 0.057 0.94 3.6
C30   -0.22  0.23   0.21  -0.03  -0.14 0.187 0.81 3.7
N31    0.60  0.04   0.00   0.00  -0.11 0.367 0.63 1.1
E32   -0.12 -0.06   0.10   0.42   0.02 0.224 0.78 1.3
O33    0.05 -0.28   0.06   0.08   0.36 0.218 0.78 2.1
A34   -0.08  0.03   0.24   0.33   0.08 0.206 0.79 2.1
C35    0.01 -0.13  -0.12  -0.09  -0.15 0.075 0.93 3.6
```

Figure 5.8: Section of the output

When we do this, the majority of the output is a DataFrame with 240 rows labeled `Standardized loadings`. Each of the rows of this data frame corresponds to a column of our original data frame, such as **N1**. Remember that these are the questions on the personality profile test that is the source of our data. The first five columns of this data frame are labeled **PA1** through **PA5**. These correspond to each of the five factors we are looking for. The number for a particular personality question and a particular factor is called a loading. So, for example, we have the entry 0.54 in our data frame, corresponding to personality question **N1**, and factor **PA1**. We say that question **N1** has

loading 0.54 on factor **PA1**.

`We can interpret loadings as contributors to an overall score. To get the final score, you can multiply each particular loading by the survey respondent's answers to each question, and sum up the results. In equation form, we can write this as follows:

Respondent 1's Factor 1 score =

(Factor 1 loading on Question 1) * (Respondent 1's answer to question 1) +

(Factor 1 loading on Question 2) * (Respondent 1's answer to question 2) +

....

(Factor 1 loading on Question 240) * (Respondent 1's answer to question 240)

So, if a factor 1 loading for a particular question is high, then the respondent's answer

to that question will have a large contribution to the total factor 1 score. If a loading is low, then the answer to that question doesn't contribute as much to the factor 1 score, or in other words it doesn't matter as much for factor 1. This means that each loading is a measurement of how much each particular question matters in the measurement of a factor.

Each factor has 240 total loadings – one for each question in the personality survey. If you look at the loading matrix, you can see that many questions have a large loading on one factor, and small loadings (close to zero) on all other factors. Researchers frequently attempt to hypothesize an interpretation for each factor based on which questions have the highest loadings for each factor.

In our case, we can see that the first factor, called PA1, has a high loading (0.54) for the first question (labeled N1). It also has a relatively high loading (0.45) for the sixth question (N6), and a high loading (0.62) for the eleventh question (N11). It is easy to see a pattern here – the questions labeled N tend to have a high loading for this first factor. It turns out that these N questions on the original test were all meant to measure something psychologists call "neuroticism." Neuroticism is a fundamental personality trait that leads people to have strong negative reactions to difficulties, among other things. The N questions in the survey are all different, but each is intended to measure this personality trait. What we have found in our factor analysis is that this first factor tends to have high loadings for these neuroticism questions – so we would be justified in calling this factor a "neuroticism factor."

We can see similar patterns in the other loadings:

- Factor 2 seems to have high loadings for "A" questions, which measure agreeableness.

- Factor 3 seems to have high loadings for "E" questions, which measure extroversion.

- Factor 4 seems to have high loadings for "C" questions, which measure conscientiousness.

- Factor 5 seems to have high loadings for "O" questions, which measure openness.

These labels correspond to the "Big 5" theory of personality, which states that these five personality traits are the most important and most fundamental aspects of a person's personality. In this case, our five-factor analysis has yielded patterns of factor loadings that match the pre-existing labels in our dataset. However, we do not need labeled questions in order to learn from factor analysis. If we had obtained data with unlabeled questions, we could still run factor analysis, and still find patterns in the loadings of particular questions with particular factors. After finding those patterns, we would have to look closely at the questions that had high loadings on the same factors, and try to find what those questions have in common.

Linear Algebra behind Factor Analysis

Factor analysis is a powerful and flexible method that can be used in a variety of ways. In the following exercise, we will change some of the details of the factor analysis commands we have used in order to get a better sense of how factor analysis works.

Please note: the following exercise builds on the previous factor analysis code. You will have to run the previously highlighted code, especially `big_cor <- cor(big5)`, in order to successfully run the code in the following exercise.

Exercise 36: More Exploration with Factor Analysis

In this exercise, we will explore factor analysis in detail:

1. We can change several of the arguments in our **fa** function to obtain a different result. Remember that last time we ran the following code to create our solution:

    ```
    solution <- fa(r = big_cor, nfactors = 5, rotate = "oblimin", fm = "pa")
    ```

    This time, we can change some of the parameters of the **fa** function, as follows:

    ```
    solution <- fa(r = big_cor, nfactors = 3, rotate = "varimax", fm =
    "minres")
    ```

    In this case, we have changed the rotation method to **varimax** and the factoring method to **minres**. These are changes to the behind-the-scenes methods used by the function. Most importantly for us, we have changed the number of factors (**nfactors**) to 3 rather than 5. Examine the factor loadings in this model:

    ```
    print(solution)
    ```

The output is as follows:

```
               PA1            PA4            PA2            PA3            PA5
N1     2.881238e-02   8.670579e-04  -3.040204e-03   7.314594e-03   0.0145400299
E2    -4.617340e-03  -1.835249e-03   1.498291e-02   2.122914e-02  -0.0116023314
O3     2.426148e-03  -6.258903e-03  -1.242467e-02   1.407778e-03   0.0497856169
A4    -8.959417e-03   6.497288e-04   4.158095e-02   1.868088e-02  -0.0149398935
C5    -7.711196e-03   2.157890e-02   8.675828e-03  -2.041749e-02   0.0277668768
N6     2.190748e-02   5.824713e-03  -2.491382e-02  -2.649121e-03   0.0047750369
E7    -1.556929e-02  -1.322104e-02  -4.031547e-03   3.387525e-02  -0.0202769952
O8     1.753012e-02   1.921573e-02   3.786774e-03   9.157273e-03   0.0376477185
A9     2.978894e-03   3.322950e-03   3.830723e-02   1.717055e-02  -0.0053211261
C10    1.254014e-02   2.655267e-02  -1.503292e-02  -8.659995e-03  -0.0133281548
N11    3.662707e-02   1.035695e-02  -1.240881e-03  -1.425144e-02   0.0312693793
E12   -2.599546e-02   2.540984e-02  -6.392001e-02   3.070693e-02  -0.0057103637
O13    1.414654e-02   8.537017e-03  -6.818238e-03   1.599520e-02   0.0317023984
A14   -1.672476e-02   9.509720e-03   6.121387e-02  -4.965671e-04   0.0132508173
C15    4.935832e-04   1.934411e-02   2.081504e-02   3.863660e-03   0.0096609759
N16    1.879551e-02   1.311568e-02   6.006537e-03  -1.621107e-02   0.0043428587
E17    1.630781e-02   4.126107e-03  -7.359349e-03  -1.977539e-03   0.0014600032
O18   -9.600614e-03  -1.067392e-02  -4.602948e-03  -1.305665e-02   0.0123377536
A19   -3.769541e-03  -1.995543e-03   3.311415e-02   1.799977e-02   0.0134641454
C20    4.235881e-04   2.573445e-02  -5.186867e-03   1.800068e-02  -0.0121188467
N21    4.341721e-03  -8.527928e-03  -1.035717e-02   2.709653e-02  -0.0003692319
E22   -7.689687e-04  -1.582864e-02  -1.073823e-02   1.291507e-02   0.0176404242
O23   -1.753918e-02  -1.571162e-02  -1.023660e-02  -4.684526e-02   0.0803286275
A24    3.211651e-04  -7.093895e-03   5.069256e-02  -7.695827e-03  -0.0154206718
C25   -6.921068e-03   3.859124e-02  -1.877422e-03   6.328299e-03   0.0069902781
N26    5.554152e-02  -3.868361e-03  -1.021338e-02   1.222294e-02  -0.0130603015
E27    2.385429e-03   1.852003e-04   1.473539e-03   4.243108e-02   0.0098817470
O28   -3.739258e-03  -2.084281e-02   7.751884e-03  -2.879907e-04   0.0292258995
A29    2.487800e-03  -3.350833e-03   9.095477e-03  -1.020894e-02   0.0193551576
C30   -1.431393e-02   5.489632e-03   1.537105e-02  -8.009814e-03  -0.0142113588
N31    4.830967e-02   1.467822e-02   1.234340e-03   1.500907e-02  -0.0152494634
E32   -4.251237e-03  -6.093333e-03   6.060609e-03   2.044216e-02  -0.0055899979
O33   -1.386843e-03  -1.678646e-02   2.053727e-03   2.469049e-03   0.0435236032
```

Figure 5.9: Section of the output

You can try to find patterns in these loadings as well. If you find that there is a striking pattern of loadings for three or four or some other number of loadings, you may even have a new theory of personality psychology on your hands.

2. Determine the number of factors to use in factor analysis. A natural question to ask at this point is: how should we go about choosing the number of factors we look for? The simplest answer is that we can use another command in R's **psych** package, called **fa.parallel**. We can run this command with our data as follows:

```
parallel <- fa.parallel(big5, fm = 'minres', fa = 'fa')
```

Again, we have made choices about the behind-the-scenes behavior of the function. You can experiment with different choices for the **fm** and **fa** arguments, but you should see substantially similar results each time.

One of the outputs of the **fa.parallel** command is the following scree plot:

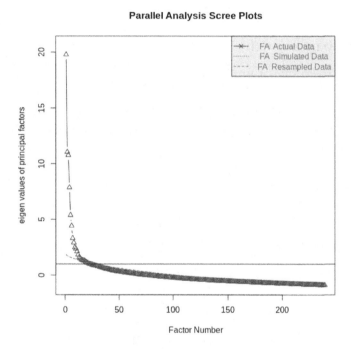

Figure 5.10: Parallel analysis scree plot

We discussed scree plots in *Chapter 4, Dimension Reduction*. The y axis, labeled **eigen values of principal factors**, shows a measurement of how important each factor is in explaining the variance of our model. In most factor analyses, the first several factors have relatively high eigenvalues, and then there is a sharp drop off in eigenvalues and a long plateau. The sharp drop off and long plateau together from an image that looks like an elbow. Common practice in factor analysis is to choose a number of factors that are close to the elbow created by this pattern. Psychologists have collectively chosen five as the number of factors that is commonly used for personality inventories. You can examine this scree plot to see whether you agree that that is the right number to use, and feel free to try factor analysis with different numbers of factors.

The final important outcome of the exercise we have just performed is the scree plot.

You may have noticed that factor analysis seems to have some things in common with principal component analysis. In particular, both rely on scree plots that plot eigenvalues as a way to measure the importance of different vectors.

A full comparison between factor analysis and principal component analysis is beyond the scope of this book. Suffice it to say that they have similar linear algebraic foundations: both are designed to create approximations of covariance matrices, but each accomplishes this in a slightly different way. The factors we have found in factor analysis are analogous to the principal components that we found in principal component analysis. You are encouraged to try both factor analysis and principal component analysis on the same dataset, and to compare the results. The results are usually substantially similar, though not identical. In most real-world applications, either approach can be used – the specific method you use will depend on your own preference and your judgment of which approach best fits the problem at hand.

Activity 13: Performing Factor Analysis

In this activity, we will use factor analysis on a new dataset. You can find the dataset at https://github.com/TrainingByPackt/Applied-Unsupervised-Learning-with-R/tree/master/Lesson05/Activity13.

> **Note**
>
> This dataset is taken from the UCI Machine Learning Repository. You can find the dataset at http://archive.ics.uci.edu/ml/machine-learning-databases/00484/tripadvisor_review.csv. We have downloaded the file and saved it at https://github.com/TrainingByPackt/Applied-Unsupervised-Learning-with-R/tree/master/Lesson05/Activity13/factor.csv.

This dataset was compiled by Renjith, Sreekumar, and Jathavedan and is available on the UCI Machine Learning Repository. This dataset contains information about reviews that individuals wrote of tourist destinations. Each row corresponds to a particular unique user, for a total of 980 users. The columns correspond to categories of tourist sites. For example, the second column records each user's average rating of art galleries, and the third column records each user's average rating of dance clubs. There are 10 total categories of tourist sites. You can find the documentation of what each column records at http://archive.ics.uci.edu/ml/datasets/Travel+Reviews.

Through factor analysis, we will seek to determine the relationships between the user ratings of different categories. For example, it could be that user ratings of juice bars (column 4) and restaurants (column 5) are similar because both are determined by the same latent factor – the user's interest in food. Factor analysis will attempt to find these latent factors that govern the users' ratings. We can follow these steps to conduct our factor analysis:

1. Download the data and read it into R.

2. Load the **psych** package.

3. Select the subset of the columns that record the user ratings.

4. Create a correlation matrix for the data.

5. Determine the number of factors that should be used.

6. Perform factor analysis using the **fa** command.

7. Examine and interpret the results of the factor analysis.

The output should be similar to the following:

```
Factor Analysis using method =  minres
Call: fa(r = ratings_cor, nfactors = 1)
Standardized loadings (pattern matrix) based upon correlation matrix
                MR1      h2   u2 com
Category.1    -0.02 0.00027 1.00   1
Category.2     0.16 0.02454 0.98   1
Category.3     0.68 0.46025 0.54   1
Category.4     0.30 0.08942 0.91   1
Category.5     0.43 0.18654 0.81   1
Category.6     0.61 0.37424 0.63   1
Category.7     0.88 0.77276 0.23   1
Category.8    -0.13 0.01718 0.98   1
Category.9     0.05 0.00257 1.00   1
Category.10   -0.74 0.55225 0.45   1

                  MR1
SS loadings      2.48
Proportion Var   0.25
```

Figure 5.11: Expected outcome of factor analysis

Note

The solution for this activity can be found on page 231.

Summary

In this chapter, we covered topics related to data comparisons. We started by discussing the idea of a data fingerprint. In order to illustrate a data fingerprint, we introduced a hash function that can take any string and convert it to a number in a fixed range. This kind of hash function is useful because it enables us to ensure that data has the right identity – just like a fingerprint in real life. After introducing hash functions, we talked about the need for data signatures. A data signature or analytic signature is useful because it enables us to see whether two datasets are approximate matches – fingerprints require exact matches. We illustrated the use of analytic signatures with image data. We concluded the chapter by covering latent variable models. The latent variable model we discussed was factor analysis. We discussed an application of factor analysis that uses psychological survey data to determine differences between people's personalities. In the next chapter, we will discuss anomaly detection, which will enable us to find observations that do not fit with the rest of a dataset.

Anomaly Detection

Learning Objectives

By the end of this chapter, you will be able to:

- Use parametric and non-parametric methods to find outliers in univariate and multivariate data

- Use data transformations to identify outliers in univariate and multivariate data

- Work with Mahalanobis distances

- Improve anomaly detection performance by incorporating a model of seasonality

In this chapter, we will have a look at different anomaly detection techniques.

Introduction

Data analysis often begins with an implicit assumption that all observations are valid, accurate, and trustworthy. But this is not always a reasonable assumption. Consider the case of credit card companies, who collect data consisting of records of charges to an individual's credit card. If they assumed that all charges were valid, they would open the door to thieves and fraudsters to take advantage of them. Instead, they examine their transaction datasets and look for anomalies – transactions that deviate from the general observed pattern. Since fraudulent transactions are not labeled, they have to use unsupervised learning to find these anomalies and prevent criminal activity.

There are many other situations in which anomaly detection is useful. For example, manufacturers may use anomaly detection methods to find defects in their products. Medical researchers may look for anomalies in otherwise regular heartbeat patterns to diagnose illnesses. IT security professionals try to find anomalous activities on servers or computers to identify malware. In each case, unsupervised learning methods can help separate the valid observations from the anomalous ones.

This chapter will cover several anomaly detection techniques. We will begin by using parametric and non-parametric methods to find outliers in univariate and multivariate data. We will then discuss using data transformations to identify outliers in univariate and multivariate data. Next, we will have a look at Mahalanobis distances, a multivariate tool for anomaly detection. We will conclude the chapter with a discussion of using regression modeling to improve anomaly detection performance by incorporating a model of seasonality, and detection of contextual and collective anomalies.

Univariate Outlier Detection

Anomaly detection is simplest in the univariate case, that is, when each observation is only one number. In this case, we might start by doing a common-sense check for anomalies by checking whether observations are missing, NULL, NA, or recorded as infinity or something that doesn't match the type of the rest of the observations. After performing this check, we can apply true unsupervised learning.

For univariate data, anomaly detection consists of looking for outliers. R's built-in `boxplot` function makes an initial exploratory check for outliers quite easy, as can be seen in the following exercise.

Exercise 37: Performing an Exploratory Visual Check for Outliers Using R's boxplot Function

For univariate data, anomaly detection consists of looking for outliers. R's built-in boxplot function makes an initial exploratory check for outliers quite easy, as demonstrated in this exercise. We will use a dataset called `mtcars`, which is built into R.

In this exercise, we will create a boxplot that you can see in Figure 6.3. A boxplot is an important type of univariate plot. Here, the thick horizontal line around 3 indicates the median value in the data. The box surrounding this median line has a lower limit at the first quartile (the 25th percentile) and an upper limit at the third quartile (the 75th percentile). The vertical dotted lines extend to the lower and upper ends of all of the non-outlier data. These dotted lines are called the whiskers of the plot, so this type of plot is sometimes called a "box and whiskers" plot. Finally, the two observations that are represented as circular points near the top of the plot are (at least, according to R) outliers.

Percentiles can also be called **quantiles**, and we'll refer to them as such in this boxplot. A quantile is a point in the data that is greater than some fixed proportion of all data points. For example, a 0.1 quantile is an observation in the data that is greater than 10% of all observations, and less than the rest. The 0.25 quantile is also called the 25th percentile or the first quartile, and it is greater than 25% of the data, and the 75th percentile or 0.75 quantile is greater than 75% of the data. When we take an observation and find what proportion of observations it is greater than, that is called finding its quantile. When we take a quantile such as 0.25 and try to find an observation that corresponds to that quantile, we can call that taking an inverse quantile.

To perform an exploratory visual check for outliers using R's **boxplot** function, perform the following steps:

1. To load the data, open the R console and enter the following command:

   ```
   data(mtcars)
   ```

2. Execute the following command to view the first six rows of the dataset:

   ```
   head(mtcars)
   ```

The output is as follows:

```
                     mpg cyl disp  hp drat    wt  qsec vs am gear carb
Mazda RX4           21.0   6  160 110 3.90 2.620 16.46  0  1    4    4
Mazda RX4 Wag       21.0   6  160 110 3.90 2.875 17.02  0  1    4    4
Datsun 710          22.8   4  108  93 3.85 2.320 18.61  1  1    4    1
Hornet 4 Drive      21.4   6  258 110 3.08 3.215 19.44  1  0    3    1
Hornet Sportabout   18.7   8  360 175 3.15 3.440 17.02  0  0    3    2
Valiant             18.1   6  225 105 2.76 3.460 20.22  1  0    3    1
```

Figure 6.1: Top six rows of the mtcars dataset

3. You can find details about this dataset by executing the following in the R console:

```
?mtcars
```

The documentation is as follows:

R: Motor Trend Car Road Tests ▾ | Find in Topic

mtcars

Format

A data frame with 32 observations on 11 (numeric) variables.

[, 1] mpg   Miles/(US) gallon
[, 2] cyl   Number of cylinders
[, 3] disp Displacement (cu.in.)
[, 4] hp   Gross horsepower
[, 5] drat Rear axle ratio
[, 6] wt   Weight (1000 lbs)
[, 7] qsec 1/4 mile time
[, 8] vs   Engine (0 = V-shaped, 1 = straight)
[, 9] am   Transmission (0 = automatic, 1 = manual)
[,10] gear Number of forward gears
[,11] carb Number of carburetors

Source

Henderson and Velleman (1981), Building multiple regression models interactively. *Biometrics*, **37**, 391–411.

Examples

```
require(graphics)
pairs(mtcars, main = "mtcars data", gap = 1/4)
coplot(mpg ~ disp | as.factor(cyl), data = mtcars,
      panel = panel.smooth, rows = 1)
## possibly more meaningful, e.g., for summary() or bivariate plots:
```

Figure 6.2: Section of output

4. Create a boxplot of the weights of cars as follows:

```
boxplot(mtcars$wt)
```

The output will look like this:

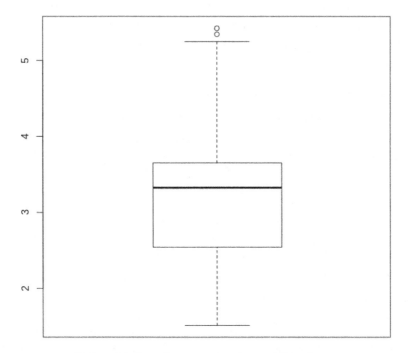

Figure 6.3: Boxplot representing weight of cars

5. There appear to be two observations that R has classified as outliers that appear to have values higher than 5. Note that these weights are measured in thousands of pounds, so actually these are weights higher than 5,000 pounds. We can determine these observations by running a simple filter on our data:

```
highest<-mtcars[which(mtcars$wt>5),]
```

```
print(highest)
```

The output is as follows:

```
                   mpg cyl disp  hp drat    wt  qsec vs am gear carb
Cadillac Fleetwood 10.4   8  472 205 2.93 5.250 17.98  0  0    3    4
Lincoln Continental 10.4  8  460 215 3.00 5.424 17.82  0  0    3    4
Chrysler Imperial   14.7  8  440 230 3.23 5.345 17.42  0  0    3    4
```

Figure 6.4: Cars with weights greater than 5,000 pounds

We can see that there are three models of car whose weights are higher than 5,000 pounds. Since we only observed two outliers, we conclude that the Cadillac Fleetwood, the car model with the third-highest weight, is not one of the outliers. This leaves the other two: the Lincoln Continental and the Chrysler Imperial, as the car models that apparently have outlier weights. These car models, when compared to the other car models, constitute anomalies. A potential next step for a researcher is to investigate why these car models appear to have anomalously high car weights.

In *Chapter 3, Probability Distributions*, we discussed different distributions that datasets tend to follow. Many datasets have so-called long tails or fat tails, meaning that a disproportionate amount of observations are very far from the mean – not necessarily because they are anomalous outliers, but only because of the nature of their distribution. Our standard for defining an outlier should change if we happen to be working with a dataset that follows a fat-tailed distribution.

In the following exercise, we will transform a dataset that follows a fat-tailed distribution and observe the changes in which observations are reported as outliers.

Exercise 38: Transforming a Fat-Tailed Dataset to Improve Outlier Classification

In the following exercise, we will transform a dataset that follows a fat-tailed distribution and observe the changes in which observations are reported as outliers. We will use the **rivers** dataset, which comes pre-loaded into R:

1. Load the dataset as follows:

   ```
   data(rivers)
   ```

2. Execute the following command to view the first six observations of the dataset:

   ```
   head(rivers)
   ```

   The output is as follows:

   ```
   [1] 735 320 325 392 524 450
   ```

3. You can see that the **rivers** dataset is a vector. You can find out more about it by typing this:

   ```
   ?rivers
   ```

The documentation is as follows:

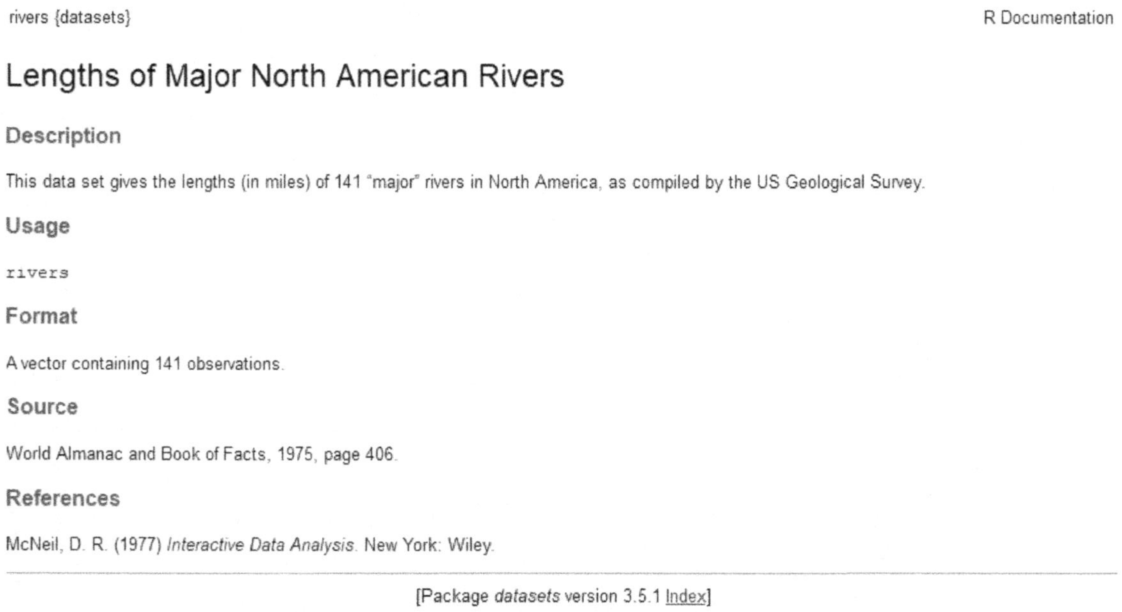

rivers {datasets}   R Documentation

Lengths of Major North American Rivers

Description

This data set gives the lengths (in miles) of 141 "major" rivers in North America, as compiled by the US Geological Survey.

Usage

`rivers`

Format

A vector containing 141 observations.

Source

World Almanac and Book of Facts, 1975, page 406.

References

McNeil, D. R. (1977) *Interactive Data Analysis*. New York: Wiley.

[Package *datasets* version 3.5.1 Index]

Figure 6.5: Information of the rivers dataset

4. Observe the distribution of outliers. First, try a boxplot of the rivers data by running the following command:

```
boxplot(rivers)
```

The boxplot looks like this:

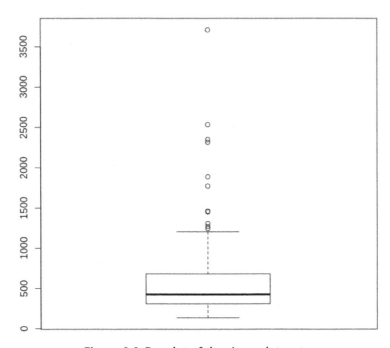

Figure 6.6: Boxplot of the rivers dataset

You can see that this boxplot looks different from the `mtcars` boxplot that we looked at previously. In particular, the box and whiskers take up a smaller portion of the plot, and a huge amount of the plot consists of observations that R has classified as outliers. However, outliers are not supposed to be extremely numerous in any datasets – by definition, they are supposed to be rare. When we observe a boxplot such as this, that presents many outliers that take up a large portion of the plot, we can reasonably conclude that our distribution is fat-tailed.

5. In order to get a better classification of outliers, it could be helpful to transform the data. Many datasets related to nature and natural phenomena are known to follow a log-normal distribution. If we take the logarithm of every observation, the resulting distribution will be normal (and therefore not fat-tailed). To transform the data, you can use the following command:

```
log_rivers<-log(rivers)
```

6. Observe the boxplot of the transformed data. Finally, we can execute the following command to see the boxplot of the transformed data:

```
boxplot(log_rivers)
```

The boxplot will look as follows:

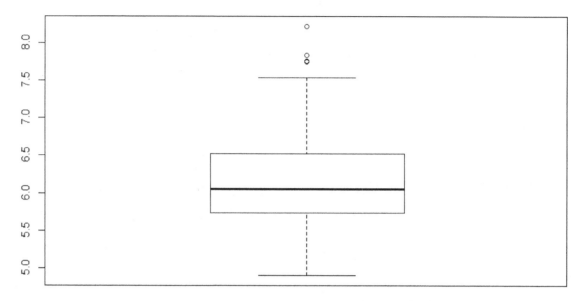

Figure 6.7: Boxplot of transformed dataset

As expected, the box and whiskers take up a greater proportion of the plot, and there are fewer observations that are classified as outliers. In this case, we can use the **log_rivers** plot instead of the **rivers** plot to classify outliers.

The preceding exercise shows the importance of data preparation in anomaly detection. We can also attempt anomaly detection on a raw dataset. But sometimes, like in the example of **rivers** that we looked at, we can get different and better results by performing some simple data preparation. One thing to keep in mind is that there are

many possible transformations of data. We have used the log transformation, but there are many others that could work. Another thing to keep in mind is that data preparation can be harmful as well as helpful: some data preparation methods, such as averaging and data smoothing, can cause us to throw out valuable information that will make our anomaly detection less effective.

So far, we have relied on R's built-in outlier detection methods, and we have done simple visual inspections of boxplots to determine which observations were outliers. In the next exercise, we will determine which observations are outliers ourselves without using R's built-in outlier classification. We will be finding quantiles of the data – specifically the 0.25 and 0.75 quantiles.

Exercise 39: Finding Outliers without Using R's Built-In boxplot Function

In this exercise, we will determine which observations are outliers ourselves without using R's built-in outlier classification. We will be finding quantiles of the data – specifically the .25 and .75 quantiles. We will use the **rivers** data again, which we used in the preceding exercise:

1. Load the data by executing the following command:

   ```
   data(rivers)
   ```

2. The interquartile range is the difference between the first quartile (the 25th percentile) and the third quartile (the 75th percentile). So, we can store the interquartile range in a variable called **interquartile_range** by running the following:

   ```
   interquartile_range<-unname(quantile(rivers,.75)-quantile(rivers,.25))
   ```

   In this case, we use **unname** to make sure that **interquartile_range** is just a number instead of a DataFrame or list or other data type. This will make it easier and more reliable to work with later.

3. Use the following command to check the interquartile range:

   ```
   print(interquartile_range)
   ```

   The output is as follows:

   ```
   [1] 370
   ```

4. The standard method in R's boxplot function is to use 1.5 times the interquartile range as a limit to how far non-outlier observations can be dispersed. Then the upper limit of non-outliers is the third quartile plus 1.5 times the interquartile range, and the lower limit of non-outliers is the first quartile minus 1.5 times the interquartile range. We can calculate this as follows:

   ```
   upper_limit<-unname(quantile(rivers,.75)+1.5*interquartile_range)
   lower_limit<-unname(quantile(rivers,.25)-1.5*interquartile_range)
   ```

5. Our outliers are the observations that are above our **upper_limit** or below our **lower_limit**. We can determine these as follows:

```
rivers[which(rivers>upper_limit | rivers<lower_limit)]
```

This will output a list of observations that we classify as outliers:

```
[1] 1459 1450 1243 2348 3710 2315 2533 1306 1270 1885 1770
```

> **Note**
>
> This exercise uses the method that is used in R's boxplot function. But with unsupervised learning, there is always flexibility about the details of the methods.

6. Another way to look for outliers would be to use the method in the preceding exercise, but to use a different value for the upper and lower limits. We could do this by changing the coefficient that we multiply by **interquartile_range**, as follows:

```
upper_limit<-unname(quantile(rivers,.75)+3*interquartile_range)
lower_limit<-unname(quantile(rivers,.25)-3*interquartile_range)
```

We have changed the coefficient from 1.5 to 3. This change makes our method less likely to classify any particular observation as an outlier, because it increases the upper limit and decreases the lower limit.

In general, you can try to be creative about changing unsupervised learning methods in ways that you believe are reasonable and will lead to good results.

The method in the preceding exercise is what is called a **non-parametric method**. In statistics, there are some methods that are called parametric and others that are called non-parametric. Parametric methods make assumptions about the underlying distribution of data, for example, the assumption that the data follows a normal distribution. Non-parametric methods are meant to be free of these constraining assumptions. The method in the preceding exercise relies only on quantiles, so it does not make any assumptions about the distribution of the data or the parameters (such as mean and variance) that go with them. Because of this, we call it a non-parametric method. A parametric anomaly detection method, by contrast, is one that makes assumptions about the distribution of the data or its parameters (such as mean and variance). Please note, non-parametric methods and parametric methods are always looking for the same anomalies: there is no such thing as a parametric anomaly or a non-parametric anomaly, but only parametric methods and non-parametric methods. We will discuss a parametric anomaly detection method in the next exercise.

We will calculate something called a **z-score**. A z-score is a standardized measurement of how far an observation is from the mean. Each z-score is measured in units of standard deviations. So, a z-score of 0 means that an observation is 0 standard deviations away from the mean; in other words, it is equal to the mean. A z-score of 1 means that an observation is 1 standard deviation above the mean. A z-score of -2.5 means that an observation is 2.5 standard deviations below the mean. It is conventional in some contexts to consider observations that are more than two standard deviations away from the mean unusual or anomalous.

Exercise 40: Detecting Outliers Using a Parametric Method

In this exercise, we will investigate anomalies by looking for observations whose z-scores are greater than 2 or less than -2. We will use the rivers dataset used in previous exercise:

1. Load the data and determine the standard deviation as follows:

   ```
   data(rivers)
   standard_deviation<-sd(rivers)
   ```

2. Determine z-scores for every observation by calculating how many standard deviations each observation is away from the mean:

   ```
   z_scores<-(rivers-mean(rivers))/ standard_deviation
   ```

3. Determine which observations are outliers by selecting observations whose z-scores are greater than 2 or less than -2:

   ```
   outliers<-rivers[which(z_scores>2 | z_scores<(-2))]
   outliers
   ```

   The output is as follows:

   ```
   [1] 2348 3710 2315 2533 1885 1770
   ```

   In this case, we can see that there are six rivers that are classified as outliers – all of them with z-scores higher than 2. Here, **outliers** is perhaps a strong word for these anomalies, since a z-score of 2 is not particularly enormous. There is no strict rule about what defines an outlier, and whether to use the term will depend on the particular situation and context.

Parametric anomaly detection, as shown in this exercise, is common practice. However, its applicability depends on whether the parametric assumptions behind it are valid. In this case, we calculated a standard deviation and looked for outliers more than two standard deviations away from the mean. This practice is justified if the data comes from a Gaussian (normal) distribution. In this case, some evidence indicates that the rivers data does not come from a Gaussian distribution. For cases in which there is doubt about the distribution of the underlying data, a non-parametric or transformed

method (as used in the previous exercises) could be more suitable.

Multivariate Outlier Detection

All of the methods so far have focused on univariate outlier detection. However, in practice such data is actually rare. Most datasets contain observations about multiple attributes of data. In these cases, it is not clear how to calculate whether a point is an outlier or not. We can calculate a z-score on each individual dimension, but what should be done about observations whose z-scores are high on one dimension and low in the other, or relatively large in one dimension and average in the other? There is no easy answer. In these cases, we can calculate a multidimensional analogue of a z-score using something called **Mahalanobis distance**. Mahalanobis distance is a multidimensional analogue of a z-score. What that means is that it measures the distance between two points, but in special units that, just like a z-score, depend on the variance of the data. We will be better able to understand the meaning of a Mahalanobis distance after going through the following exercise.

Exercise 41: Calculating Mahalanobis Distance

In this exercise, we will learn a new measurement that will eventually help us find which individuals are outliers compared to the general population when considering both their height and their weight. The expected output of this exercise will be a Mahalanobis distance for a single data point, measuring how far from the center of the data it is.

> **Note**
>
> For all the exercises and activities where we are importing external CSV files or images, go to **RStudio**-> **Session**-> **Set Working Directory**-> **To Source File Location**. You can see in the console that the path is set automatically.

In a later exercise, we will find the Mahalanobis distance for all the points in the dataset. We will then be able to use these measurements to classify which individuals are outliers compared to the general population when considering both their height and their weight:

> **Note**
>
> This dataset is taken from the Statistics Online Computational Resource. You can find the dataset at http://wiki.stat.ucla.edu/socr/index.php/SOCR_Data_Dinov_020108_HeightsWeights. We have downloaded the file and saved it at https://github.com/TrainingByPackt/Applied-Unsupervised-Learning-with-R/tree/master/Lesson06/Exercise41-42/heightsweights.csv. We have used the first 200 rows of the data.

1. Start by loading this in R. First, download it from our GitHub repository at https://github.com/TrainingByPackt/Applied-Unsupervised-Learning-with-R/tree/master/Lesson06/Exercise41-42/heightsweights.csv. Then, save it to your computer in R's working directory. Then, load it into R as follows:

   ```
   filename<-'heightsweights.csv'
   raw<-read.csv(filename, stringsAsFactors=FALSE)
   ```

2. We have given the dataset the name **raw**. You can make sure the columns have the right names as follows:

   ```
   names(raw)<-c('index','height','weight')
   ```

3. Plot the data and observe the patterns:

   ```
   plot(raw$height,raw$weight)
   ```

The plot appears as follows:

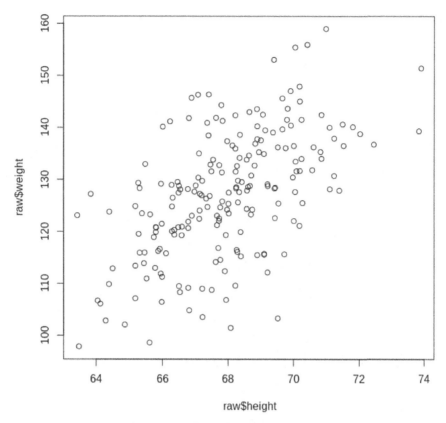

Figure 6.8: Plot of height and weight

We can see that there is great variation in both heights and weights in this sample. Note that our univariate methods will not work in a straightforward way in this data. We could calculate a standard deviation or interquartile range for height, and find outliers for height. But the outliers for height will not necessarily be outliers for weight – they might be a normal weight, or exactly what is expected for weight. Similarly, outliers for weight might have completely average or expected heights. It is not immediately obvious how we should calculate "complete outliers," or observations that are outliers in some holistic sense, taking into account both height and weight.

4. Next, we will calculate the multidimensional equivalent of the mean, called **centroid**:

```
centroid<-c(mean(raw$height),mean(raw$weight))
```

5. Calculate the distance between any given point and the centroid. As an example, we will choose the first observation in the dataset:

```
example_distance<-raw[1,c('height','weight')]-centroid
```

6. Calculate the inverse of the covariance matrix of our data. First, we calculate the covariance matrix of our height and weight data:

```
cov_mat<-cov(raw[,c('height','weight')])
```

7. Calculate its inverse using the **solve** function, which calculates matrix inverses in R:

```
inv_cov_mat<-solve(cov_mat)
```

8. Calculate the Mahalanobis distance between our point and the centroid of our dataset:

```
mahalanobis_dist<-t(matrix(as.numeric(example_distance)))%*% matrix(inv_
cov_mat,nrow=2) %*% matrix(as.numeric(example_distance))
```

In this case, we use **%*%** because it indicates matrix multiplication, which is what we want to perform, and we likewise need to turn every argument into a numeric matrix.

The output of this exercise is a Mahalanobis distance, which is a generalization of a z-score in multiple dimensions: that is, a generalized measure of how many standard deviations each point is away from the mean. In this case, the Mahalanobis distance we found is 1.71672. Mahalanobis distances are like any type of distance measurement – 0 is the lowest possible measurement and the higher the number, the farther the distance. Only the centroid will have a measured Mahalanobis distance of 0. The advantage of Mahalanobis distances is that they are standardized in a way that takes into account the variances of each variable and makes them effective for outlier detection. Later on in this chapter, we will see how to use this type of measurement to find outliers in this multi-dimensional dataset.

Detecting Anomalies in Clusters

In the first two chapters, we discussed the different clustering methods. The method we are discussing now, Mahalanobis distances, could be used fruitfully in clustering applications, if you imagine that the data we are looking at is the data corresponding to one particular cluster. For example, in divisive clustering, the point with the highest Mahalanobis distance could be selected as the point to remove from a cluster. Also, the range of Mahalanobis distances could be used to express the dispersion of any given cluster.

Other Methods for Multivariate Outlier Detection

There are other methods for multivariate outlier detection, including some that are known as **non-parametric** methods. Non-parametric methods, like some of the preceding exercises, may rely on quantiles, or in other words, the rank of each observation from largest to smallest, in order to classify outliers. Some non-parametric methods use the sums of such rankings to understand the distribution of data. However, such methods are not common and are not more effective than Mahalanobis distances in general, so we recommend relying on Mahalanobis distance for multivariate outlier detection.

Exercise 42: Classifying Outliers based on Comparisons of Mahalanobis Distances

In this exercise, we will use a comparison of Mahalanobis distances to classify outliers. This exercise is a continuation of the previous exercise, and it will rely on the same dataset and some of the same variables. In that exercise, we found the Mahalanobis distance for one data point; now we're going to find it for all the data points. Before executing the following exercise, you should run all of the code in the previous exercise and make sure you are familiar with the ideas presented there:

> **Note**
>
> This dataset is taken from the UCI Machine Learning Repository. You can find the dataset at http://wiki.stat.ucla.edu/socr/index.php/SOCR_Data_Dinov_020108_HeightsWeights. We have downloaded the file and saved it at https://github.com/TrainingByPackt/Applied-Unsupervised-Learning-with-R/tree/master/Lesson06/Exercise41-42/heightsweights.csv. We have used the first 200 rows of the data.

1. Create a **NULL** variable that will hold each of our calculated distances:

   ```
   all_distances<-NULL
   ```

2. Loop through each observation and find the Mahalanobis distance between it and the centroid of the data. The code inside this loop is taken from the previous exercise, where we learned how to calculate Mahalanobis distances:

   ```
   k<-1
   while(k<=nrow(raw)){
   the_distance<-raw[k,c('height','weight')]-centroid
   mahalanobis_dist<-t(matrix(as.numeric(the_distance)))%*% matrix(inv_cov_
   mat,nrow=2) %*% matrix(as.numeric(the_distance))
   all_distances<-c(all_distances,mahalanobis_dist)
   k<-k+1
   }
   ```

   After running this loop, we have a measured Mahalanobis distance for each of the points in our data.

3. Plot all observations that have particularly high Mahalanobis distances. In this case, we will say that particularly high means the highest 10% of Mahalanobis distances. This means all Mahalanobis distances that are higher than the 0.9 quantile of Mahalanobis distances, which we select in the following code:

   ```
   plot(raw$height,raw$weight)
   points(raw$height[which(all_distances>quantile(all_
   distances,.9))],raw$weight[which(all_distances>quantile(all_
   distances,.9))],col='red',pch=19)
   ```

The output is as follows:

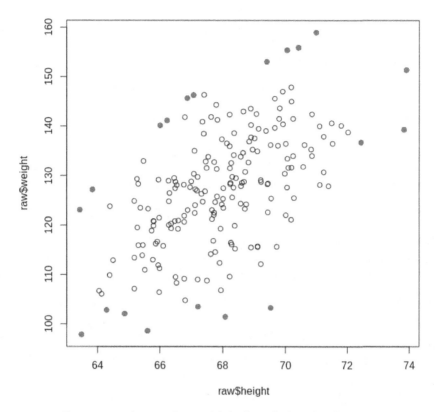

Figure 6.9: Observations with high Mahalanobis distances

This plot shows solid red points for each point that is in the top 10% of Mahalanobis distances. We can see that some of them appear to be outliers both for height and for weight, and could be observed simply by performing our univariate outlier detection methods. However, many of the red points in the plot above are neither univariate outliers for height nor for weight. They are outliers only relative to the entire cloud of points, and Mahalanobis distances enable us to quantify and detect that.

Detecting Outliers in Seasonal Data

So far, we have only discussed outlier detection as a way to detect anomalies. However, anomaly detection consists of more than only outlier detection. Some anomalies cannot easily be detected as raw outliers. Next, we will look at seasonal, trended data. In this data, we want to find anomalies that occur specifically in the context of a seasonal trend or cycle.

We will use data from the **expsmooth** package in R.

The data we will use records the monthly number of visitors to Australia between 1985 and 2005, measured in thousands of people.

In the following exercise, we will be working with data that has a **time trend**. By time trend, we mean that over time, the observations tend to increase or decrease (in this case, they tend to increase). In order to detect outliers, we want to do something called **de-trending**. To de-trend data means to remove, as much as possible, its time trend so that we can find how much each observation deviates from the expected values.

Exercise 43: Performing Seasonality Modeling

In this exercise, we will attempt to model this data to establish what we should regard as the expected values of the data, and what we should regard as deviations from expectations. The expected output is a set of error values, which we will use in a future exercise to classify outliers – the observations with the largest errors will be classified as the dataset's outliers:

1. First, load this data into R by executing the following commands:

    ```
    install.packages("expsmooth")
    library(expsmooth)
    data(visitors)
    plot(visitors)
    ```

The output is as follows:

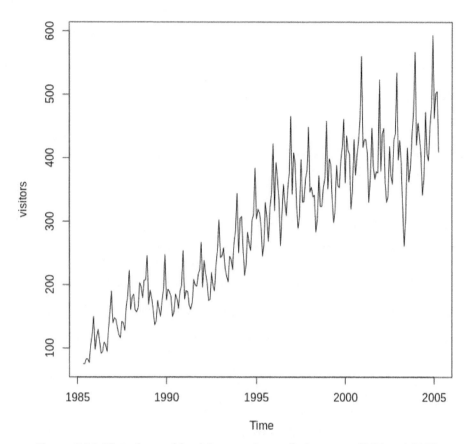

Figure 6.10: Plot of monthly visitors to Australia between 1985 and 2005

2. Check the first six observations of the data as follows:

```
head(visitors)
```

The output is as follows:

```
        May    Jun    Jul    Aug    Sep    Oct
1985   75.7   75.4   83.1   82.9   77.3  105.7
```

Check the last six observations as follows:

```
tail(visitors)
```

The output is as follows:

```
         Jan    Feb    Mar    Apr May Jun Jul Aug Sep Oct    Nov    Dec
2004                                                        479.9  593.1
2005 462.4 501.6 504.7 409.5
```

3. Since dates can be hard to work with, we can assign a numeric variable that tracks the dates in order. We will call this variable **period** and define it as follows:

   ```
   period<-1:length(visitors)
   ```

4. Combine the **visitors** data with the **period** variable we just created by putting them both into one DataFrame called **raw**:

   ```
   raw<-data.frame(cbind(visitors,period))
   ```

5. This step is technically supervised, rather than unsupervised, learning. In this case, we will use supervised learning, but only as an intermediate step on the way to doing unsupervised learning. To find the time trend in the data, we can run a linear regression relating the sales figures to the numeric time period as follows:

   ```
   timetrend<-lm(visitors~period+I(log(period)),data=raw)
   ```

6. Next, we can obtain fitted values for this time trend, and store them as part of the **raw** DataFrame:

   ```
   raw$timetrend<-predict(timetrend,raw)
   ```

7. The process of de-trending means we subtract the predicted trend that we found in *Step* 6. The reason we do this is that we want to find anomalies in the data. If we keep the trend in the data, something that looks like an anomaly may actually be the expected result of a trend. By removing the trend from the data, we can be sure that observed anomalies are not the result of a trend. We can accomplish de-trending as follows:

   ```
   raw$withouttimetrend<-raw$visitors-raw$timetrend
   ```

8. We can draw a simple plot of the de-trended data as follows:

```
plot(raw$withouttimetrend,type='o')
```

The plot looks as follows:

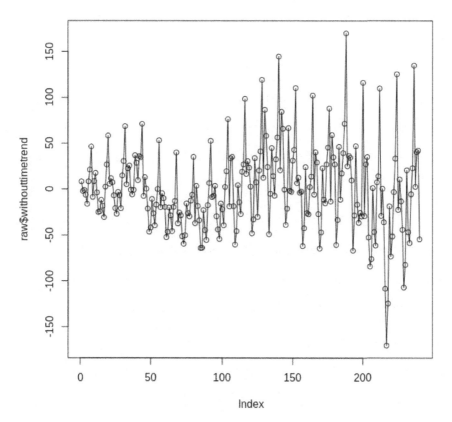

Figure 6.11: Plot of the de-trended data

In this plot, you should notice that there is no apparent left-to-right trend in the data, showing that we have successfully de-trended it.

Our data records the monthly number of visitors to Australia. There are variations in temperature and weather across seasons in Australia, and it is reasonable to hypothesize that tourist visits could increase or decline depending on how favorable the weather tends to be in a particular month. There could even be variations in business or diplomatic visits to Australia that relate to seasons and weather changes throughout the year. So, it is reasonable to suppose that there are yearly patterns in visits to Australia. Our next step will be to remove these yearly patterns from our data.

9. First, we create a matrix where each of the columns contains de-trended visitor data about a separate month of the year:

```
seasonsmatrix = t(matrix(data = raw$withouttimetrend, nrow = 12))
```

10. Take the mean of each column to get the mean of de-trended visitors in that particular month:

```
seasons = colMeans(seasonsmatrix, na.rm = T)
```

11. This gives us a vector with 12 values – one for each month of the year. Since we have 20 years of data, we repeat this vector 20 times:

```
raw$seasons<-c(rep(seasons,20))
```

12. Finally, we can obtain our de-trended, de-cycled data, which we will name **error** because random error is the only thing remaining after removing the time trends and yearly cycles in the data:

```
raw$error<-raw$visitors-raw$timetrend-raw$seasons
```

13. We can plot this to see what it looks like:

```
plot(raw$error,type='o')
```

The plot looks as follows:

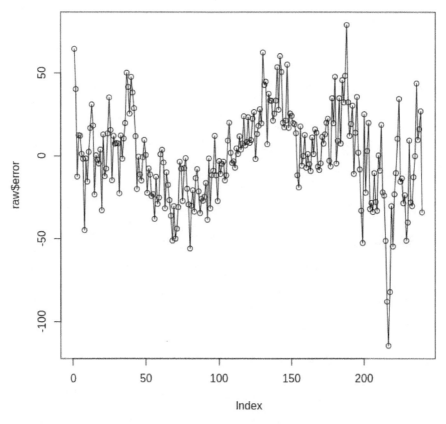

Figure 6.12: Plot of the de-trended data

14. Plot all elements of seasonality modeling together. Finally, we can show all of the elements we have isolated from our seasonal data: a time trend, a yearly cycle, and random error:

```
par(mfrow=c(3,1))
plot(raw$timetrend,type='o')
plot(raw$seasons,type='o')
plot(raw$error,type='o')
```

The output is as follows:

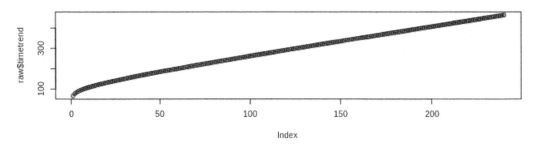

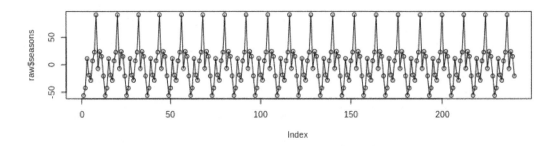

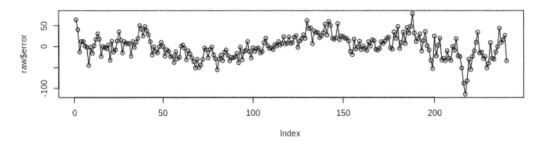

Figure 6.13: Plot of elements of seasonality modelling

The three plots shown together in Figure 6.13 show a decomposition of the original data. The first plot shows the time trend, or in other words the overall pattern observed in the data that each month tends to have more visitors than the previous month. Of course, this is an oversimplification of the data, because there are also seasonal patterns: certain months tend to have more or fewer visitors than other months, irrespective of the overall trend. The second plot shows these seasonal patterns, which repeat in the same way year after year. Finally, the third plot shows the error, which is all of the variation in the data that is not captured by an overall time trend or by a seasonal pattern within each year. If you take the sum of all the data presented in these three plots, you will recover the original dataset. But in these three plots, we can see these elements decomposed, and this decomposition gives us a better understanding of how time trends, seasonality, and error interact to constitute the observed data.

This exercise enabled us to create a variable called **error** that we added to the raw data frame. Now that we have created the error vector, we can use standard anomaly detection to find anomalies in the data frame.

Exercise 44: Finding Anomalies in Seasonal Data Using a Parametric Method

In this exercise, we will do anomaly detection by finding the largest deviations from expected values:

1. Calculate the standard deviation of the error data calculated in the previous exercise:

   ```
   stdev<-sd(raw$error)
   ```

2. Find which data points are more than two standard deviations away from the mean value:

   ```
   high_outliers<-which(raw$error>(mean(raw$error)+2*sd(raw$error)))
   low_outliers<-which(raw$error<(mean(raw$error)-2*sd(raw$error)))
   ```

3. Examine the observations that we have classified as outliers:

   ```
   raw[high_outliers,]
   ```

The output is as follows:

```
    visitors period timetrend withouttimetrend   seasons     error
1      75.7      1  67.18931          8.510688 -55.94655 64.45724
130   392.7    130 305.93840         86.761602  24.35847 62.40313
142   408.0    142 323.44067         84.559332  24.35847 60.20086
147   397.4    147 330.70509         66.694909  11.55558 55.13933
188   559.9    188 389.78579        170.114205  91.11673 78.99748
```

Low outliers are classified as follows:

```
raw[low_outliers,]
```

The output is as follows:

```
    visitors period timetrend withouttimetrend    seasons       error
80     266.8     80 231.4934          35.30663   91.11673  -55.81010
216    321.5    216 429.7569        -108.25691  -20.46137  -87.79553
217    260.9    217 431.1801        -170.28007  -55.94655 -114.33352
218    308.3    218 432.6029        -124.30295  -42.40371   -81.8992
```

4. We can plot these points as follows:

```
plot(raw$period,raw$visitors,type='o')
points(raw$period[high_outliers],raw$visitors[high_
outliers],pch=19,col='red')
points(raw$period[low_outliers],raw$visitors[low_
outliers],pch=19,col='blue')
```

The plot looks as follows:

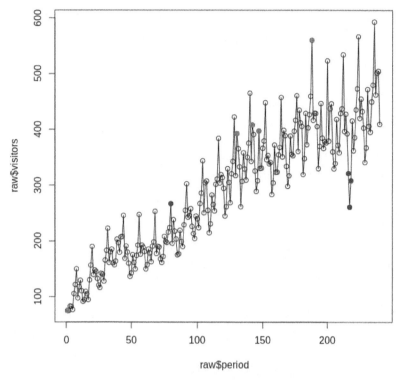

Figure 6.14: Plot of data classified as anomalies

The plot shows all of our data and the points that we have classified as anomalies, with high anomalies plotted in red and low anomalies plotted in blue. You should note that not all of these points are immediately obvious as outliers. We have only been able to recognize them as outliers after doing the seasonality modeling exercise earlier, and determining expected values that the anomalies depart from.

Next, we will introduce two more types of anomalies: contextual and collective anomalies. In order to introduce these concepts, we will generate an artificial dataset that contains both contextual and collective anomalies.

Contextual and Collective Anomalies

At around x=1 in Figure 6.15, you can see a single point that is quite far from its neighbors. This is an example of a **contextual anomaly**, and we will discuss what that means and how to detect these types of anomalies first. At around x=3.6, you can see a region where y is flat, with every value equal to 0. Zero values are not anomalous in this data, but having so many of them together is anomalous. So, this collection of data is referred to as a **collective anomaly**.

We will consider contextual anomalies first. Contextual anomalies are observations that are considered anomalies only because of their neighbors. In the dataset we have just generated, there is one point at x=1 where y=0. However, the values of y for x=0.99 and x=1.01 are close to 0.84, very far from 0 in this context. Contextual anomalies can be detected by finding observations that have anomalous distance from their neighbors, as we will see in the following exercise.

Exercise 45: Detecting Contextual Anomalies

The following exercise shows how to detect contextual anomalies in the dataset we have just introduced. Since contextual anomalies are observations that are very different from their neighbors, we need to do an explicit comparison of each observation with its neighbor. In order to do this, we calculate a first difference. A first difference is simply the value of an observation minus the value of the observation before it.

The expected outcome of this exercise will be the observations in the dataset that are contextual anomalies:

1. We will generate an artificial dataset that contains both contextual and collective anomalies. The dataset can be generated by running the following code in the R console:

   ```
   x<-1:round(2*pi*100+100)/100
   y<-rep(0,round(2*pi*100)+100)
   y[1:314]<-sin(x[1:314])
   y[415:728]<-sin(x[315:628])
   y[100]<-0
   ```

2. You can see what this data looks like by plotting **x** and **y** as follows:

```
plot(x,y,type='o')
```

The output is as follows:

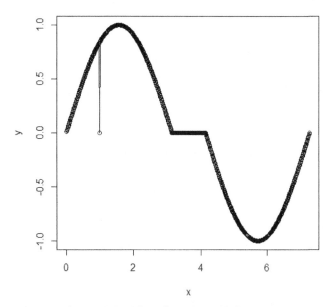

Figure 6.15: Plot of generated dataset

This plot shows a sine curve: a simple type of curve that begins at 0, and slopes gently upward and downward, finally returning to 0 again. This data is artificially generated; however, we might imagine that it represents observations of temperature: low in some months, climbing higher in some months, high in some months, and climbing downward in other months. Temperature and weather data often follow a pattern that can be modeled with a trigonometric curve such as a sine or cosine. We have altered our sine curve so that it includes some anomalous data.

3. Find the first difference for every observation at the same time as follows:

```
difference_y<-y[2:length(y)]-y[1:(length(y)-1)]
```

4. Create a boxplot of the first difference data:

```
boxplot(difference_y)
```

The resulting boxplot looks as follows:

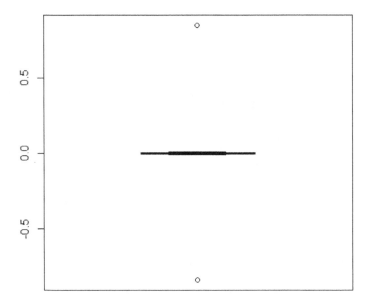

Figure 6.16: Boxplot of the first difference data

This boxplot shows that nearly all first differences are very close to zero, while two outlier differences are far away from the rest. We can see from the first difference boxplot that the single high outlier is larger than 0.5.

You may notice that there are two apparent outliers in Figure 6.16, but only one single outlier apparent in Figure 6.15. The reason for this is that Figure 6.16 shows first difference data, and the single outlier in the data leads to two large first differences: the difference between the 99th and the 100th values, and the difference between the 100th and 101st values. One outlier observation in the original data has led to two outlier observations in the first difference data.

5. Determine which observation corresponds to this outlier by using R's useful **which** function:

```
which(difference_y>0.5)
```

which returns the value 100, indicating that it is the 100th observation that is a contextual anomaly. If we check, **y[100]** is equal to 0, and its neighbors are not, so we have successfully found the contextual anomaly.

Next, we will discuss collective anomalies. In our x-y plot, we pointed out the 100 observations that were all equal to 0 around x=3.64. A zero value is not in itself an anomaly in this dataset, but having 100 observations all equal to 0 is anomalous. The collection of 100 zero values together here is referred to as a collective anomaly. Collective anomalies are more difficult to detect than contextual anomalies, but we will attempt to detect them anyway in the following exercise.

Exercise 46: Detecting Collective Anomalies

In the following exercise, we will detect collective anomalies in the dataset we created earlier. The expected outcome of this exercise is a list of observations that constitute collective anomalies:

1. In order to detect this kind of anomaly, we need to look for groups of observations, or neighborhoods, that contain no variation or only small variations. The following loop accomplishes this. It creates a vector that consists of the maximum value of two differences: the difference between an observation and the observation 50 periods before, and the difference between an observation and the observation 50 periods later. If the maximum of these differences is zero or very small, then we have detected a neighborhood that is extremely flat, a sign of this kind of collective anomaly. Here is the loop we will use:

    ```
    changes<-NULL
    ks<-NULL
    k<-51
    while(k<(length(y)-50)){
    changes<-c(changes,max(abs(y[k-50]),abs(y[k+50])))
    ks<-c(ks,k)
    k<-k+1
    }
    ```

    This loop has created a vector called **changes**. Each element of this vector measures the maximum difference observed between an observation and its neighbors 50 observations away. Especially small values of the **changes** vector will indicate that we could have a collective anomaly consisting of a flat neighborhood.

2. Now that we have a vector measuring neighborhood changes, we can create a simple boxplot, the same as we have done in previous exercises:

    ```
    boxplot(changes)
    ```

    The output is as follows:

    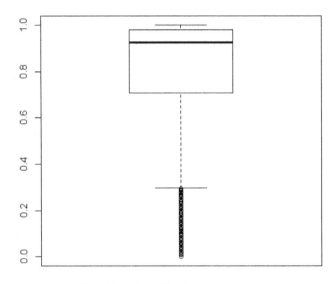

    Figure 6.17: Boxplot of neighborhood changes

    We can see that there are many observations classified as outliers, which shows evidence of very low neighborhood changes.

3. We can find which observation leads to this collective anomaly as follows:

    ```
    print(ks[which(changes==min(changes))])
    ```

    The output is 364.

4. We can verify that this is an index corresponding to the collective anomaly by checking the y value at that index:

    ```
    print(y[ks[which(changes==min(changes))]])
    ```

    So, y is 0, which is the value of y at the collective anomaly, providing evidence that we have found the right point.

Kernel Density

To conclude the chapter, we will discuss using kernel density estimates to perform outlier detection on a set of blood samples. **Kernel density** estimation provides a natural way to test whether a particular set of blood results are anomalous, even without having specialized knowledge of the particular blood test being used or even of medicine in general.

Suppose that you are working at a doctor's office and your boss asks you to do a new type of blood test on patients. Your boss wants to know if any of the patients have anomalous test results. However, you are not familiar with this new blood test and you do not know what normal and anomalous results are supposed to look like. All you have is a record of previous blood tests that your boss assures you are from normal patients. Suppose that these tests had the following results:

```
normal_results<-c(100,95,106,92,109,190,210,201,198)
```

Now suppose that your boss wants you to find anomalies (if any) in the following new blood test results:

```
new_results<-c(98,35,270,140,200)
```

In kernel density estimation, we model a dataset with a collection of kernels. For our purposes, the kernels will just be normal distributions with different means and variances. You can learn more about the normal distribution in *Chapter 3*, *Probability Distributions*. We will suppose that our data has a density that is captured by a sum of normal distributions. Then, any data that appears to be inconsistent with the sum of normal distributions that we specify can be classified as an anomaly.

When we calculate kernel density, we will have to specify something called **bandwidth**. Here, the bandwidth will be a measure of the variance of the normal distributions that we are using to model our data. If we specify a high bandwidth, we are assuming that the data is widely dispersed, and if we specify a low bandwidth, we are assuming that the data is largely contained in a relatively narrow range. This should become more clearer to you as you work through the following exercise.

Exercise 47: Finding Anomalies Using Kernel Density Estimation

In this exercise, we will cover how to find anomalies using kernel density estimation. The expected output of this exercise is a list of observations that constitute anomalies according to a kernel density estimation method:

1. Specify our data and our parameters. For our data, we will use the **normal results** and **new results** we specified earlier:

    ```
    normal_results<-c(100,95,106,92,109,190,210,201,198)
    new_results<-c(98,35,270,140,200)
    ```

2. Kernel density estimation relies on a parameter called **bandwidth**. For that, we will start with 25. The choice of bandwidth will depend on your own preferences and also on the original data. If you are not sure, you can choose a bandwidth that is about the same size as the standard deviation of your data. In this case, we will choose 25, which is lower than the standard deviation of our data. You can set the bandwidth at 25 as follows:

    ```
    bandwidth<-25
    ```

    > **Note**
    >
    > You can feel free to experiment with other bandwidth values if you like.

3. Use R's **density** function to obtain a kernel density estimate:

    ```
    our_estimate<-density(normal_results, bw=bandwidth)
    ```

4. Plot the density estimate:

    ```
    plot(our_estimate)
    ```

The resulting plot appears as follows:

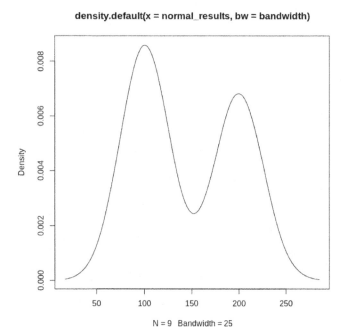

density.default(x = normal_results, bw = bandwidth)

Figure 6.18: Plot of density estimate

5. The shape of the graph in Figure 6.18 represents the distribution of our original data. You can learn more about probability distributions in *Chapter 3, Probability Distributions*. This distribution is called **bimodal**, which means that the data appears to cluster mainly around two points: most of the observations are close to either 100 or 200. We will interpret an observation as an anomaly if its corresponding point on the distribution shown in Figure 6.18 shows that it is particularly unlikely.

6. We can obtain density estimates for each of our new results. For each of the observations in **new_results**, we will calculate the density estimate according to the kernel illustrated in Figure 6.18. We will store each of these density estimates in new variables as follows:

```
new_density_1<-density(normal_results,bw=25,n=1,from=new_
results[1],to=new_results[1])$y
new_density_2<-density(normal_results,bw=25,n=1,from=new_
results[2],to=new_results[2])$y
new_density_3<-density(normal_results,bw=25,n=1,from=new_
results[3],to=new_results[3])$y
new_density_4<-density(normal_results,bw=25,n=1,from=new_
results[4],to=new_results[4])$y
new_density_5<-density(normal_results,bw=25,n=1,from=new_
results[5],to=new_results[5])$y
```

The output will be the heights on the graph from *Step* 3 that corresponds to each of the x-values specified in the **new_results** vector. We can observe each of these values by printing them. Print **new_density_1** as follows:

```
print(new_density_1)
```

The output is as follows:

```
[1] 0.00854745
```

Print **new_density_2** as follows:

```
print(new_density_2)
```

The output is as follows:

```
[1] 0.0003474778
```

Print **new_density_3** as follows:

```
print(new_density_3)
```

The output is as follows:

```
[1] 0.0001787185
```

Print **new_density_4** as follows:

```
print(new_density_4)
```

The output is as follows:

```
[1] 0.003143966
```

Print **new_density_5** as follows:

```
print(new_density_5)
```

The output is as follows:

```
[1] 0.006817359
```

7. We can plot these points on our density plot as follows:

```
plot(our_estimate)
points(new_results[1],new_density_1,col='red',pch=19)
points(new_results[2],new_density_2,col='red',pch=19)
points(new_results[3],new_density_3,col='red',pch=19)
points(new_results[4],new_density_4,col='red',pch=19)
points(new_results[5],new_density_5,col='red',pch=19)
```

8. The result of executing these commands is the following plot:

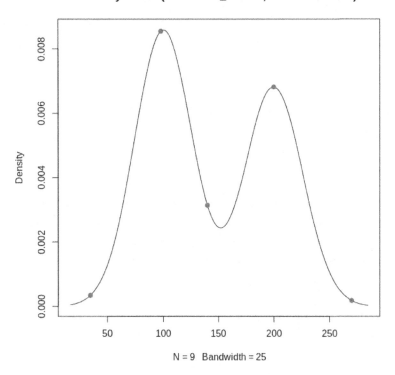

Figure 6.19: Points mapped on density plot

This shows the same density plot we examined earlier, with five points added – one for each of the new results that we are examining to find anomalies. Each of the points shows the relative likelihood of each particular observation: points that have a higher estimated density value are more likely to be observed, while points that have a lower estimated density value are less likely to be observed and are therefore more likely to be anomalies. There is no strict rule about which observations are anomalies and which are not, but in general the observations whose estimated densities are closest to zero are most likely to be anomalies.

9. Interpret the results to classify anomalies.

Each of the density values appear quite close to zero. However, some are much closer to zero than others. In this case, the closer the density estimate is to zero, the more confident we are that the observation is an anomaly. In this case, we will choose a threshold value and say that blood test results whose kernel density estimates are lower than the threshold are anomalous, and results whose kernel density estimates are higher than the threshold are not anomalous. It seems that 0.001 is a reasonable threshold, since it separates the high-density values from the lowest-density values – the observations whose density values are lower than 0.001 appear on the plot shown in *Step* 6 to be very unlikely. So, we will classify the blood test results 35 and 270 as anomalous results, and all of the others as reasonable, because we saw in step 4 that 35 and 270 corresponded to density estimates that were lower than 0.001.

So, the final output of our exercise is the conclusion that the blood test results 35 and 270 are anomalies, while the rest of the blood test results are reasonable.

Continuing in Your Studies of Anomaly Detection

If you continue to learn about anomaly detection, you will find that there are a huge number of different anomaly detection techniques. However, all of them follow the same basic pattern that we have seen in our seasonality modeling example. Specifically, advanced anomaly detection usually consists of the following:

- Specifying a model of what is expected

- Calculating the difference between what is expected based on the model, and what is observed – this is called the error

- Using univariate outlier detection on the error vector to determine anomalies

The biggest difficulty comes in the first step: specifying a useful model of what is expected. In this case, we specified a seasonal model. In other cases, it will be necessary to specify models that take into account multi-dimensional image data, audio recordings, or complicated economic indicators or other complex attributes. The right way to set up models for those cases will require study of the particular domains from which the data is drawn. However, in each case, anomaly detection will follow the three-step bulleted pattern listed earlier.

Activity 14: Finding Univariate Anomalies Using a Parametric Method and a Non-parametric Method

The aim of the activity is to find univariate anomalies using a parametric method. For this activity, we will use a dataset that is built in to R, called **islands**. If you execute **?islands** in R, you can find the documentation of this dataset. In this documentation, you can notice that this dataset contains the areas in thousands of square miles of landmasses on Earth that exceed 10,000 square miles.

This might be a dataset that would be of interest to a geologist who studied the formation of landmasses on earth. According to scientists, there are numerous ways that islands can form: sometimes through volcanic activity, sometimes through coral growth, and sometimes in other ways. A geologist might be interested in finding islands that are anomalously large or small – these islands might be the best places to do further research to try to understand the natural processes of island formation. In this activity, we will find anomalies in the **islands** dataset.

These steps will help you complete the activity:

1. Load the data called **islands** in R's built-in datasets and create a boxplot of this data. What do you notice about the distribution of data and outliers?

2. Transform the **islands** data with a logarithm transformation and create a boxplot of this transformed data. How has this changed the data points that are classified as outliers?

3. Calculate the outliers in the islands dataset manually using a non-parametric method (the method that defines outliers as points lying more than 1.5 times the interquartile range above or below the first and third quartiles, respectively). Do the same for the log transformation of the islands data.

4. Classify outliers in the **islands** dataset using a parametric method by calculating the mean and standard deviation of the data and classifying outliers as observations that are more than two standard deviations away from the mean. Do the same for the logarithm transformation of the islands data.

5. Compare the results of each of these outlier detection methods.

> **Note**
>
> The solution for this activity can be found on page 234.

Activity 15: Using Mahalanobis Distance to Find Anomalies

In the following activity, we will examine data related to the speed and stopping distance of cars. This data might be useful to an automotive engineer who is trying to research which cars perform the best. Cars that have especially low stopping distance relative to their speeds can be used as examples of high-performing cars, while those that have anomalously high stopping distance relative to their speeds may be candidates for further research to find areas for improvement. In this activity, we will find anomalies based on both speed and stopping distance. Because we are working with multivariate data, it makes sense to use Mahalanobis distance to find anomalies.

These steps will help you complete this activity:

1. Load the **cars** dataset from R's built-in datasets. This dataset contains the speed of some very old cars together with the distance required to stop at that speed. Plot the data.

2. Calculate the centroid of this data, and calculate the Mahalanobis distance between each point and the centroid. Find the outliers (points whose Mahalanobis distance from the centroid is the highest). Draw a plot showing all the observations and the outliers plotted together.

The plot will look as follows:

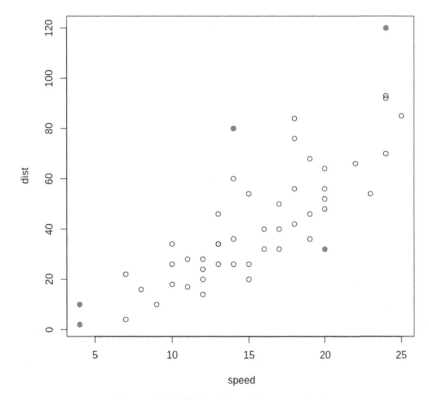

Figure 6.20: Plot with outliers marked

Note

The solution for this activity is on page 237.

Summary

In this chapter, we have discussed anomaly detection. We began with univariate anomaly detection, including non-parametric and parametric approaches. We discussed performing data transformations to obtain better classifications of outliers. We then discussed multivariate anomaly detection using Mahalanobis distances. We completed more advanced exercises to classify anomalies related to seasonally varying data. We discussed collective and contextual anomalies, and concluded the chapter with a discussion of how to use kernel density estimation in anomaly detection.

Appendix

About

This section is included to assist the students to perform the activities in the book.
It includes detailed steps that are to be performed by the students to achieve the objectives of
the activities.

Chapter 1: Introduction to Clustering Methods

Activity 1: k-means Clustering with Three Clusters

Solution:

1. Load the Iris dataset in the **iris_data** variable:

    ```
    iris_data<-iris
    ```

2. Create a **t_color** column and make its default value **red**. Change the value of the two species to **green** and **blue** so the third one remains **red**:

    ```
    iris_data$t_color='red'
    iris_data$t_color[which(iris_data$Species=='setosa')]<-'green'
    iris_data$t_color[which(iris_data$Species=='virginica')]<-'blue'
    ```

    > **Note**
    >
    > Here, we change the **color** column of only those values whose species is **setosa** or **virginica**)

3. Choose any three random cluster centers:

    ```
    k1<-c(7,3)
    k2<-c(5,3)
    k3<-c(6,2.5)
    ```

4. Plot the **x**, **y** plot by entering the sepal length and sepal width in the **plot()** function, along with color:

    ```
    plot(iris_data$Sepal.Length,iris_data$Sepal.Width,col=iris_data$t_color)
    points(k1[1],k1[2],pch=4)
    points(k2[1],k2[2],pch=5)
    points(k3[1],k3[2],pch=6)
    ```

Here is the output:

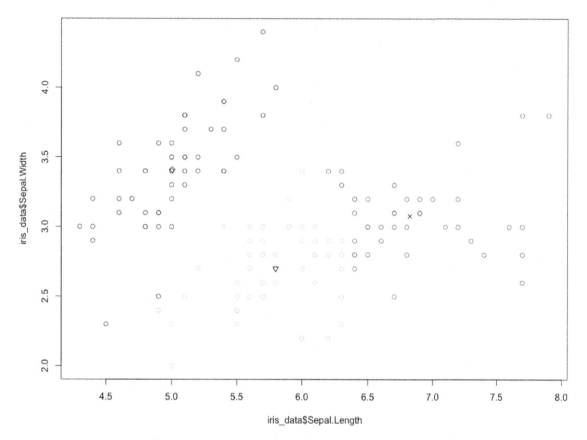

Figure 1.36: Scatter plot for the given cluster centers

5. Choose a number of iterations:

    ```
    number_of_steps<-10
    ```

6. Choose an the initial value of **n**:

    ```
    n<-1
    ```

7. Start the **while** loop for finding the cluster centers:

    ```
    while(n<number_of_steps){
    ```

8. Calculate the distance of each point from the current cluster centers. We're calculating the Euclidean distance here using the **sqrt** function:

```
iris_data$distance_to_clust1 <- sqrt((iris_data$Sepal.Length-
k1[1])^2+(iris_data$Sepal.Width-k1[2])^2)
iris_data$distance_to_clust2 <- sqrt((iris_data$Sepal.Length-
k2[1])^2+(iris_data$Sepal.Width-k2[2])^2)
iris_data$distance_to_clust3 <- sqrt((iris_data$Sepal.Length-
k3[1])^2+(iris_data$Sepal.Width-k3[2])^2)
```

9. Assign each point to a cluster to whose center it is closest:

```
   iris_data$clust_1 <- 1*(iris_data$distance_to_clust1<=iris_
data$distance_to_clust2 & iris_data$distance_to_clust1<=iris_
data$distance_to_clust3)
   iris_data$clust_2 <- 1*(iris_data$distance_to_clust1>iris_data$distance_
to_clust2 & iris_data$distance_to_clust3>iris_data$distance_to_clust2)
   iris_data$clust_3 <- 1*(iris_data$distance_to_clust3<iris_data$distance_
to_clust1 & iris_data$distance_to_clust3<iris_data$distance_to_clust2)
```

10. Calculate new cluster centers by calculating the mean **x** and **y** coordinates of each center with the **mean()** function in R:

```
k1[1]<-mean(iris_data$Sepal.Length[which(iris_data$clust_1==1)])
k1[2]<-mean(iris_data$Sepal.Width[which(iris_data$clust_1==1)])
k2[1]<-mean(iris_data$Sepal.Length[which(iris_data$clust_2==1)])
k2[2]<-mean(iris_data$Sepal.Width[which(iris_data$clust_2==1)])
k3[1]<-mean(iris_data$Sepal.Length[which(iris_data$clust_3==1)])
k3[2]<-mean(iris_data$Sepal.Width[which(iris_data$clust_3==1)])
n=n+1
}
```

11. Choose the color for each center to plot a scatterplot:

```
iris_data$color='red'
iris_data$color[which(iris_data$clust_2==1)]<-'blue'
iris_data$color[which(iris_data$clust_3==1)]<-'green'
```

12. Plot the final plot:

```
plot(iris_data$Sepal.Length,iris_data$Sepal.Width,col=iris_data$color)
points(k1[1],k1[2],pch=4)
points(k2[1],k2[2],pch=5)
points(k3[1],k3[2],pch=6)
```

The output is as follows:

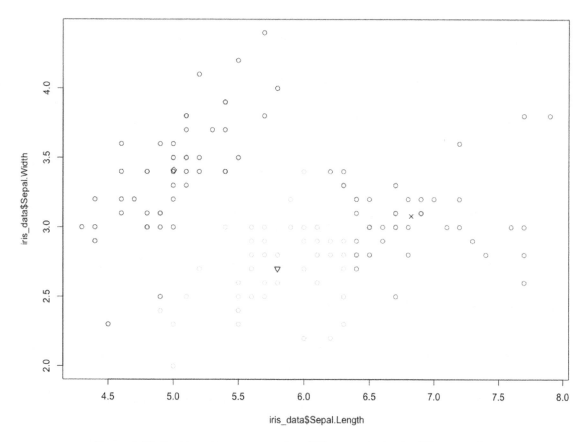

Figure 1.37: Scatter plot representing different species in different colors

Activity 2: Customer Segmentation with k-means

Solution:

1. Download the data from https://github.com/TrainingByPackt/Applied-Unsupervised-Learning-with-R/tree/master/Lesson01/Activity02/wholesale_customers_data.csv.

2. Read the data into the **ws** variable:

   ```
   ws<-read.csv('wholesale_customers_data.csv')
   ```

3. Store only column 5 and 6 in the **ws** variable by discarding the rest of the columns:

   ```
   ws<-ws[5:6]
   ```

4. Import the **factoextra** library:

   ```
   library(factoextra)
   ```

5. Calculate the cluster centers for two centers:

   ```
   clus<-kmeans(ws,2)
   ```

6. Plot the chart for two clusters:

   ```
   fviz_cluster(clus,data=ws)
   ```

   The output is as follows:

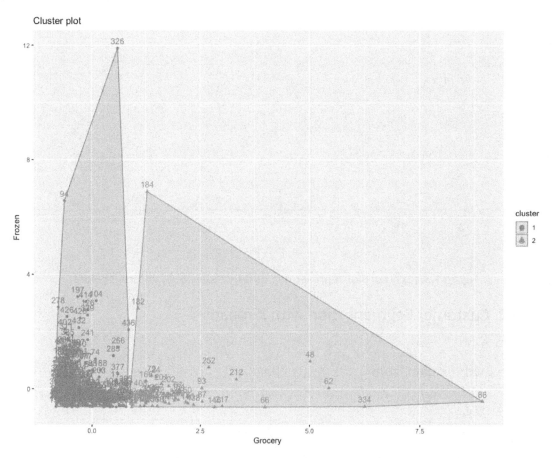

Figure 1.38: Chart for two clusters

Notice how outliers are also part of the two clusters.

7. Calculate the cluster centers for three clusters:

   ```
   clus<-kmeans(ws,3)
   ```

8. Plot the chart for three clusters:

```
fviz_cluster(clus,data=ws)
```

The output is as follows:

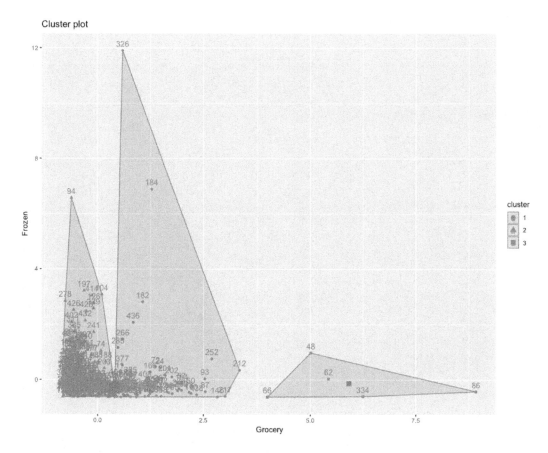

Figure 1.39: Chart for three clusters

Notice some outliers are now a part of a separate cluster.

9. Calculate the cluster centers for four centers:

```
clus<-kmeans(ws,4)
```

10. Plot the chart for four clusters:

```
fviz_cluster(clus,data=ws)
```

The output is as follows:

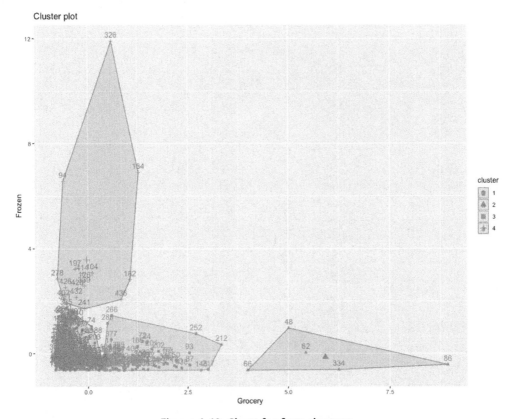

Figure 1.40: Chart for four clusters

Notice how outliers have started separating in two different clusters.

11. Calculate the cluster centers for five clusters:

```
clus<-kmeans(ws,5)
```

12. Plot the chart for five clusters:

```
fviz_cluster(clus,data=ws)
```

The output is as follows:

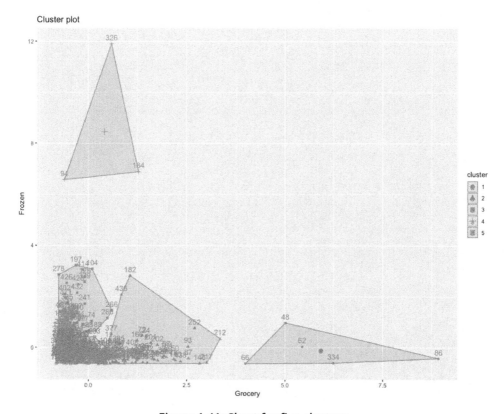

Figure 1.41: Chart for five clusters

Notice how outliers have clearly formed two separate clusters in red and blue, while the rest of the data is classified in three different clusters.

13. Calculate the cluster centers for six clusters:

```
clus<-kmeans(ws,6)
```

14. Plot the chart for six clusters:

```
fviz_cluster(clus,data=ws)
```

The output is as follows:

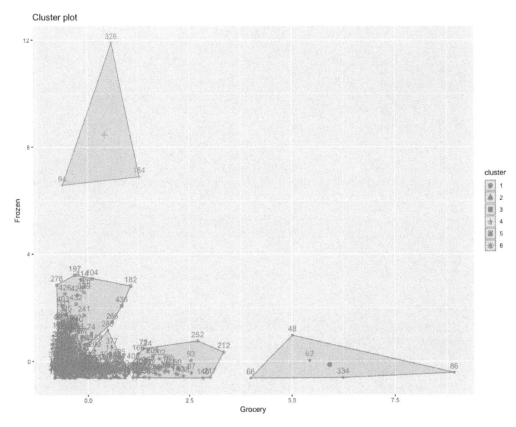

Figure 1.42: Chart for six clusters

Activity 3: Performing Customer Segmentation with k-medoids Clustering

Solution:

1. Read the CSV file into the **ws** variable:

```
ws<-read.csv('wholesale_customers_data.csv')
```

2. Store only columns 5 and 6 in the **ws** variable:

```
ws<-ws[5:6]
```

3. Import the **factoextra** library for visualization:

```
library(factoextra)
```

4. Import the **cluster** library for clustering by PAM:

    ```
    library(cluster)
    ```

5. Calculate clusters by entering data and the number of clusters in the **pam** function:

    ```
    clus<-pam(ws,4)
    ```

6. Plot a visualization of the clusters:

    ```
    fviz_cluster(clus,data=ws)
    ```

    The output is as follows:

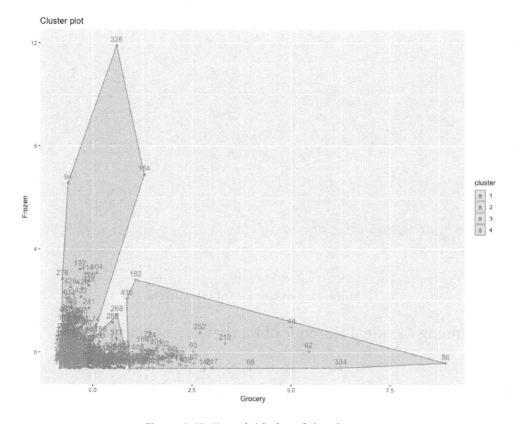

Figure 1.43: K-medoid plot of the clusters

7. Again, calculate the clusters with k-means and plot the output to compare with the output of the **pam** clustering:

    ```
    clus<-kmeans(ws,4)
    fviz_cluster(clus,data=ws)
    ```

The output is as follows:

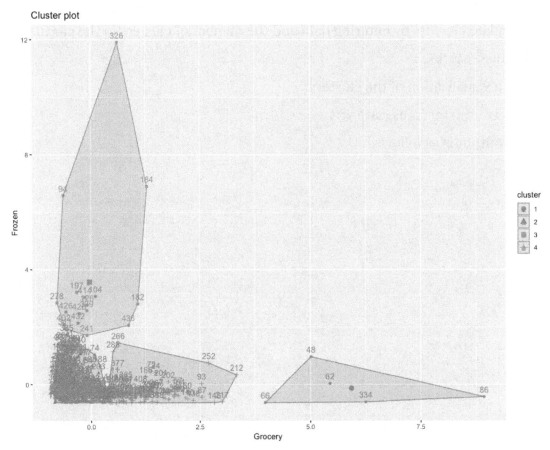

Figure 1.44: K-means plot of the clusters

Activity 4: Finding the Ideal Number of Market Segments

Solution:

1. Read the downloaded dataset into the **ws** variable:

    ```
    ws<-read.csv('wholesale_customers_data.csv')
    ```

2. Store only columns 5 and 6 in the variable by discarding other columns:

    ```
    ws<-ws[5:6]
    ```

3. Calculate the optimal number of clusters with the silhouette score:

```
fviz_nbclust(ws, kmeans, method = "silhouette",k.max=20)
```

Here is the output:

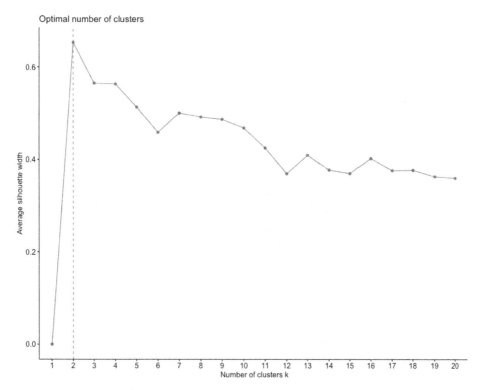

Figure 1.45: Graph representing optimal number of clusters with the silhouette score

The optimal number of clusters, according to the silhouette score, is two.

4. Calculate the optimal number of clusters with the WSS score:

```
fviz_nbclust(ws, kmeans, method = "wss", k.max=20)
```

Here is the output:

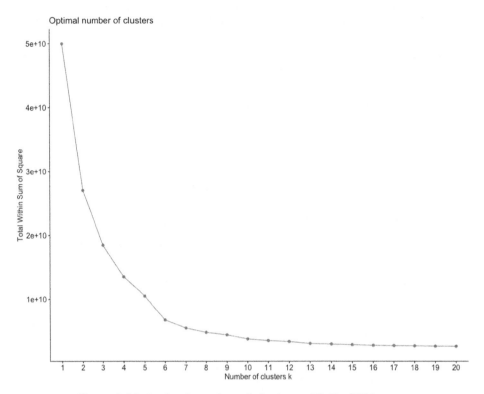

Figure 1.46: Optimal number of clusters with the WSS score

The optimum number of clusters according to the WSS elbow method is around six.

5. Calculate the optimal number of clusters with the Gap statistic:

```
fviz_nbclust(ws, kmeans, method = "gap_stat",k.max=20)
```

Here is the output:

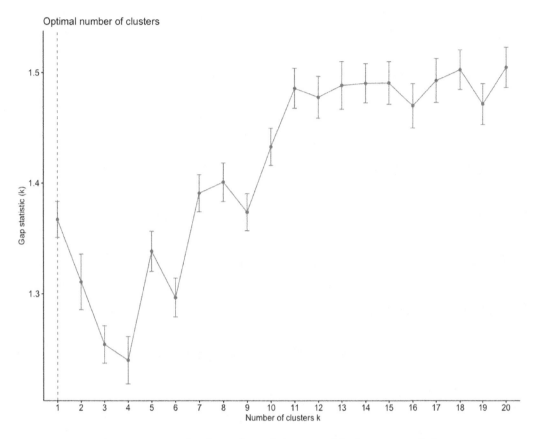

Figure 1.47: Optimal number of clusters with the Gap statistic

The optimal number of clusters according to the Gap statistic is one.

Chapter 2: Advanced Clustering Methods

Activity 5: Implementing k-modes Clustering on the Mushroom Dataset

Solution:

1. Download **mushrooms.csv** from https://github.com/TrainingByPackt/Applied-Unsupervised-Learning-with-R/blob/master/Lesson02/Activity05/mushrooms.csv.

2. After downloading, load the **mushrooms.csv** file in R:

   ```
   ms<-read.csv('mushrooms.csv')
   ```

3. Check the dimensions of the dataset:

   ```
   dim(ms)
   ```

   The output is as follows:

   ```
   [1] 8124    23
   ```

4. Check the distribution of all columns:

   ```
   summary.data.frame(ms)
   ```

   The output is as follows:

```
 class    cap.shape cap.surface  cap.color    bruises        odor      gill.attachment
 e:4208   b: 452    f:2320     n    :2284   f:4748   n    :3528     a: 210
 p:3916   c:   4    g:   4     g    :1840   t:3376   f    :2160     f:7914
          f:3152    s:2556     e    :1500            s    : 576
          k: 828    y:3244     y    :1072            y    : 576
          s:  32               w    :1040            a    : 400
          x:3656               b    : 168            l    : 400
                               (Other): 220         (Other): 484
 gill.spacing gill.size  gill.color   stalk.shape stalk.root stalk.surface.above.ring
 c:6812       b:5612    b    :1728   e:3516      ?:2480     f: 552
 w:1312       n:2512    p    :1492   t:4608      b:3776     k:2372
                        w    :1202               c: 556     s:5176
                        n    :1048               e:1120     y:  24
                        g    : 752               r: 192
                        h    : 732
                        (Other):1170
 stalk.surface.below.ring stalk.color.above.ring stalk.color.below.ring veil.type veil.color
 f: 600                   w    :4464             w    :4384           p:8124    n:  96
 k:2304                   p    :1872             p    :1872                     o:  96
 s:4936                   g    : 576             g    : 576                     w:7924
 y: 284                   n    : 448             n    : 512                     y:   8
                          b    : 432             b    : 432
                          o    : 192             o    : 192
                          (Other): 140          (Other): 156
 ring.number ring.type spore.print.color population habitat
 n:  36      e:2776    w    :2388        a: 384     d:3148
 o:7488      f:  48    n    :1968        c: 340     g:2148
 t: 600      l:1296    k    :1872        n: 400     l: 832
             n:  36    h    :1632        s:1248     m: 292
             p:3968    r    :  72        v:4040     p:1144
                       b    :  48        y:1712     u: 368
                       (Other): 144                 w: 192
```

Figure 2.29: Screenshot of the summary of distribution of all columns

Each column contains all the unique labels and their count.

5. Store all the columns of the dataset, except for the final label, in a new variable, **ms_k**:

```
ms_k<-ms[,2:23]
```

6. Import the **klaR** library, which has the **kmodes** function:

```
install.packages('klaR')
library(klaR)
```

7. Calculate **kmodes** clusters and store them in a **kmodes_ms** variable. Enter the dataset without **true** labels as the first parameter and enter the number of clusters as the second parameter:

```
kmodes_ms<-kmodes(ms_k,2)
```

8. Check the results by creating a table of **true** labels and **cluster** labels:

```
result = table(ms$class, kmodes_ms$cluster)
result
```

The output is as follows:

```
       1     2
 e    80  4128
 p  3052   864
```

As you can see, most of the edible mushrooms are in cluster 2 and most of the poisonous mushrooms are in cluster 1. So, using k-modes clustering has done a reasonable job of identifying whether each mushroom is edible or poisonous.

Activity 6: Implementing DBSCAN and Visualizing the Results

Solution:

1. Import the **dbscan** and **factoextra** library:

```
library(dbscan)
library(factoextra)
```

2. Import the **multishapes** dataset:

```
data(multishapes)
```

3. Put the columns of the **multishapes** dataset in the **ms** variable:

```
ms<-multishapes[,1:2]
```

4. Plot the dataset as follows:

```
plot(ms)
```

The output is as follows:

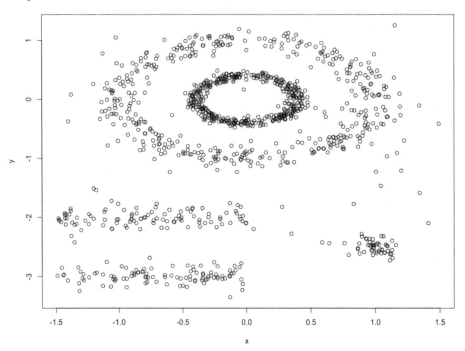

Figure 2.30: Plot of the multishapes dataset

5. Perform k-means clustering on the dataset and plot the results:

```
km.res<-kmeans(ms,4)
fviz_cluster(km.res, ms,ellipse = FALSE)
```

The output is as follows:

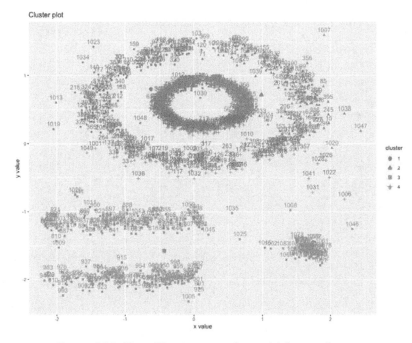

Figure 2.31: Plot of k-means on the multishapes dataset

6. Perform DBSCAN on the **ms** variable and plot the results:

```
db.res<-dbscan(ms,eps = .15)
fviz_cluster(db.res, ms,ellipse = FALSE,geom = 'point')
```

The output is as follows:

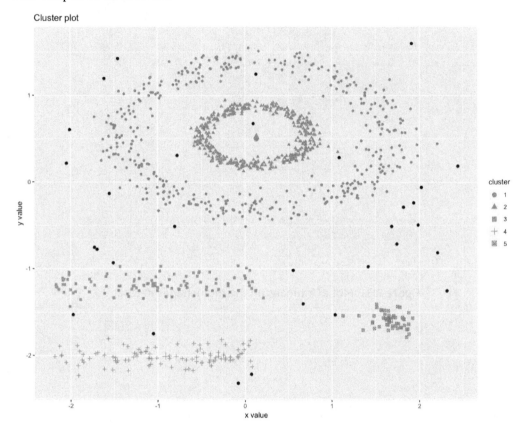

Figure 2.32: Plot of DBCAN on the multishapes dataset

Here, you can see all the points in black are anomalies and are not present in any cluster, and the clusters formed in DBSCAN are not possible with any other type of clustering method. These clusters have taken all types of shapes and sizes, whereas in k-means, all clusters are of a spherical shape.

Activity 7: Performing a Hierarchical Cluster Analysis on the Seeds Dataset

Solution:

1. Read the downloaded file into the **sd** variable:

   ```
   sd<-read.delim('seeds_dataset.txt')
   ```

   > **Note**
   >
   > Make changes to the path as per the location of the file on your system.

2. First, put all the columns of the dataset other than final labels into the **sd_c** variable:

   ```
   sd_c<-sd[,1:7]
   ```

3. Import the **cluster** library:

   ```
   library(cluster)
   ```

4. Calculate the hierarchical clusters and plot the dendrogram:

   ```
   h.res<-hclust(dist(sd_c),"ave")
   plot(h.res)
   ```

The output is as follows:

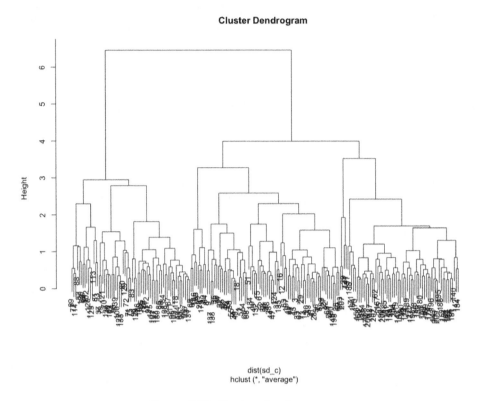

Figure 2.33: Cluster dendrogram

5. Cut the tree at **k=3** and plot a table to see how the results of the clustering have performed at classifying the three types of seeds:

```
memb <- cutree(h.res, k = 3)
results<-table(sd$X1,memb)
results
```

The output is as follows:

```
      memb
         1   2   3
    1   65   3   1
    2    6   0  64
    3    9  61   0
```

Figure 2.34: Table classifying the three types of seeds

6. Perform divisive clustering on the **sd_c** dataset and plot the dendrogram:

```
d.res<-diana(sd_c,metric ="euclidean",)
plot(d.res)
```

The output is as follows:

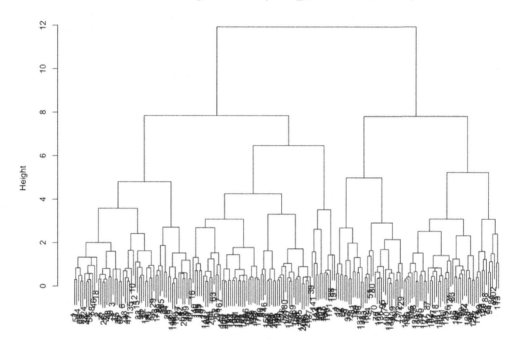

Figure 2.35: Dendrogram of divisive clustering

7. Cut the tree at **k=3** and plot a table to see how the results of the clustering have performed at classifying the three types of seeds:

```
memb <- cutree(h.res, k = 3)
results<-table(sd$X1,memb)
results
```

The output is as follows:

```
          memb
           1   2   3
      1 65   3   1
      2  6   0  64
      3  9  61   0
```

Figure 2.36: Table classifying the three types of seeds

You can see that both types of clustering methods have produced identical results. These results also demonstrate that divisive clustering is the reverse of hierarchical clustering.

Chapter 3: Probability Distributions

Activity 8: Finding the Standard Distribution Closest to the Distribution of Variables of the Iris Dataset

Solution:

1. Load the Iris dataset into the **df** variable:

   ```
   df<-iris
   ```

2. Select rows corresponding to the setosa species only:

   ```
   df=df[df$Species=='setosa',]
   ```

3. Import the **kdensity** library:

   ```
   library(kdensity)
   ```

4. Calculate and plot the KDE from the **kdensity** function for sepal length:

   ```
   dist <- kdensity(df$Sepal.Length)
   plot(dist)
   ```

The output is as follows:

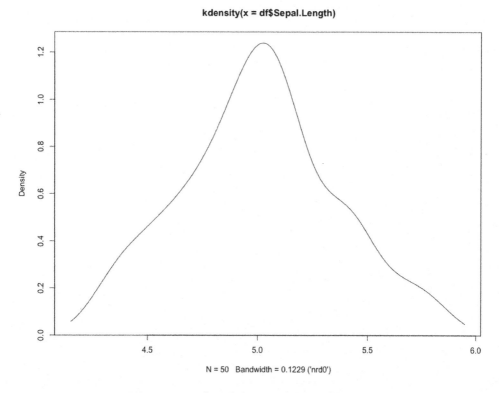

Figure 3.36 Plot of the KDE for sepal length

This distribution is closest to the normal distribution, which we studied in the previous section. Here, the mean and median are both around 5.

5. Calculate and plot the KDE from the **kdensity** function for sepal width:

```
dist <- kdensity(df$Sepal.Width)
plot(dist)
```

The output is as follows:

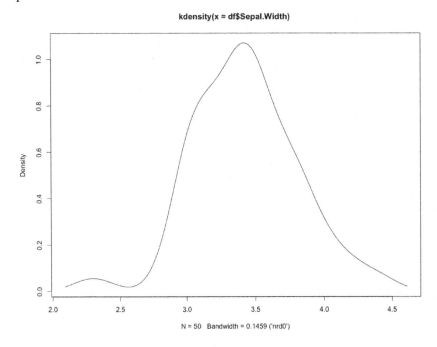

Figure 3.37 Plot of the KDE for sepal width

This distribution is also closest to normal distribution. We can formalize this similarity with a Kolmogorov-Smirnov test.

Activity 9: Calculating the CDF and Performing the Kolmogorov-Simonov Test with the Normal Distribution

Solution:

1. Load the Iris dataset into the **df** variable:

   ```
   df<-iris
   ```

2. Keep rows with the setosa species only:

   ```
   df=df[df$Species=='setosa',]
   ```

3. Calculate the mean and standard deviation of the sepal length column of **df**:

   ```
   sdev<-sd(df$Sepal.Length)
   mn<-mean(df$Sepal.Length)
   ```

4. Generate a new distribution with the standard deviation and mean of the sepal length column:

```
xnorm<-rnorm(100,mean=mn,sd=sdev)
```

5. Plot the CDF of both **xnorm** and the sepal length column:

```
plot(ecdf(xnorm),col='blue')
plot(ecdf(df$Sepal.Length),add=TRUE,pch = 4,col='red')
```

The output is as follows:

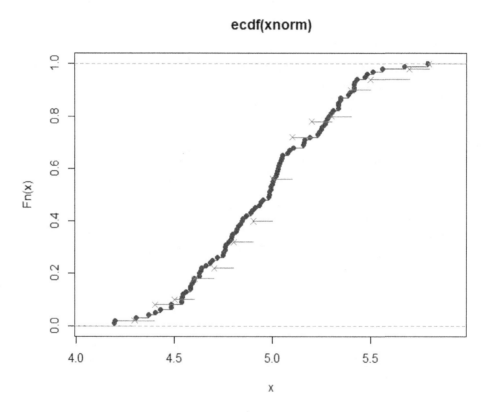

Figure 3.38: The CDF of xnorm and sepal length

The samples look very close to each other in the distribution. Let's see, in the next test, whether the sepal length sample belongs to the normal distribution or not.

6. Perform the Kolmogorov-Smirnov test on the two samples, as follows:

```
ks.test(xnorm,df$Sepal.Length)
```

The output is as follows:

```
        Two-sample Kolmogorov-Smirnov test
    data: xnorm and df$Sepal.Length
    D = 0.14, p-value = 0.5307
    alternative hypothesis: two-sided
```

Here, **p-value** is very high and the **D** value is low, so we can assume that the distribution of sepal length is closely approximated by the normal distribution.

7. Repeat the same steps for the sepal width column of **df**:

```
sdev<-sd(df$Sepal.Width)
mn<-mean(df$Sepal.Width)
xnorm<-rnorm(100,mean=mn,sd=sdev)
plot(ecdf(xnorm),col='blue')
plot(ecdf(df$Sepal.Width),add=TRUE,pch = 4,col='red')
```

The output is as follows:

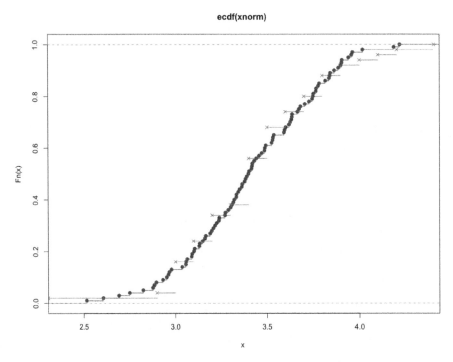

Figure 3.39: CDF of xnorm and sepal width

8. Perform the Kolmogorov-Smirnov test as follows:

```
ks.test(xnorm,df$Sepal.Length)
```

The output is as follows:

```
        Two-sample Kolmogorov-Smirnov test

data: xnorm and df$Sepal.Width
D = 0.12, p-value = 0.7232
alternative hypothesis: two-sided
```

Here, also, the sample distribution of sepal width is closely approximated by the normal distribution.

Chapter 4: Dimension Reduction

Activity 10: Performing PCA and Market Basket Analysis on a New Dataset

Solution:

1. Before starting our main analysis, we will remove one variable that will not be relevant to us:

```
Boston<-Boston[,-12]
```

2. We will create dummy variables. We will end up with one original dataset, and one dummy variable dataset. We do that as follows:

```
Boston_original<-Boston
```

Next, we will create dummy variables for each of the measurements in the original dataset. You can find out the meaning of each of the variables in the dataset in the documentation of the MASS package, available at https://cran.r-project.org/web/packages/MASS/MASS.pdf.

3. Create dummy variables for whether a town has high or low crime per capita:

```
Boston$highcrim<-1*(Boston$indus>median(Boston$crim))
Boston$lowcrim<-1*(Boston$indus<=median(Boston$crim))
```

Create dummy variables for whether a town has a high or low proportion of land zoned for lots over 25,000 feet:

```
Boston$highzn<-1*(Boston$zn>median(Boston$zn))
Boston$lowzn<-1*(Boston$zn<=median(Boston$zn))
```

Create dummy variables for whether a town has a high or low proportion of non-retail business acres per town:

```
Boston$highindus<-1*(Boston$indus>median(Boston$indus))
Boston$lowindus<-1*(Boston$indus<=median(Boston$indus))
```

Create dummy variables for whether a town borders the Charles River:

```
Boston$highchas<-(Boston$chas)
Boston$lowchas<-(1-Boston$chas)
```

Create dummy variables for whether a town has a high or low nitrogen oxide concentration:

```
Boston$highnox<-1*(Boston$nox>median(Boston$nox))
Boston$lownox<-1*(Boston$nox<=median(Boston$nox))
```

Create dummy variables for whether a town has a high or low average number of rooms per dwelling:

```
Boston$highrm<-1*(Boston$rm>median(Boston$rm))
Boston$lowrm<-1*(Boston$rm<=median(Boston$rm))
```

Create dummy variables for whether a town has a high or low proportion of owner-occupied units built prior to 1940:

```
Boston$highage<-1*(Boston$age>median(Boston$age))
Boston$lowage<-1*(Boston$age<=median(Boston$age))
```

Create dummy variables for whether a town has a high or low average distance to five of Boston's employment centers:

```
Boston$highdis<-1*(Boston$dis>median(Boston$dis))
Boston$lowdis<-1*(Boston$dis<=median(Boston$dis))
```

Create dummy variables for whether a town has a high or low index of accessibility to radial highways:

```
Boston$highrad<-1*(Boston$rad>median(Boston$rad))
Boston$lowrad<-1*(Boston$rad<=median(Boston$rad))
```

Create dummy variables for whether a town has a high or low full-value property tax rate:

```
Boston$hightax<-1*(Boston$tax>median(Boston$tax))
Boston$lowtax<-1*(Boston$tax<=median(Boston$tax))
```

Create dummy variables for whether a town has a high or low pupil-teacher ratio:

```
Boston$highptratio<-1*(Boston$ptratio>median(Boston$ptratio))
Boston$lowptratio<-1*(Boston$ptratio<=median(Boston$ptratio))
```

Create dummy variables for whether a town has a high or low proportion of lower-status population:

```
Boston$highlstat<-1*(Boston$lstat>median(Boston$lstat))
Boston$lowlstat<-1*(Boston$lstat<=median(Boston$lstat))
```

Create dummy variables for whether a town has a high or low median home value:

```
Boston$highmedv<-1*(Boston$medv>median(Boston$medv))
Boston$lowmedv<-1*(Boston$medv<=median(Boston$medv))
```

4. Create a dataset that consists entirely of the dummy variables we have just created:

```
Bostondummy<-Boston[,14:ncol(Boston)]
```

5. Finally, we will restore our **Boston_2** dataset to its original form before all of the dummy variables were added:

```
Boston<-Boston_original
```

6. Calculate the eigenvalues and eigenvectors of the covariance matrix of the dataset, as follows:

```
Boston_cov<-cov(Boston)
Boston_eigen<-eigen(Boston_cov)
print(Boston_eigen$vectors)
```

The output is as follows:

```
                  [,1]          [,2]          [,3]          [,4]          [,5]
 [1,]    2.964674e-02 -0.015003651 -0.0268303390  0.3105083975  0.9159233539
 [2,]   -4.492354e-02  0.631037941 -0.7639084529  0.0914984764 -0.0419675589
 [3,]    2.939532e-02 -0.088515154  0.0130376306  0.0541523272 -0.1258473131
 [4,]   -5.070965e-05 -0.000906056 -0.0009292491 -0.0055661084  0.0009662470
 [5,]    4.615941e-04 -0.001817055 -0.0006921813  0.0002758662 -0.0003315697
 [6,]   -1.225450e-03  0.005008013 -0.0063668357 -0.0463339423  0.0208901648
 [7,]    8.630861e-02 -0.752355714 -0.6397040816 -0.0812146848 -0.0035253723
 [8,]   -6.760251e-03  0.044759063 -0.0017451705  0.0325596672 -0.0278668129
 [9,]    4.670538e-02  0.002571526  0.0181608586 -0.0234532588  0.2379011114
[10,]    9.926372e-01  0.101541990  0.0199846897 -0.0305981550 -0.0272793198
[11,]    5.910888e-03 -0.011370960  0.0329866611  0.0589679625 -0.0184675768
[12,]    2.321636e-02 -0.096883535 -0.0409221274  0.4586710733 -0.0858251068
[13,]   -2.565800e-02  0.076330017 -0.0528757677 -0.8167640810  0.2778687767
                  [,6]          [,7]          [,8]          [,9]         [,10]
 [1,]   -0.155644295 -0.158326612  0.111224831  0.025486508 -0.0227333012
 [2,]   -0.038206577 -0.006260425 -0.057018732  0.017656920  0.0318490448
 [3,]   -0.860395716 -0.075885802 -0.465215293  0.009900762 -0.0977504102
 [4,]   -0.006737114  0.005445449 -0.006327226 -0.009680569 -0.0052830397
 [5,]   -0.004868223  0.001270763 -0.003446759 -0.015765167  0.0154002725
 [6,]    0.011854493 -0.009388874 -0.006015218 -0.009814883 -0.0007255794
 [7,]    0.078477626 -0.061457820 -0.007848599  0.009174481 -0.0238738299
 [8,]    0.110677220 -0.041812471  0.013583151  0.116127372 -0.9839320643
 [9,]    0.358117027  0.407606104 -0.793550182 -0.126111107 -0.0106763230
[10,]    0.003158506 -0.016277550  0.044752857  0.001579001 -0.0006268944
[11,]    0.088474600 -0.046285998 -0.146719744  0.973113016  0.1268199497
[12,]   -0.170432847  0.807481699  0.287200268  0.071157157 -0.0279765721
[13,]   -0.224240115  0.378038741  0.178558244  0.130435940 -0.0545477337
                 [,11]         [,12]         [,13]
 [1,]   -3.579451e-03 -1.386274e-03  7.168469e-04
 [2,]   -2.722109e-03 -1.079790e-04  1.021309e-05
 [3,]    1.260538e-03  8.190011e-03 -4.138848e-03
 [4,]   -2.085826e-02 -9.995483e-01 -1.406496e-02
 [5,]   -3.828993e-04 -1.392499e-02  9.996394e-01
 [6,]    9.982814e-01 -2.054663e-02  2.645536e-05
 [7,]   -5.357718e-03  1.068461e-03 -8.705608e-04
 [8,]    7.023865e-04  2.505075e-03  1.772891e-02
 [9,]   -1.221601e-02  6.746324e-03 -3.164339e-03
[10,]    7.268209e-05 -4.231324e-04 -4.147717e-05
[11,]    1.046531e-02 -1.078571e-02  1.320768e-02
[12,]    3.536485e-02 -6.651794e-05  3.293986e-04
[13,]   -3.579491e-02  6.976225e-03  2.455507e-03
```

Figure 4.17: Eigenvectors of the covariance matrix

7. Print eigen values as follows:

```
print(Boston_eigen$values)
```

The output is as follows:

```
[1]  2.881882e+04 8.260671e+02 2.673629e+02 7.984006e+01 4.733876e+01
[6]  1.706442e+01 1.359537e+01 8.961253e+00 2.761729e+00 1.103303e+00
[11] 2.233296e-01 5.914172e-02 2.930149e-03
```

Figure 4.18: Eigenvalues of the covariance matrix

8. For the third part, we create a simple scree plot based on the eigenvalues:

```
plot(Boston_eigen$values,type='o')
```

The output is as follows:

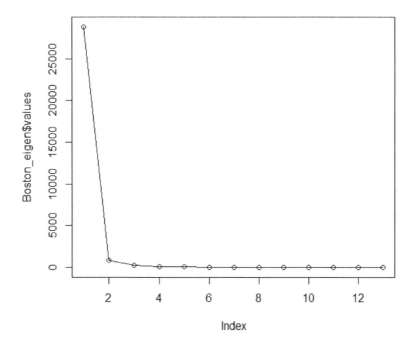

Figure 4.19: Plot of the eigenvalues

9. Next, we choose the number of eigenvectors we will use (I chose 10), and we transform the dataset to be 10-dimensional, as follows:

```
neigen<-10
transformed<-t(t(as.matrix(Boston_eigen$vectors[,1:neigen])) %*% t(as.matrix(Boston)))
```

10. Then, we restore the dataset as much as possible:

```
restored<- t(as.matrix(Boston_eigen$vectors[,1:neigen]) %*% t(as.
matrix(transformed)))
```

11. Finally, we can check how close our restoration is to the original dataset, as follows:

```
print(head(restored-Boston))
```

12. Here, we need to specify a **support** threshold (for example, 20%), and complete the first pass through the data:

```
support_thresh<-0.2
firstpass<-unname(which(colMeans(Bostondummy,na.rm=TRUE)>support_thresh))
```

13. Here, we complete the second pass through the data:

```
secondcand<-t(combn(firstpass,2))
secondpass<-NULL
k<-1
while(k<=nrow(secondcand)){
support<-mean(Bostondummy[,secondcand[k,1]]*Bostondummy[,secondcand[k,2]]
,na.rm=TRUE)
if(support>support_thresh){
secondpass<-rbind(secondpass,secondcand[k,])
}
k<-k+1
}
```

14. Here, we complete the third pass, and then do filtering based on the **confidence** and **lift** thresholds:

```
thirdpass<-NULL
k<-1
while(k<=nrow(secondpass)){
j<-1
while(j<=length(firstpass)){
n<-1
product<-1
while(n<=ncol(secondpass)){
product<-product*Bostondummy[,secondpass[k,n]]
n<-n+1
}
if(!(firstpass[j] %in% secondpass[k,])){
product<-product*Bostondummy[,firstpass[j]]
```

```
support<-mean(product,na.rm=TRUE)
if(support>support_thresh){
thirdpass<-rbind(thirdpass,c(secondpass[k,],firstpass[j]))
}
}
j<-j+1
}
k<-k+1
}


thirdpass_conf<-NULL
k<-1
while(k<=nrow(thirdpass)){

support<-mean(Bostondummy[,thirdpass[k,1]]*Bostondummy[,thirdpass[k,2]]*Bo
stondummy[,thirdpass[k,3]],na.rm=TRUE)
confidence<-mean(Bostondummy[,thirdpass[k,1]]*Bostondummy[,
thirdpass[k,2]]*Bostondummy[,thirdpass[k,3]],na.rm=TRUE)/
mean(Bostondummy[,thirdpass[k,1]]*Bostondummy[,thirdpass[k,2]],na.rm=TRUE)

lift<-confidence/mean(Bostondummy[,thirdpass[k,3]],na.rm=TRUE)

thirdpass_conf<-rbind(thirdpass_
conf,unname(c(thirdpass[k,],support,confidence,lift)))
k<-k+1
}
```

15. Our final output is the list of three-item baskets that have passed the **support**, **confidence**, and `lift` thresholds:

```
print(head(thirdpass_conf))
```

The output is as follows:

	[,1]	[,2]	[,3]	[,4]	[,5]	[,6]
[1,]	1	3	6	0.2588933	0.9776119	1.917332
[2,]	1	3	8	0.2509881	0.9477612	1.018189
[3,]	1	3	10	0.2411067	0.9104478	1.693701
[4,]	1	3	14	0.2332016	0.8805970	1.761194
[5,]	1	3	15	0.2371542	0.8955224	1.791045
[6,]	1	3	18	0.2015810	0.7611940	1.254606

Figure 4.20: Output of the three-item basket

Chapter 5: Data Comparison Methods

Activity 11: Create an Image Signature for a Photograph of a Person

Solution:

1. Download the Borges photo to your computer and save it as **borges.jpg**. Make sure that it is saved in R's working directory. If it is not in R's working directory, then change R's working directory using the **setwd()** function. Then, you can load this image into a variable called **im** (short for image), as follows:

    ```
    install.packages('imager')
    library('imager')
    filepath<-'borges.jpg'
    im <- imager::load.image(file =filepath)
    ```

    The rest of the code we will explore will use this image, called **im**. Here, we have loaded a picture of the Alamo into **im**. However, you can run the rest of the code on any image, simply by saving the image to your working directory and specifying its path in the **filepath** variable.

2. The signature we are developing is meant to be used for grayscale images. So, we will convert this image to grayscale, using functions in the **imager** package:

    ```
    im<-imager::rm.alpha(im)
    im<-imager::grayscale(im)
    im<-imager::imsplit(im,axis = "x", nb = 10)
    ```

    The second line of this code is the conversion to grayscale. The last line performs a split of the image into 10 equal sections.

3. The following code creates an empty matrix that we will fill with information about each section of our 10x10 grid:

    ```
    matrix <- matrix(nrow = 10, ncol = 10)
    ```

Next, we will run the following loop. The first line of this loop uses the `imsplit` command. This command was also used previously to split the x axis into 10 equal parts. This time, for each of the 10 x-axis splits, we will do a split along the y-axis, also splitting it into 10 equal parts:

```
for (i in 1:10) {
  is <- imager::imsplit(im = im[[i]], axis = "y", nb = 10)
  for (j in 1:10) {
    matrix[j,i] <- mean(is[[j]])
  }
}
```

The output so far is the `matrix` variable. We will use this in *step 4*.

4. Get the signature of the Borges photograph by running the following code:

```
borges_signature<-get_signature(matrix)
borges_signature
```

The output is as follows:

```
 [1]  0  0  0  0  0  0  0  0  0  0  1  0  1  1  0  0  0 -1  0  1  1  1  0  0  0 -1  0  1  1  0  0  0  0  0  0  1  1 -1  0  0  0  1  1  1  1  1  0  0
0 -1  1  1  1  1
 [55]  0  0  0 -1  0  0  0  1  0  1  0 -1  0  0  0  1  1  1  0  0  0  0  0  0  0  0  0  0 -1  0  0  0  1  1  1  1  0  0  0 -1 -1  0  0  1  1
0  0 -1 -1  0  0
[109]  1  1  0 -1 -1 -1 -1  0  0  0 -1 -1 -1  0  0  0  0  0 -1 -1 -1  0  0  0  0  0  0 -1 -1  0  0  0  0  0  0  0  0  0  0  0  0 -1 -1 -1 -1  0  1  0  0
0  0  0 -1  0  0
[163]  0  1  1  0 -1  0  0  0  1  1  1  0  0 -1 -1  0  1  0 -1  0  0  0 -1  0  0 -1  0  1  1  0 -1 -1 -1 -1  0  0  0  0  0  0 -1  0 -1  0  0  0  0  1
1 -1 -1  0  0  0
[217]  0  0 -1 -1 -1  0  0  0  0  0 -1 -1 -1  0  0  0  1  1  0  0  0  0  0  0  0  0  0  1  1  1 -1 -1 -1 -1  0  1 -1  0 -1 -1 -1  0  1 -1 -1 -1  0  0
1  1  1  1  1  1
[271]  1  1  0 -1  1  0 -1  1  1  1  1  0 -1 -1 -1 -1 -1  0  1  1 -1  0 -1 -1  1  1  1  1  1  0 -1  1  1  1  1 -1 -1 -1 -1  0  0  1  1  0 -1 -1  0  0
0  0  0  0  0  0
[325]  1  0  0 -1  0  0  0 -1 -1 -1  0  1  1  1  1  0  0 -1  1  1  0  1  0  0  1  1 -1 -1 -1 -1 -1 -1 -1  1  0  1  1  1  0  0  1  1  1  1 -1 -1 -1 -
1 -1 -1  0  1  1
[379]  0 -1 -1 -1  1  0  1  1 -1  0  0  1  1  1  1 -1 -1 -1  0  0  0  1  0  0  0  0 -1  0  0  0 -1  0  0 -1  0 -1 -1  0  1  1  0  1 -1 -1 -1 -1 -1  0  1
1 -1 -1  0  1  0
[433]  0  0 -1 -1 -1 -1 -1  1  1  1 -1 -1 -1  0  1  0  0  0 -1 -1 -1 -1  0  1  1  1 -1  0  0  1  1  1  1  0  0  0  0  0  1  0  0  0 -1  0  0  0  0  1
0  0  0 -1 -1 -1
[487]  0  0  1  1  0 -1  0  1  0  1  0 -1 -1 -1 -1 -1 -1 -1  1  1  1  1 -1  0  1  1  1  0  1 -1  0 -1  1  1  1  1 -1  0  1 -1  1  1  1  1  1  1  1  1
1  1  1 -1  1  1
[541]  1  0  0  0  0  0  1 -1  0  1  1  0  0 -1 -1 -1  0  0  0  0  0  0 -1 -1 -1  0  1  1  1  0 -1 -1  1  1  1  1  0 -1 -1 -1  0  0 -1  1  1  0 -1 -1 -
1 -1 -1 -1  1  1
[595]  1  1  0  1  1  1  0 -1  1 -1 -1  1 -1  0 -1 -1 -1 -1 -1 -1 -1 -1 -1 -1  1 -1 -1 -1 -1 -1 -1 -1  1  1 -1 -1  0  1  1  1  0 -1 -1 -1  0  0  0  1  0  0
0  1 -1 -1  0  1
[649]  1  1  1  0 -1 -1  1  1  1  1  1  0  0  1  1  1  0 -1 -1 -1 -1 -1 -1  1  1  1 -1  0 -1 -1 -1 -1 -1  0  1  1  1  0  0  1  1  1  0  1 -1  0 -1  1  1
1  1  0  0  0 -1
[703]  1  1  1  1  1  1  1  1  1  1  1  0 -1 -1  1  0  0  0  1  0  0  0  0  0 -1 -1 -1  1  1  0  0  0 -1 -1  0  1  1  0  0  0  0  1  0  0  0  0  0  1
1  1  1 -1  0  0
[757]  0 -1 -1  0  1  1  0  0  0 -1 -1 -1  1  1  0  0  0  0  0  1  0  0  0  0  0  0 -1  0  0  0  0  0  0  1  1 -1 -1 -1 -1  0  0  0  0  0 -1
```

Figure 5.12: Matrix of borges_signature

5. Next, we will start calculating a signature using a 9x9 matrix, instead of a 10x10 matrix. We start with the same process we used before. The following lines of code load our Borges image like we did previously. The final line of this code splits the image into equal parts, but instead of 10 equal parts, we set **nb=9** so that we split the image into 9 equal parts:

```
filepath<-'borges.jpg'
im <- imager::load.image(file =filepath)
im<-imager::rm.alpha(im)
im<-imager::grayscale(im)
im<-imager::imsplit(im,axis = "x", nb = 9)
```

6. The following code creates an empty matrix that we will fill with information about each section of our 9x9 grid:

```
matrix <- matrix(nrow = 9, ncol = 9)
```

Note that we use **nrow=9** and **ncol=9** so that we have a 9x9 matrix to fill with our brightness measurements.

7. Next, we will run the following loop. The first line of this loop uses the `imsplit` command. This command was also used earlier to split the x axis into 9 equal parts. This time, for each of the 9 x axis splits, we will do a split along the y axis, also splitting it into 9 equal parts:

```
for (i in 1:9) {
  is <- imager::imsplit(im = im[[i]], axis = "y", nb = 9)
  for (j in 1:9) {
    matrix[j,i] <- mean(is[[j]])
  }
}
```

The output so far is the **matrix** variable. We will repeat *Step 4*.

8. Get a 9x9 signature of the Borges photograph by running the following code:

```
borges_signature_ninebynine<-get_signature(matrix)
borges_signature_ninebynine
```

The output is as follows:

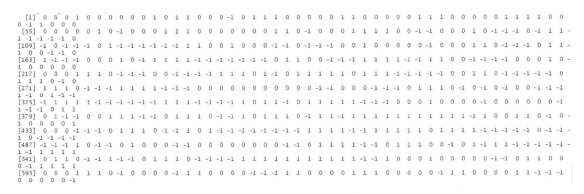

Figure 5.13: Matrix of borges_signature_ninebynine

Activity 12: Create an Image Signature for the Watermarked Image

Solution:

1. Download the watermarked photo to your computer and save it as **alamo_marked. jpg**. Make sure that it is saved in R's working directory. If it is not in R's working directory, then change R's working directory using the **setwd()** function. Then, you can load this image into a variable called **im** (short for image), as follows:

```
install.packages('imager')
library('imager')
filepath<-'alamo_marked.jpg'
im <- imager::load.image(file =filepath)
```

The rest of the code we will explore will use this image called **im**. Here, we have loaded a watermarked picture of the Alamo into **im**. However, you can run the rest of the code on any image, simply by saving the image to your working directory, and specifying its path in the **filepath** variable.

2. The signature we are developing is meant to be used for grayscale images. So, we will convert this image to grayscale by using functions in the **imager** package:

    ```
    im<-imager::rm.alpha(im)
    im<-imager::grayscale(im)
    im<-imager::imsplit(im,axis = "x", nb = 10)
    ```

    The second line of this code is the conversion to grayscale. The last line performs a split of the image into 10 equal sections.

3. The following code creates an empty matrix that we will fill with information about each section of our 10x10 grid:

    ```
    matrix <- matrix(nrow = 10, ncol = 10)
    ```

    Next, we will run the following loop. The first line of this loop uses the **imsplit** command. This command was also used earlier to split the x axis into 10 equal parts. This time, for each of the 10 x-axis splits, we will do a split along the y axis, also splitting it into 10 equal parts:

    ```
    for (i in 1:10) {
      is <- imager::imsplit(im = im[[i]], axis = "y", nb = 10)
      for (j in 1:10) {
        matrix[j,i] <- mean(is[[j]])
      }
    }
    ```

    The output so far is the **matrix** variable. We will use this in *Step 4*.

4. We can get the signature of the watermarked photograph by running the following code:

    ```
    watermarked_signature<-get_signature(matrix)
    watermarked_signature
    ```

The output is as follows:

```
  [1] 0  0  0  0  0  0  0  0  0  0  0  0  0  0  0  0  0  0  0  0  0  0  0  0  0  0  0  0  0  0  0  0  0  0  0  0  0  0  0  0  0  0  0  0  0  0  0  0  0  0  0  0  0  0
 0  0  0  0  0  0
 [55] 0  0  0  0  0  0  0 -1 -1  0  0  0  1  1 -1 -1 -1  0  0  0  1  0 -1  0  0  0  0  0  0  0  0  0  0  0  0  0  0  0  0  0  0  1  0  0  0  0  0  0  0  0  0  0  0  0
 1  0  0  0  0  0
[109] 0  0  0  0  0  0  0  0  0  0  0  0  0  0  0  0  0  0  0  0  0  0  0  0  0  0 -1  0  0  0  0  0  0 -1 -1 -1 -1  0  1  1  1  0 -1 -1  0  1  1  1  1  0
 0  0  0  1  0  0
[163] 0  0  0  0  0  0  0  0  0  0  0  0  0  0 -1  0  0  0  0  0  0  0  0  0  0  0  0  0  0  0  0  0  0  0  0  0  0  0  0  0  0  0  0  0  0  0  0  0  0  0  0  0  0
 0  0 -1  0  0  0
[217] 1  0  1  0 -1 -1 -1  1  1  1  1 -1 -1 -1 -1  0  1  1  0 -1  0  0  0  0  0  0  0  0  0  0  0  0 -1  0  0  0  0  0  0  0  0  0 -1  0  0  0
 0  0 -1 -1 -1  0
[271] 0  0  0  0 -1 -1  0  0  0  0  0  0 -1  0  0  0  0  0  0  0  0  0 -1 -1 -1  0  1  1  1  0 -1 -1 -1  0  1  1  1  1 -1 -1  0  1  1  1  1 -1  0  0
 0  1  0  0  0 -1
[325] -1  0  1  0  0  0 -1 -1 -1  0  0  0  0  0 -1  0 -1  0  1  0  1  0  0 -1 -1  0  1  1  1  0 -1 -1 -1  0  1  1  0  0 -1 -1 -1  0  0  0  0  0 -1 -1 -
 1  0 -1  0  1  0
[379] -1 -1 -1 -1 -1  0  1  1  1  1 -1 -1 -1 -1  1  1  1  1  0  0  0  1  0  0  0 -1  0  1  1  1  1 -1 -1 -1 -1  0  1  1  1  0 -1 -1 -1 -1  0  1  1  1
 0 -1  0  0  1  1
[433] 1  0 -1  0  0  0  1  1  1  0 -1 -1 -1  0  1  1  1  0 -1 -1 -1  0  1  1  1  0 -1 -1 -1 -1 -1  1  1  1 -1 -1 -1 -1 -1 -1  1  1 -1  0  0  0 -1
 0  0  0 -1  1  1
[487] 1  1  0 -1 -1 -1  0  1  1  1  0 -1 -1 -1 -1  0  1  1  1  0 -1 -1  1  1  1  0 -1 -1 -1  0  0  1  0  0  0 -1  0 -1 -1  1  1  1  1  1  0  0  0
[541] -1 -1  1  1  1  1  0 -1 -1  1  1  1  1  1 -1  0  0  0  1  0  0  0 -1  1  1  1  1 -1 -1 -1 -1 -1  0  1  1  1  0 -1 -1 -1 -1  0  1  1  1 -1 -1
 0  1  1  1  1 -1
[595] -1 -1  0  1  1  1  0 -1 -1 -1 -1 -1 -1  0  1  1  0  0 -1  0 -1  0  0  0  0  0 -1 -1 -1  0  1  1  1  0 -1 -1 -1  0  1  1  1  1  0  0  0  1  0  0
 0  1  1  1  1  1
[649] -1 -1 -1 -1  1  1  1  1  1 -1 -1 -1 -1 -1  1  1  1  1  0  0  0  1  1  1  0 -1 -1 -1 -1  1  1  1  0 -1 -1 -1 -1  0  0  1  1  0 -1 -1 -1 -1  0  0
 1  1 -1 -1 -1 -1
[703] -1  0  1  1  1  0  0 -1 -1  0  1  1  1  1  0  0  0 -1  0  0  0  0  0  0  1 -1 -1  0  0  0  0  0  1  1  1  0  0  0  0  0  0  1  1  0  0  0  0  0
 1  0  0  0  0  0
[757] 0  0  1  1  1  0  0  0  0  0  1  1  1  0  0  0  0  0  1  1  1  1  0  0  0 -1 -1  1  1  1  0  0  0  0 -1  0  0  0  0  0  0  0  0  0 -1
```

Figure 5.14: Signature of watermarked image

The final output of this activity is the `watermarked_signature` variable, which is the analytic signature of the watermarked Alamo photo. If you have completed all of the exercises and activities so far, then you should have three analytic signatures: one called `building_signature`, one called `borges_signature`, and one called `watermarked_signature`.

5. After completing this activity, we have stored this signature in a variable called `watermarked_signature`. Now, we can compare it to our original Alamo signature, as follows:

```
comparison<-mean(abs(watermarked_signature-building_signature))
comparison
```

In this case, the result we get is 0.015, indicating a very close match between the original image signature and this new image's signature.

What we have seen is that our analytic signature method returns similar signatures for similar images, and different signatures for different images. This is exactly what we want a signature to do, and so we can judge this method a success.

Activity 13: Performing Factor Analysis

Solution:

1. The data file can be downloaded from https://github.com/TrainingByPackt/ Applied-Unsupervised-Learning-with-R/tree/master/Lesson05/Data/factor. csv. Save it to your computer and make sure that it is in R's working directory. If you save it as **factor.csv**, then you can load it in R by executing the following command:

```
factor<-read.csv('factor.csv')
```

2. Load the **psych** package as follows:

```
library(psych)
```

3. We will be performing factor analysis on the user ratings, which are recorded in columns 2 through 11 of the data. We can select these columns as follows:

```
ratings<-factor[,2:11]
```

4. Create a correlation matrix of the ratings data as follows:

```
ratings_cor<-cor(ratings)
```

5. Determine the number of factors we should use by creating a scree plot. A scree plot is produced as one of the outputs of the following command:

```
parallel <- fa.parallel(ratings_cor, fm = 'minres', fa = 'fa')
```

6. The scree plot looks like the following:

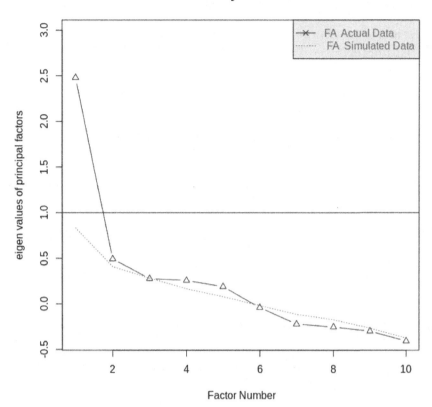

Figure 5.15: Parallel Analysis Scree Plots

The scree plot shows one factor whose eigenvalue is much higher than the others. While we are free to choose any number of factors in our analysis, the single factor that is much larger than the others provides good reason to use one factor in our analysis.

7. We can perform factor analysis as follows, specifying the number of factors in the **nfactors** parameter:

```
factor_analysis<-fa(ratings_cor, nfactors=1)
```

This stores the results of our factor analysis in a variable called **factor_analysis**:

8. We can examine the results of our factor analysis as follows:

```
print(factor_analysis)
```

The output looks as follows:

```
Factor Analysis using method =  minres
Call: fa(r = ratings_cor, nfactors = 1)
Standardized loadings (pattern matrix) based upon correlation matrix
               MR1      h2    u2 com
Category.1   -0.02 0.00027 1.00   1
Category.2    0.16 0.02454 0.98   1
Category.3    0.68 0.46025 0.54   1
Category.4    0.30 0.08942 0.91   1
Category.5    0.43 0.18654 0.81   1
Category.6    0.61 0.37424 0.63   1
Category.7    0.88 0.77276 0.23   1
Category.8   -0.13 0.01718 0.98   1
Category.9    0.05 0.00257 1.00   1
Category.10  -0.74 0.55225 0.45   1

                 MR1
SS loadings     2.48
Proportion Var  0.25
```

Figure 5.16: Result of factor analysis

The numbers under MR1 show us the factor loadings for each category for our single factor. Since we have only one explanatory factor, all of the categories that have positive loadings on this factor are positively correlated with each other. We could interpret this factor as general positivity, since it would indicate that if people rate one category highly, they will also rate other categories highly, and if they rate one category poorly, they are likely to rate other categories poorly.

The only major exception to this rule is Category 10, which records users' average ratings of religious institutions. In this case, the factor loading is large and negative. This indicates that people who rate most other categories highly tend to rate religious institutions poorly, and vice versa. So, maybe we can interpret the positivity factor we have found as positivity about recreational activities, instead since religious institutions are arguably not places for recreation but rather for worship. It seems that, in this dataset, those who are positive about recreational activities are negative about worship, and vice versa. For the factor loadings that are close to 0, we can also conclude that the rule about positivity about recreation holds less strongly. You can see that factor analysis has enabled us to find relationships between the observations in our data that we had not previously suspected.

Chapter 6: Anomaly Detection

Activity 14: Finding Univariate Anomalies Using a Parametric Method and a Non-parametric Method

Solution:

1. Load the data as follows:

```
data(islands)
```

2. Draw a boxplot as follows:

```
boxplot(islands)
```

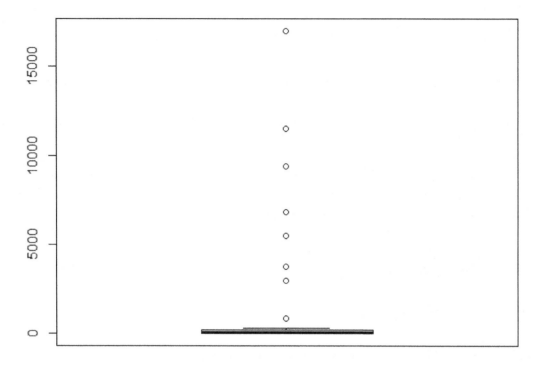

Figure 6.21: Boxplot of the islands dataset

You should notice that the data is extremely fat-tailed, meaning that the median and interquartile range take up a relatively tiny portion of the plot compared to the many observations that R has classified as outliers.

3. Create a new log-transformed dataset as follows:

```
log_islands<-log(islands)
```

4. Create a boxplot of the log-transformed data as follows:

```
boxplot(log_islands)
```

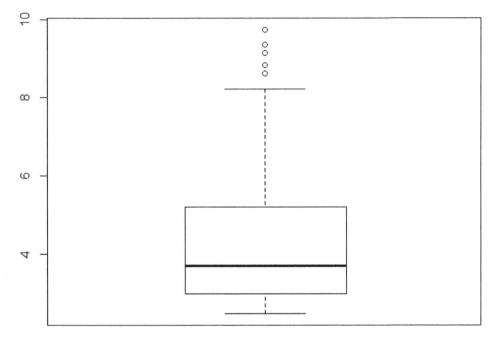

Figure 6.22: Boxplot of log-transformed dataset

You should notice that there are only five outliers after the log transformation.

5. Calculate the interquartile range:

```
interquartile_range<-quantile(islands,.75)-quantile(islands,.25)
```

6. Add 1.5 times the interquartile range to the third quartile to get the upper limit of the non-outlier data:

```
upper_limit<-quantile(islands,.75)+1.5*interquartile_range
```

7. Classify outliers as any observations above this upper limit:

```
outliers<-islands[which(islands>upper_limit)]
```

8. Calculate the interquartile range for the log-transformed data:

```
interquartile_range_log<-quantile(log_islands,.75)-quantile(log_
islands,.25)
```

9. Add 1.5 times the interquartile range to the third quartile to get the upper limit of the non-outlier data:

```
upper_limit_log<-quantile(log_islands,.75)+1.5*interquartile_range_log
```

10. Classify outliers as any observations above this upper limit:

```
outliers_log<-islands[which(log_islands>upper_limit_log)]
```

11. Print the non-transformed outliers as follows:

```
print(outliers)
```

For the non-transformed outliers, we obtain the following:

```
   Africa    Antarctica      Asia    Australia      Europe    Greenland North America South America
    11506          5500     16988         2968        3745          840          9390          6795
```

Figure 6.23: Non-transformed outliers

Print the log-transformed outliers as follows:

```
print(outliers_log)
```

For the log-transformed outliers, we obtain the following:

```
   Africa    Antarctica            Asia North America South America
    11506          5500           16988          9390          6795
```

Figure 6.24: Log-transformed outliers

12. Calculate the mean and standard deviation of the data:

```
island_mean<-mean(islands)
island_sd<-sd(islands)
```

13. Select observations that are more than two standard deviations away from the mean:

```
outliers<-islands[which(islands>(island_mean+2*island_sd))]
outliers
```

We obtain the following outliers:

```
   Africa                Asia North America
    11506               16988          9390
```

Figure 6.25: Screenshot of the outliers

14. First, we calculate the mean and standard deviation of the log-transformed data:

```
island_mean_log<-mean(log_islands)
island_sd_log<-sd(log_islands)
```

15. Select observations that are more than two standard deviations away from the mean:

```
outliers_log<-log_islands[which(log_islands>(island_mean_log+2*island_sd_log))]
```

16. We print the log-transformed outliers as follows:

```
print(outliers_log)
```

The output is as follows:

```
    Africa    Antarctica          Asia North America South America
  9.350624      8.612503      9.740262       9.147401       8.823942
```

Figure 6.26: Log-transformed outliers

Activity 15: Using Mahalanobis Distance to Find Anomalies

Solution:

1. You can load and plot the data as follows:

```
data(cars)
plot(cars)
```

The output plot is the following:

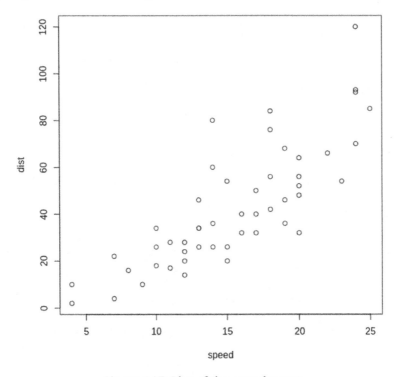

Figure 6.27: Plot of the cars dataset

2. Calculate the centroid:

```
centroid<-c(mean(cars$speed),mean(cars$dist))
```

3. Calculate the covariance matrix:

```
cov_mat<-cov(cars)
```

4. Calculate the inverse of the covariance matrix:

```
inv_cov_mat<-solve(cov_mat)
```

5. Create a **NULL** variable, which will hold each of our calculated distances:

```
all_distances<-NULL
```

6. We can loop through each observation and find the Mahalanobis distance between them and the centroid of the data:

```
k<-1
while(k<=nrow(cars)){
the_distance<-cars[k,]-centroid
mahalanobis_dist<-t(matrix(as.numeric(the_distance)))%*% matrix(inv_cov_
mat,nrow=2) %*% matrix(as.numeric(the_distance))
all_distances<-c(all_distances,mahalanobis_dist)
k<-k+1
}
```

7. Plot all observations that have particularly high Mahalanobis distances to see our outliers:

```
plot(cars)
points(cars$speed[which(all_distances>quantile(all_
distances,.9))], cars$dist[which(all_distances>quantile(all_
distances,.9))],col='red',pch=19)
```

We can see the output plot as follows, with the outlier points shown in red:

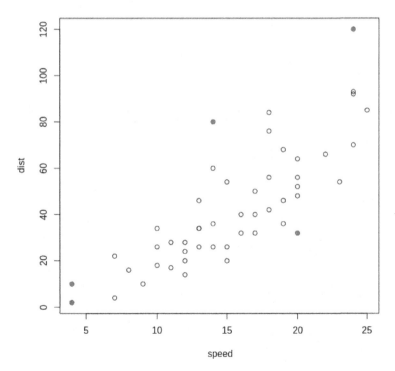

Figure 6.28: Plot with outliers marked

Index

About

All major keywords used in this book are captured alphabetically in this section. Each one is accompanied by the page number of where they appear.

Made in United States
North Haven, CT
14 June 2022